Managing people

influencing behavior

Managing people
influencing behavior

DAVID THOMPSON, Ph.D.

MTR Corp.

Glenview, Illinois   1986

Printed in the United States of America

MTR Corp.
1807 Glenview Road, Glenview, Illinois 60025

Library of Congress Cataloging in Publication Data

Thompson, David Wilson, 1935-
    Managing people, influencing behavior.

    Bibliography: p.
    Includes index.
    1. Psychology, Industrial.   2. Personnel
management.   I. Title.
HF5548.8.T486   158.7   77-15993
ISBN 0-8016-4933-1

GW/M/M 9 8 7 6 5 4 3 2 1

To

Kristen, Erik, and Bradley,
from whom I have learned so much,

and

*to all people who sincerely like and respect
themselves so much that they seek out as friends
people who are confident, competent, and happy*

Certainly the pragmatism of both approach and content will find responsiveness in the activist manager. Dr. Thompson knows what it's all about—he understands "where the manager lives." Profits, action and results are no foreigners to him.

> William B. Johnson
> Chairman, Illinois Central Industries

The chapter on interviewing is the best I have read on this subject. It is must reading and should be reviewed before every important interview.

> Frederick C. Langenberg
> Interlake, Inc.

If 'The Manager' helps to spread this gospel to a large group of managers throughout the country, the results can only be beneficial for the business community and perhaps, as suggested in the final chapter, for the country as a whole.

> John D. Ong
> Chairman, B.F. Goodrich Co.

I believe the lack of observation of these principles accounts for more business inefficiency than any other single factor.

> Michael E. Tobin
> Chairman, American National Bank

FORWARD

The Manager is a book setting forth the principles or rules of reinforcement theory. It defines them, describes them and offers numerous examples of application within the work environment. Dr. Thompson is a good writer. His book is for the layman; one does not require the services of a psychologist to interpret its function or meaning.

The probability is great, it seems to me, that those who read *The Manager* and apply its rules will find this book one of their better investments in management and self-development. It has been my observation that those who manage best use the principles intuitively; all of us are not so fortunate, however. Reinforcement theory describes in the most precise terms I have seen the behavior of those who have been able to elicit the best from others.

One of the great benefits of reinforcements theory is that it forces the individual to assess himself constantly. Since the behavior of others is so heavily dependent on our own behavior, it becomes difficult to blame others without, at the same time, becoming acutely aware of our own contribution to their faults. This increased self-awareness can be of great importance to managers, who receive so little constructive criticism from others.

A good deal of time and effort must be put into reinforcement principles if one is both to understand and to apply them properly. Most businessmen want to improve, but those who look for quick and easy changes will not gain much from reinforcement theory. It is complex. Its implementation requires extensive practice and trial and error learning. It can lead to the frustrating realization of one's own inadequacies in dealing effectively with other people. Nevertheless, the time and effort required are absolutely worth it!

Reinforcement theory elicits controversy because of its precision. If the behavior of others can be so readily influenced, one must ask who will determine the ultimate goal of the influence. Reinforcement principles do not answer this question—nor should they be expected to do so. This issue involves values and ethics, not scientific principles. Can these principles be used destructively? Certainly —just as knowledge on any issue can be so used. Are we then to ignore the knowledge? Those who would use it destructively will not ignore it, as the history of mankind so often proves.

While reinforcement theory does not answer the question of ethics and mores, it does point the way to the true implementation of ethical standards by people in their daily lives. This may well be the more important issue. The commonality of basic ethical standards held by people around the world is surprising. In the darkest hours of mankind, people have still felt a need to rationalize or in some way justify their atrocities toward their fellow man. They have been aware of basic standards of decency; why their behavior was not influenced by these standards would seem, therefore, a more important question than developing the standards. It is a question I feel reinforcement theory can answer to a large degree.

This book provides business managers with many resources to achieve their own potential by developing the potential of their subordinates. Perhaps because of my "conditioning," I am a true believer. I hope the reader will, as Dr. Thompson occasionally does, apply these principles to areas outside the business arena. For we all are not only managers, but citizens, friends, spouses, and parents as well.

Alan S. Boyd
Chairman
Airbus Industries of North America

AUTHOR'S PREFACE

Truth is an elusive quality for two reasons. First, appearances to the contrary, it is intellectually difficult to determine the relevant variables influencing a given event. The most effective approach seems to be scientific experimentation. This book is based on principles derived from rigidly controlled experiments; its conclusions, therefore, should not fall victim to the frequent and realistic criticism that they represent a transient fad in the management development arena.

Second, truth is elusive because it sometimes conflicts emotionally with ideals and attitudes we have long held to be "good." This book is based on the experimental work of Pavlov and Skinner, two names that strike emotional terror in the hearts of many people. One might well ask whether such terror results from a confrontation with truth. The answer is an emphatic yes, as Socrates, Copernicus, and Galileo could attest. Indeed, Diogenes might have searched in vain not only for someone who spoke truth, but also for someone who sought truth.

It is hoped that the reader will judge this book by the criterion of truth—by the workability of the concepts presented, not by their compatability with values he has held most of his life.

Few standards of truth are more stringent than whether a concept actually works. Yet few institutions in our society are concerned about a concept working. It seems to this writer that managers in private industry are more concerned with a concept working than are people in any other sector, be it government, non-profit organizations, or academic and military institutions.

The best prediction of future behavior is past behavior. The history of mankind is a history of war and conflict. Yet, while the future may be a repetition of the past behaviorally, it will not be a repetition in its effects. This is because we have developed technology in the physical sciences that allows us to start a war that will indeed end all wars, be it by bomb or by germ. The only hope would seem to lie in developing and applying scientific principles in the behavioral sciences that are as effective as those in the physical sciences. These principles are now known. The survival of mankind may well rest on our acceptance of them and our determination to apply them toward socially constructive, rather than destructive, ends.

David Thompson, Ph.D.

CONTENTS

CHAPTER 1

Managing people

Commerce links all mankind in one common brotherhood of mutual dependence and interests.

JAMES A. GARFIELD

Survival depends on profits. Survival is the basic goal of any organization. In political organizations, it depends on votes. In private industrial or business corporations, it depends on profits.

Profits, however, are an effect, a consequence. As such, there is little anyone can do about them directly. The manager, therefore, should be concerned with those things that *cause* profits to rise, fall, or stay the same. Recognition of, and attention to, these relevant causes will have a dramatic impact on subsequent profits.

FACTORS INFLUENCING PROFITS

Profits are, to a large extent, a reflection of the behavior of the people in an organization in a free enterprise economy. This is because the activities that determine the profits—judgments, decisions, changes in policy, new product lines, effective sales calls, and other meaningful events—originate ultimately in the behavior (attitudes and feelings) of the people in the organization. *For this reason, one of the primary responsibilities of managers in private in-dustry is the behavior of their subordinates.*

Many managers are reluctant to focus their attention on the behavior of subordinates and the causes of that behavior. Too often they concentrate solely on the results of the behavior, for example, the number of sales calls made, the errors in a submitted report, or the inadequate design or assembly of a particular product. Even profits are the *result* of behavior. To focus on profits is to focus on a past event, an event that has occurred and can never be changed by direct action.

These results or consequences of behavior, however, can be a managerial starting point. The manager should use quantitative measures of profits such as production and sales as an indication of effective or noneffective behavior patterns of people in his organization. Many managers assume that developing quantitative performance measures of their people constitutes managerial responsibility. This is merely the first (and probably the easiest) step in the managerial process. The next step is determining the behavioral factors that caused the quantitative measures; this is done in terms of the constructive (or nonconstructive) behavior of the people in the organization. Herein lies the manager's principal responsibility. This can be emotionally difficult and, therefore, is often avoided.

Why do managers tend to avoid responsibility for the behavior of subordinates? In the first place, in a society in which all people are created equal, accepting responsibility to judge and change the behavior of someone else is akin to playing God, and that can be frightening. The mere fact of authority over others makes many managers uncomfortable. Second, one of the most powerful factors influencing an individual's behavior in the work setting is the behavior of his immediate superior. Changing the behavior of the subordinate, therefore, is often dependent upon changing one's own managerial behavior. Third, there are enormous complexities involved in the behavior of people. It is much easier to focus on a written report than on the vagaries that lead an individual to slant that report one way or another.

There are, however, as many complex variables in determining and measuring the objectives and effects of behavior as there are in measuring behavior itself. Some of these variables are controllable; many are not. Suppose, for example, two salesmen are achieving only 80 percent of their sales quota. Many competent managers will focus on the "missing 20 percent." By complaining about it they can create a good deal of motivation in their two subordinates—motivation that, unfortunately, lasts about three days. The subordinates, on the other hand, will focus on the uncontrolled variables (factors beyond their control) that are influencing their poor performance. Perhaps their best customer moved, or a competitor has a close relative on a customer's staff. These statements may be true, but there is little one can do about them.

Discussions dealing only with the 20 percent itself or with the uncontrolled variables have little long-term effect and waste valuable time. They merely serve the purpose (for the salesman) of shifting the manager's attention away from the shortcomings of the salesman to innocuous factors that the manager can do little about. The manager's proper focus should be on the behavior of the subordinate that is contributing to the "missing 20 percent." The manager may determine, for example, that one salesman loses sales because he is too abrasive with customers, another because he is too meek and passive. These are variables that the manager can influence. Toning down abrasiveness and replacing meekness with confidence, even to a small degree, should help bridge the gap between sales and quota. More important, sales should improve for the long term; the manager should no longer have to deal constantly with new problems caused by the same old ineffectual behavior of his salesmen.

To summarize: Many variables influence the profits of an organization. While a number of these variables cannot be controlled (e.g., the actions of people in government, weather conditions), one of the most important—the behavior of the people in the organization—is always susceptible to managerial influence. Too many managers focus solely on the effects of behavior (e.g., profit, production, sales figures) or spend too much time on causative factors over which they have little control. *Many managers could increase profits substantially by recognizing the impact their own behavior has on the behavior of people below them.*

MANAGING PEOPLE IS EMOTIONALLY DIFFICULT

Managing people is a task more difficult emotionally than intellectually. This can be demonstrated by looking at three basic functions of a manager.

No decision a manager makes is more important than the selection-promotion decision. At the highest levels of an organization, the selection of a chief executive officer may determine the fate of the entire organization for years to come. The manager is expected to surround himself with highly competent subordinates—people who are independent, attack problems aggressively, and take the initiative in speaking up for their ideas. Managers may give lip service to selecting such people, but it is emotionally difficult for them actually to do so. Most managers, consciously or not, tend to surround themselves with people who won't cause trouble, who will follow orders with a minimum of back talk, and who avoid mistakes that will reflect on the manager. Most managers are reluctant to select or promote the subordinate who is ideal from a profit point of view because such an individual can be personally threatening to them.

Another basic managerial function is to fire incompetent subordinates quickly. The inability to carry out this responsibility at high levels within large organizations probably accounts for more business failures than all other factors combined. The cause, of course, is that firing someone is the most emotionally difficult task required of managers. The idea of an organization layoff of one hundred production people is much easier for the sales manager to accept than is personally firing three incompetent salesmen, even though the salesmen's incompetence may well be the cause of the production department layoffs.

A third basic function of managers is the development of subordinates (changing their behavior). This requires external feedback to the subordinate. Discussing personal shortcomings with another human being is again one of the most emotionally difficult managerial responsibilities. Indeed, it is assiduously avoided. (This is why most companies insist on a performance review every six or twelve months. Little is known, however, about what actually takes place during the performance review. At best, little behavioral change will occur as a result of talking with a subordinate about his behavior and attitudes as infrequently as once or twice a year.)

MANAGING PEOPLE IS INCREASINGLY IMPORTANT

Management, therefore, consists of many emotionally difficult tasks that are often avoided by the manager, and most of these responsibilities involve personal interactions. Oddly enough, advanced technology has further emphasized this important area in recent years. Most interactions used to be of a man-machine variety. Automation in the plant and computerization in the office, however, have led to an enormous increase in the need for person-person interactions. The primary effect of the enormous technological advances made in recent years is to increase the consequences of the behavior of an individual. Because of automation, one factory worker can now produce 2,000 units instead of fifty per day. Because of computerization, one office worker can now handle effectively many more paper transactions than before.

These factors have had the effect of placing much more responsibility on people in lower level positions. This increased responsibility requires more frequent manager-subordinate interactions because small behavioral errors can have far greater consequences. In short, because of its multiplying effect through computers and automation, the behavior of a given individual can have much more impact than formerly, and the need for managerial monitoring and influence is correspondingly increased.

Yet the abuse of managerial power in private industry has stemmed more from its lack of use than from its misuse. Because of the emotional difficulties involved, many managers shrink from judgments and interactions involving people. But judgments involving millions of dollars of inventory, capital investments, or potential mergers also involve and have a direct impact on people. In fact, the judgment, whether it concerns inventory or people, is intrinsic to a managerial position and can never be avoided. When a manager refuses to respond to subordinates or to fire incompetent people, he is actually making a judgment and having an impact on the behavior of not only his subordinates, but also others in the organization.

Indeed, the constructive, profit-enhancing behavioral impact on others, especially subordinates, should be the primary criterion upon which many managerial selection-promotion decisions are made. Like most management decisions, selection-promotion judgments are intrinsically subjective. No amount of quantification or performance-related measures (objective objectives do not exist in the real world) can rid the manager of his subjective responsibilities. To select or promote people into management positions because of number of years with a company or technical expertise may lead to more objective, but often more destructive, decisions in the long run.

MANAGING PEOPLE THROUGH PERSONALITY THEORIES

The manager, then, is faced with a dilemma. The often distasteful use of managerial power is not only increasingly necessary; it is also unavoidable. This situation has given rise to numerous personality theories intended to help the manager cope with the behavior of his subordinates. These theories, however, often suffer from two shortcomings. First, they are so abstract as to be meaningless in day-to-day affairs. Lecturing a manager on "self-actualization" leaves him with little real grasp of what he should do about a constantly complaining subordinate. Second, most theories describe the ideal of human behavior but give little information on how to achieve it. Few would disagree with the thought that "relationships of trust and respect" are goals to strive for; how to reach those goals with an overly suspicious subordinate is another question.

SPECIFICITY IN PRINCIPLES OF BEHAVIOR

The purpose of this book is to set forth specific principles by which the behavior of people is influenced. Consciously using these principles implies manipulation—the shaping of people's behavior. Labeling a set of principles as manipulative, however, does not deny their validity. Much of the behavior of all people is directed toward influencing the behavior of others. We can call this influence education, persuasion, enlightenment, or, if we do not like it, manipulation. Suffice it to say, scientific principles are not manipulative, people are; and people are manipulative whether or not they know and consciously use the principles. Politicians, teachers, advertisers, parents, labor leaders, and managers all influence behavior in order to achieve their goals. Moreover, a statement of principles is not an attempt to tell a manager how he *should* manage, but rather, how he *does* manage. The purpose here is not necessarily to describe the ideal; it is to describe reality.

IMPORTANCE OF MANAGERIAL BEHAVIOR

Like it or not, the most important factor influencing an individual's on-the-job be-

havior is his manager's behavior. Most people at the managerial level, consciously or not, are deeply concerned with those things that will please or anger their immediate superior, and their behavior reflects this concern. For example, most vice presidents are intent on pleasing their immediate superior, the president. To change in one way or another the behavior of all the vice presidents, one merely has to bring in a new president; and a frank employee might even admit that he is quite a different person working for the new man from what he was for his predecessor.

Yet most people—and, particularly, most managers—seldom recognize the dramatic impact of their own behavior on that of their subordinates. The same vice president who admits he is different under the new president will still minimize and, indeed, scoff at the supposed impact he has on people below him. We are often more readily aware of the influence other people have on us than we are of the influence we have on other people.

LIMITATIONS

This book attempts to specify the principles that control a human being's behavior. A word of caution: Managerial-subordinate interactions are complex. Although the principles themselves seem simple, their different combinations in real-life situations, the difficulty of diagnosing actual behavior, and the manager's own emotional involvement in a given situation make their use difficult. Fortunately, the manager is not expected to be thinking constantly of these principles as he deals with subordinates. He should apply the principles when a subordinate obviously and frequently displays an ineffective behavior pattern. The manager is most effective in applying principles where he is least involved emotionally. Thus, for example, the manager should plan his own behavior when he is dealing with frequent indecisiveness on the part of a subordinate much as he would plan his own behavior in dealing with less important matters, such as inventory. Such planning and detachment are impossible in an emotionally traumatic situation, such as might occur should a subordinate insult the manager in the presence of others. In this situation, the manager will inevitably respond spontaneously according to the immediate dictates of his own feelings. There are limits, then, to a manager's ability to influence behavior.

SINCERITY

Inevitably, the question of sincerity arises when the manager is expected to plan his behavior so that its impact on his subordinate's behavior will increase profits. This book will assume sincerity on the manager's part. If, for example, the manager is asked to compliment his subordinate, it is assumed that the manager will select an area in which he feels the subordinate actually deserves a compliment. Sincerity is self-revealing, and so is its opposite. If you think a man's tie is ugly it will do you no good to compliment him falsely on his good taste in haberdashery. There

are too many subtle ways by which your insincerity is revealed. Always be aware that many attempts to manipulate the behavior of others are doomed to failure if in any way your own behavior is incompatible with your convictions.

Perhaps the most important function of this book is to offer a manager the tools to "know thyself." As he grows in an understanding of the principles by which behavior is influenced, he will enhance his insight into his own behavior. This is self-diagnosis. It can be frightening. It can also be immensely rewarding. The manager will then be better able to adapt his own behavior so that its impact on his subordinates will help them in developing greater self-awareness and effectiveness, an effectiveness that will be reflected in the increased profits of the organization.

CLASSROOM EXERCISES

1. The profits of an organization in private industry are an indication of the value people in a society place on that organization's goods or services. Profits represent a vote by the people in the most stringent sense: how they spend their money. The only alternative to profits as a criterion of the worth of a company is an arbitrary judgment by people in government. Discuss this concept.

2. Break the class into groups of four or five. Appoint one person "manager" of each group. Have the manager give each person a three-minute task, such as determining how the class as a whole could be better run. Then have the "manager" pick out the best and the worst presentation and tell the worst presenter what was wrong with the presentation. Then have the class as a whole discuss the emotional reactions of the "managers" and the "subordinates."

3. Carry out exercise 2 with a different ap-

pointed "manager" and different topic. This time have the manager "fire" the worst presenter by asking that presenter to leave the group.

4. Break the class into small groups and have each person discuss what he thinks his behavioral impact is on people with whom he interacts frequently, e.g., are they more confident, aggressive, decisive, independent after interactions with him.
5. Pick what you feel is the worst shortcoming of your instructor. Discuss it with him.
6. The only purpose of communication is to influence the behavior, thoughts, and feelings of the person(s) being communicated with. Discuss this concept.

SUGGESTED READINGS

Drucker, P. F.: The practice of management. New York, 1954, Harper & Row, Publishers.
Considered by many to be a classic in the field of management.
Maccoby, M.: The gamesman, New York, 1976, Simon and Schuster.
A best-seller that uses oversimplified generalizations, but shows the effect of personalities on organizations.
McDonald, F.: The phaeton ride, Garden City, N.Y., 1974, Doubleday & Co., Inc.
Shows the influence (often deleterious) of government actions on private industry.

CHAPTER 2

Forming attitudes, beliefs, and opinions

CLASSICAL LEARNING I

The manager directs people or misdirects them. He brings out what is in them
or he stifles them. He strengthens their integrity or he corrupts them.
He trains them to stand upright and strong or he deforms them.
Every manager does these things when he manages—whether he knows
it or not. He may do them well, or he may do them wretchedly, but he
always does them.

PETER DRUCKER
The Practice of Management

We will discuss two general methods of influencing behavioral changes in others— classical and operant learning. Classical learning involves the association of events or stimuli in the presence of an individual. (Beecroft, 1966) These associations, or pairings, have a profound impact on a person's attitudes toward situations, ideas, and people. Operant learning, on the other hand, requires the individual to respond in a given situation. (Reynolds, 1975; Skinner, 1935) The environmental consequences in relation to his behavior will influence his future behavior. The primary distinction between classical and operant learning is that the latter requires overt behavior on an individual's part before

changes in that behavior can be effected; classical learning requires no behavior to effect changes. (Bitterman, 1962; Kling & Riggs, 1971; Skinner, 1935) (This will be discussed more fully in Chapter 6.)

Classical learning is one of the most effective and frequently used ways of influencing behavior. This is because, as mentioned above, the behavior to be influenced does not have to occur. Advertisers and government officials frequently use classical learning principles to influence our behavior. For example, sitting passively in front of a television set and watching a series of ads concerning a particular product can make us decide to purchase it. Likewise, the well-publicized activities and opinions of government leaders can soon change our attitudes toward the Chinese even though we have never dealt with someone from China. To explain classical influences adequately, we must introduce and define two terms, "reinforcers" and "aversive stimuli."

REINFORCERS

Most of the stimuli or situations with which we interact in our daily lives are neutral; that is, they have little impact on our behavior. One class of stimuli has a noticeable impact on our behavior, however; these stimuli are called reinforcers. A reinforcer is any sensory external stimulus that a person seeks out and wants to experience. (Guthrie, 1934; Kling & Riggs, 1971) Hence, a reinforcer might be the sight of a beautiful woman, the taste of delicious food, the feel of a fine fabric, or the smell of an exotic perfume.

One of the most important categories of reinforcers consists of auditory stimuli, those that affect our sense of hearing. Hence the phrase, "You are doing a fine job," can be a strong reinforcer for which we will put forth a good deal of effort. *Indeed, from a profit point of view, what people say to each other and how they say it probably have more influence than any other kind of interaction in private industry. Verbal interactions can make or break a company.*

AVERSIVE STIMULI

Aversive stimuli have the opposite effect on behavior. These are external sensory stimuli we attempt to avoid. (Guthrie, 1934; Kling & Riggs, 1971) They might include the sight of blood, the taste of certain types of food, the feel of running one's fingernail down a blackboard, the smell of a noxious odor. Again, auditory stimuli are among the most important. The phrase, "You really messed that one up," directed by a manager to a subordinate can be strongly aversive.

Only overt sensory stimuli influence us. The fact that a stimulus must have an impact on an individual's sense organs if it is to influence his behavior is important for two reasons. In the first place, there are many competent people whose abilities are not matched by their self-confidence. This is often because an individual's competence frequently is unacknowledged in his own presence. The manager who speaks glowingly of his subordinate's abilities to everyone except the subordinate himself will have a competent, but insecure, subordinate. Many misunderstandings between manager and subordinate occur because the manager silently responds to his own inner positive feelings about the subordinate, who in turn responds—uncomfortably—to his manager's silence.

The second reason for emphasizing the sensory aspect of stimuli is more subtle, but just as important. Many managers discuss with other people individuals who are not present at the time of the discussion. *The only possible justification for such discussions is the manager's desire to change the behavior of the person to whom he is talking in relation to the absent third party.* The question, "How is Jim doing?" is relevant only insofar as the manager is attempting to change his listener's behavior in relation to Jim. Long conversations about Jim's shortcomings will have no impact on Jim if they occur in his absence (he can't hear them). What may be interesting gossip can also be destructive unless the manager's focus is on his listener's behavior, rather than on Jim's. This focus will be evident if the manager, during a discussion of Jim's behavior, asks his listener, "What are you doing about it?"

TURNING A NEUTRAL STIMULUS INTO A REINFORCER OR AVERSIVE STIMULUS

It is quite apparent that the same stimulus can be a reinforcer to one person and an aversive stimulus to another. Eating octopus or snake meat would be aversive to most people in our society but reinforcing to people in other societies. The question is, how does a neutral stimulus become a reinforcer or an aversive stimulus?

Any stimulus paired or associated with a reinforcer becomes a reinforcer. Any stimulus paired or associated with an aversive stimulus becomes an aversive stimulus. (Bugelski, 1938; Pavlov, 1927; Skinner, 1935)

This principle is frequently employed by advertisers. Using a particular mouthwash, for example, leads to a kiss by an attractive girl. Smoking a certain brand of cigarettes is paired with a "rugged, independent" personality. Pictures of an automobile are often paired with bikini-clad beauties. Most important pairings, however, take place during conversations. Frequently we pair a stimulus with what to our listener is a reinforcer or an aversive stimulus. Suppose, for example, one person tells another, "George Towers is trying to discredit you with the rest of the staff." The speaker has paired the stimulus "George Towers" with a stimulus aversive to the listener. He has made it less likely that the listener will react favorably to George Towers in subsequent interactions. The opposite effect will take place, of course, if the name is paired with reinforcers. The statement, "You know, John Akerman thinks you are the most effective salesman in our company," increases the probability that the listener will respond favorably to John Akerman.

DIAGNOSING ONESELF

Managers often hear such pairings from one subordinate concerning another subordinate, especially in highly competitive departments. The manager should pay attention to the aversive stimuli or reinforcers used by the speaker, who is really indicating what he feels is reinforcing or aversive to the manager; in many instances, he is right! The subordinate, for example, who tells his manager that another subordinate "went beyond his authority" may believe that initiative by subordinates is aversive to the manager. Similarly, pairing another subordinate with "not following orders" indicates that the speaker feels his manager finds independent behavior by a subordinate aversive.

FOCUSING ON OTHERS

Sensitivity to the listener is crucial. In many instances, however, the speaker pairs others with stimuli that are reinforcing or aversive to himself, without regard to his audience at the moment. Consider the following comments by a personnel director: "We just hired a fellow by the name of Clayton Smith for the area sales manager position. Clayton looks like a real comer. He's a young, aggressive guy who set sales records at Ryerton Manufacturing three years running. I think Clayton is going to move up fast in this company." Addressed to a profit-oriented president, these pairings are quite reinforcing and will lead the president to look favorably on Clayton Smith when they meet. The same comments made to an area sales manager already in the company will have the opposite effect.

A personnel director has just evaluated an applicant for a position. His comments to the line manager over the position are as follows:

I don't recommend Larry Wilson for this position. I think Larry lacks confidence in himself. As a result, he's too subservient to his superior. Larry is so intent on pleasing his boss that he doesn't make any contribution on his own. He's always trying to find out what his superior thinks before committing himself. I also think Larry is so preoccupied with avoiding mistakes that he bogs down in details. Finally, I feel Larry is uneasy with people and goes too far out of his way to avoid confrontations.

The personnel director is surprised later to find that Larry was hired. Why was he hired? The line manager said it was because Larry had good technical experience for the position. The real reason was that every comment the personnel director made actually paired Larry with an aversive stimulus to the personnel director— but a strong reinforcer to the weak line manager. "Lacking confidence," "subservient," "pleasing his boss . . ." can only

heighten a weak manager's interest in an applicant.

The president of a company is presenting the "Yearly Outstanding Salesman" award to Mike Brun in front of the company's entire sales force:

Mike Brun is being presented this award because of his unusually strong contribution to the sales of this company. Mike has shown a degree of persistence and dedication rarely found in society. Mike's ability to aggressively attack his territory sets an example we could all learn a great deal from. I hope that Mike will now share with us some of those things he does so as to help each and every one of us do a better job.

The president may have paired Mike with reinforcers to Mike, but with aversive stimuli to many other people in that room. It is axiomatic that a manager should not criticize a subordinate in front of others; praising him can eventually do as much damage (the president has developed many enemies for Mike). In sum, *developing greater sensitivity to one's audience and to one's impact on that audience is a proper goal for any manager*.

THE SPEAKER AS A STIMULUS

Since any stimulus paired with a reinforcer or an aversive stimulus becomes reinforcing or aversive, it stands to reason that the person who frequently uses reinforcers will become a reinforcer and the person who frequently uses aversive stimuli will become an aversive stimulus to others. The speaker who said, "John Akerman thinks you are the best salesman in our company," is not only pairing John Akerman with a reinforcer; he is also pairing himself with the same reinforcer. By using this reinforcer, he has increased the probability that the listener will like him and will seek him out for conversation. He has become a reinforcer to the listener.

On the other hand, the speaker who said, "George Towers is trying to discredit you with the rest of the staff," is pairing himself with the same aversive stimulus he associates with George Towers. The listener may "thank" the speaker for giving him this news, but he does not like him the more for it. Indeed, if the speaker paired the names of a few more people (and himself in the process) with aversive stimuli, the listener would soon avoid him; that is, react to him as he would to any aversive stimulus.

Being required to interact with several subordinates at the same time complicates the manager's role. By focusing his attention on the proper pairings for one subordinate the manager can inadvertently have a negative impact on another subordinate. Ben is the president of a company. His favorite subordinate and heir-apparent, Al, likes Ben's attention and the status he gets from his relationship with Ben. Jim joins the company as a new vice president and within several months has won Ben's confidence. Over a two-week period Ben makes the following comments in Al's presence:

"That was an excellent idea, Jim. Very good."
"That is an important issue; let's hold off our discussion until Jim gets here."

"Jim, could we get together for a few hours after this meeting?"
"Jim, I'll take you out to the airport tonight; I enjoy the drive."
"Refer any questions on that matter to Jim while I'm away next week."

Subsequently, Ben cannot understand why Al suddenly turns on him and fights ideas he had originally endorsed. Ben protests—correctly—that none of these comments reflects badly on Al. He also denies any change in his feelings toward Al, giving as proof the fact that he has within the last two days recommended Al as his replacement to the board of directors. Yet every comment mentioned above not only has paired Jim with aversive stimuli to Al, but also has paired the speaker, Ben, with aversive stimuli to Al. Thus, Ben himself has become aversive to Al, as evidenced by Al's sudden opposition to Ben's ideas.

PAIRINGS VERSUS LOGIC

It is important to note that such pairings can take precedence over rational considerations, including the facts or logic of a situation. All organizations experience this phenomenon frequently. There are positive and negative aspects to any idea, any situation, any person. If an individual is an aversive stimulus to us, our attention will automatically focus on the negative aspects of his ideas, since the ideas are paired with the individual presenting them. If, conversely, an individual is a strong reinforcer to us, our attention will focus on the positive aspects of his ideas. "Complete objectivity is a rare phenomenon unless the issues are of little consequence to the individual." (McGregor, 1967, p. 24) If two managers dislike each other intensely, meetings will be disrupted by their attacking each other's ideas.

A manager can almost ensure a subordinate's complete agreement with his proposal, on the other hand, if, just before a meeting on the proposal, he tells the subordinate, "You've done such an outstanding job, I've recommended you for the job in London you wanted." The subordinate is likely to focus on the positive aspects of his manager's proposal in the meeting because of this strong manager-reinforcer pairing.

The reactions of subordinates to their managers are determined, to a large extent, by whether the manager has paired himself with stimuli aversive or reinforcing to the subordinate. An indecisive manager can become an intense aversive stimulus to a fast-paced, impulsive subordinate. Such a manager incurs the subordinate's dislike by pairing himself frequently with such phrases as, "Why don't we wait for more information before we go ahead," or "Let's hold off on that until George gives us his input." To a cautious, indecisive subordinate, however, this manager is, with the same statements, pairing himself with reinforcers. In the former instance, if the manager is aversive enough, his ideas will be opposed by the impulsive subordinate; in the latter case, if the manager is reinforcing enough, his ideas will be supported by the cautious subordinate, *regardless of the content of the ideas*.

Many companies train their sales personnel to associate their product with rational, logical factors, such as low price and high quality. A more individualized approach is called for, since few people are influenced by rational, logical factors. Consider the following two examples of pairings by computer salesmen to an ambitious vice president of administration in a large company.

Salesman: If you buy our computer, we will give you the highest quality gear on the market at a price level that will save your company a good deal of money.

Salesman: I should warn you that with our computer you will become the central point of your company, since all the important information in the company will have to go through your department. So with our computer, if the president needs information, he'll have to come to you to get it.

An instructor was giving a lecture on reinforcement principles to a group of managers. He asked managers A and B to tell the group something that might be reinforcing to him.

Manager A: Well, I like praise.

Instructor (enthusiastically): Excellent! That's very insightful on your part. Obviously you have the confidence to say openly that praise is reinforcing to you.

Manager B: I guess I'd have to admit I like money.

Instructor (grimaces, looks down at the floor, then says monotonely): Well, frankly, that's superficial and trite . . . let's go on with the lecture.

Both managers evaluated this instructor's lecture differently. Even a rational explanation to B that, no matter what he said, the instructor was going to use an aversive stimulus on him had little effect on B's hurt feelings. So the instructor subsequently paired himself with a reinforcer to B, "I must admit I picked you to do that to because I felt you were more emotionally stable than anyone else in the room."

Rational, logical people are often lonely, frustrated people. This is because they live in an irrational, illogical world and the facts they use to uphold their arguments often have minimal influence on other people.

THE RANGE OF REINFORCERS AND AVERSIVE STIMULI

The greatest *intellectual* difficulty in using management psychology lies in deciding what really is a reinforcer or an aversive stimulus to an individual. The fact is, *any stimulus can be a reinforcer or an aversive stimulus* depending on the person and the situation. (Premack, 1959, 1962; Reynolds, 1975) (Correctly diagnosing a specific person or situation will be discussed in Chapter 6.) The range of reinforcers and aversive stimuli is virtually limitless, often self-destructive, and rarely compatible with reality. If the manager feels the principles set forth here do not work, it will more often than not be because he has incorrectly diagnosed reinforcers as aversive stimuli or vice versa in a given individual.

Pain as a reinforcer is not an uncommon phenomenon in human behavior. (Coleman, 1964) This is particularly true in the sexual area, in which case the people are called masochistic. Most studies show that males can be physically aggressive in sexual behavior. (Coleman, 1964) If the pain to the female resulting from this aggres-

siveness is interspersed with words of love, devotion, and an orgasm, pain will then become a reinforcer. This will be especially true if the female is in need of a good deal of affection; that is, words of love and devotion are strong reinforcers to her. (The purpose of this example is to show the wide range of reinforcers, not to elicit an angry reaction from women.)

Attention from his mother is a strong reinforcer to a child. (Bijou and Baer, 1965; Harris, Wolf, and Baer, 1967) The child only elicits his mother's attention, however, by engaging in destructive behavior. This destructive behavior elicits both a negative emotional reaction and the attention the child so desperately seeks. This pairing soon results in a negative emotional reaction from a female becoming a strong reinforcer, a reinforcer that may stay with the child into adulthood. He marries an emotional woman and the marriage consists of little more than frequent shouting matches, yet neither spouse seriously considers divorce. They are in love, for the negative emotional interactions may well be mutually reinforcing.

A father is a strong reinforcer to his daughter. Her pleas for his time and attention are met with periodic rejections and reinforcement pairings: "I can't play with you now, honey, but Sunday I'll take you for a ride in the car." "I won't be able to come home for your birthday party, but I'll get you a surprise gift you'll really love." Soon rejection becomes a reinforcer to the girl. In later years, she has little time for the individual who sends her flowers and candy along with his pleas for a date, but she actively pursues the young man who rejects her with such comments as, "I won't be able to take you to the dance Friday." By rejecting her the young man is actually pairing himself with stimuli strongly reinforcing to the girl.

All of these examples illustrate how useless and even misleading it is to assume that a wide range of reinforcers or aversive stimuli is "common" to many people. A "pat on the back," money (consider the pairings of money with aversive stimuli by some religions), attention, and so forth can be quite aversive to many people.

Nothing is reinforcing to all people and everything (including death) is reinforcing to some people. A compliment can be quite aversive to a person, and, if it is not, it can be made aversive by pairing compliments with aversive stimuli. Consider the impact of the following four comments by a new manager to his subordinate over a two-week period:

"You did an excellent job on that report, Jim, but I wish you'd pay more attention to organization; it was sloppy."

"I was really delighted that you sold Micron Company, although the order you got was much smaller than I'd anticipated."

"That was an excellent presentation, Jim; it would be a lot better, however, if you didn't talk with your hand in front of your mouth so much."

"You're one of the best salesmen we have, Jim, even though you have a lot to learn."

Soon the subordinate turns away from his manager's compliments. Indeed, he might well describe his manager as "insincere" or "a phony."

These pairings represent a common phenomenon in our society—the "but" pairing. In most cases, they represent an insidious association of natural reinforcers with aversive stimuli that destroys the impact of the reinforcer.

"That's a beautiful tie but it doesn't quite match the rest of your outfit."

"You did a good job on your test but let's see if you can do even better next time."

"We exceeded our sales quota this time but that was due to a windfall from a large account."

"The human mind is the finest instrument on earth but it has many limitations."

Managers who pair compliments with aversive stimuli are often highly competitive people, so competitive that genuine accomplishments by their subordinates are aversive rather than reinforcing to them.

At the other end of the spectrum are those people to whom winning is aversive. Despite great skill in a particular field, these people always seem to make debilitating mistakes when engaged in direct competition with another person. Such individuals almost always find "being disliked by other people" intensely aversive. In previous experiences, winning over someone else was paired with this dislike, an association that soon led to a "loser syndrome."

Consider the following comment to two different managers about a subordinate: "Jim Camden is a meek, frightened person." One manager is quick to help subordinates in trouble and has a "social worker" philosophy toward running his department. He is likely to seek out Jim Camden, to interact closely with him, to provide him with aid and support. This is because "meek, frightened" people are reinforcing to this manager and the above-mentioned comment has paired Jim Camden with reinforcers. The second manager, however, looks for independence and initiative in his subordinates, and the same comment has increased the probability he will fire Jim Camden. The same statement, therefore, can elicit opposite reactions from two different people.

Obviously, naive assumptions are often made in diagnosing what is reinforcing or aversive to a given individual. In private industry, the basic function of a salesman is to make his company and its product or service reinforcers to a given customer, and salesmen often feel they are doing an effective job when they pair their company's product with high quality, low price, and on-time delivery. Purchasing agents who have a strong practical-results orientation may indeed find these stimuli reinforcing; unfortunately, many purchasing agents do not.

Likewise, it is wrong to assume that a chief executive officer always finds profits strongly reinforcing. Many chief executives find firing an incompetent vice president far more aversive than profits are reinforcing (a fact that quickly leads to mediocrity at the top of many companies and often throughout the organization as well). Indeed, many chief executives find the admiration, awe, and respect they elicit from incompetent subordinates far more reinforcing than increased corporation profits. The assumption that profits are the most intense reinforcer to a chief executive officer is misleading, unrealistic, and often destructive to an organization.

(In my experience, one of the most in-

tense reinforcers to the greatest number of people is a positive emotional reaction from another person. Two of the most aversive stimuli, excluding physiological stimuli, are meeting new people and being alone.)

"YOU" PAIRINGS

One of the most potentially damaging or beneficial pairings is what we might term the "you" pairing. This occurs when the speaker pairs the individual directly with an aversive stimulus or a reinforcer. Bombarded with these "you" pairings, an individual will soon find the one stimulus he can never escape, himself, reinforcing or aversive to himself.

Concern has arisen in recent years as to why a rape victim feels demeaned after interactions with police officers. Why would a girl who has been attacked feel guilty about herself? Because in many cases the questions asked her by police officers involve you–aversive stimuli pairings:

> Why were you out so late?
> What were you doing in that neighborhood alone?
> Didn't you know someone was following you?
> Shouldn't you have locked your car door?

These you–aversive stimuli pairings would exact their toll from any person.

Parents can do irreparable harm by punishing their children with statements such as the following: "You are such a sloppy child." "Can't you do a better job than that?" "Why are you so frightened all the time?" "You are an ignorant child!" "Can't you do anything right?"

These unfortunate pairings also occur in private industry. Depressingly few managers are reinforced by confidence and competence in their subordinates. The defensive salesman says to his manager, "I'm a good salesman!" The manager replies, "Maybe, but you've got a lot to learn. Believe me, you have a long way to go before you stop making mistakes." A machinist was so skilled at his trade that he started his own business. It grew until he was managing twenty other machinists. He would periodically walk into his plant, pick out his best machinist, literally push him aside, and "show him how a good machinist really works." These episodes always involved a number of "you aren't nearly as good as you think" pairings. Competence in a subordinate was intensely aversive to this highly competitive entrepreneur, despite the fact that he increased his personal income on the basis of that competence.

Managers who use you–aversive stimuli pairings are capable of not only hurting company profits, but also usurping the confidence of their subordinates. Conversely, the manager who tells his subordinate, "You are certainly adept at that," when a good job has been done, is helping both the individual and his company. Indeed, the effective manager is frequently in a position to say (but rarely does), "You did a better job on that than I could have." The manager who sincerely asks his subordinate, "What do you think I should do?" cannot help but increase the confidence of that person.

Even social institutions can have a deleterious effect ("You are original sin"). Yet how can we expect people to be decisive and self-reliant when relying on themselves means relying on someone whom, deep down, they really don't like. What a person thinks of himself will often deter-

mine his fate (Thoreau). What a person thinks of himself will be determined, to a large extent, by the people with whom he interacts most frequently. A concentrated effort by managers to use you-reinforcer pairings with subordinates, given the many realistic opportunities to do so, would go a long way toward building a viable, confident team.

FACIAL-BODY GESTURES AND TONE OF VOICE

Some of the strongest reinforcers and aversive stimuli involve tone of voice and facial and body gestures. (Bijou and Baer, 1965) In fact, these are often far more intense reinforcers and aversive stimuli than are the actual words being used. The phrase, "That's pretty good," enthusiastically spoken, has quite a different impact from the same phrase spoken in an unenthusiastic monotone. To return to an earlier example: A compliment on a man's tie will be enthusiastic when the tie is truly a reinforcer to the speaker. If, on the other hand, the real reinforcer controlling the speaker is "being liked by the other person," then the compliment will not be genuinely enthusiastic, a difference the listener will quickly notice. This is the primary reason "sincerity" is so important and manipulation is so difficult. People are quite perceptive in responding to slight nuances, and the same words may be reinforcing or aversive, depending on the inflection and gestures accompanying them. "If we are intent on impressing people, that is how we impress people."

It has been mentioned that a positive *emotional* reaction is one of the strongest reinforcers to the greatest number of people. Tone of voice (inflection) and facial-body gestures are the vehicle by which emotions are conveyed. The statement "That was a nice job," given in an intense, spontaneous, and enthusiastic manner, can be a strong reinforcer; given in a perfunctory, monotone way, the same statement could be neutral at best.

THE MANAGER AS A STIMULUS

The managerial function requires a manager to pair himself with aversive stimuli. For example, he has to refuse pay raises, point out mistakes, and see that his subordinates conform to the rules and regulations of the organization. To overcome this inherent disadvantage, it is necessary for a manager to pair himself with stimuli that are reinforcing to subordinates whenever the opportunity arises. Otherwise, he will become an intense aversive stimulus to his subordinates. Lack of communication (the subordinate avoids his superior) and time wasted in bickering, backbiting, complaining, and even strikes and sabotage are the consequences of such a situation.

If managers were one half as quick to use reinforcers when dealing with subordinates as they are to use aversive stimuli, many of these problems would disappear; when a manager becomes a strong reinforcer to his subordinates, the organization's goals soon become their goals as well. As a rule of thumb, a manager should attempt to use four or five reinforcers to counteract each aversive stimulus used; reality indicates that most managers do the opposite in far greater proportions. The minimal use of reinforcers by managers often stems from the fact that the competence, confidence, and concrete accomplishments of subordinates are not really reinforcing to them.

"When the boss gives an order, asks for a job to be done, reprimands, praises, conducts an appraisal interview, deals with a mistake, holds a staff meeting, works with his subordinates in solving a problem, gives a salary increase, discusses a possible promotion, or takes any other action with subordinates, he is teaching them something." (McGregor, 1960, p. 200) What the manager is teaching the subordinate may best be defined in terms of classical learning. Hopefully, the manager, through his behavior, is encouraging constructive behavior and profit-producing goals by pairing them with reinforcers and discouraging destructive behavior and undesirable goals by pairing them with aversive stimuli. These pairings can have an immediate and critical impact on subordinates.

Consider the following statement by a manager in the presence of his subordinates. "The indecisiveness in this department is about to drive me up the wall!" The manager has paired indecisiveness with an aversive stimulus (especially his negative tone of voice) and has decreased the probability of his subordinates engaging in indecisive behavior. But, by using an aversive stimulus, the manager has also paired himself—and his department as well—with the aversive stimulus. This, too, will influence the behavior of his subordinates. Some managers are surprised by a subordinate's negative reaction to an "obvious" compliment, "You'd probably go a long way in this company if you weren't a woman."

If the manager is reinforcing, most subordinates will attempt to please him and will (often subconsciously) try to find out what is reinforcing to him and engage in that type of behavior. If, for example, their manager constantly complains about various people in the organization, his subordinates will also engage in that type of complaining behavior when they are in their immediate superior's presence. If the manager gives raises to detail-oriented people (pairing), there will be a strong shift toward details on the part of his other subordinates. Promotions are one of the strongest reinforcers available to managers. When an individual is promoted, his attitudes and style of work are being associated with strong reinforcers, and others in the department will soon start to emulate his behavior if promotions are reinforcing to them (to some, they are not).

On the other hand, if a subordinate has a strong dislike for his manager (the manager is an intense aversive stimulus to the subordinate), he may well engage in behavior patterns that are aversive to his manager. Consider the case of a superior who delegates no authority downward and blocks all communications upward. He gives no credit to his subordinates but is quick to blame them for all mistakes. He has, however, a highly independent subordinate who dislikes him intensely. This subordinate knows that his manager becomes uneasy when a subordinate goes around him and interacts with his superiors; consequently, this subordinate goes

out of his way to do just that! If this behavior were not aversive to the manager, the subordinate would be much less inclined to engage in it.

How the manager (or anyone) is reacted to by subordinates is not entirely dependent on the manager's behavior. Pairings about the manager by third parties also have an effect. Indeed, if an individual's last interaction with another person was positive and a coolness is evident in their next interaction, we can rest assured that some third party was doing pairings in the interim.

Clyde asks one of his subordinates to stay late and work on a report. The subordinate, who doesn't mind at all, calls his wife and says, "Clyde wants me to work on a report tonight, so I'll be home late for dinner." The subordinate has paired Clyde with aversive stimuli to his wife. Several days later, Clyde notices some coolness on his subordinate's part. He incorrectly attributes it to his asking the subordinate to stay late. The real cause is the wife's pairings of Clyde with aversive stimuli in the interim period: "Why does Clyde always want you to stay late? Just because he doesn't care about his family is no reason for him to think no one else does! He doesn't work half as hard as you and he makes twice as much!"

This tug of war between the wife and the superior is not an uncommon phenomenon. A person's success in the work setting may lead him to talk excitedly about it at home. This enthusiasm may be quite reinforcing to the speaker but quite aversive to a spouse who feels left out. Subtle "work-aversive" pairings by the spouse often follow. Success does sometimes contain within it the seeds of ultimate failure (principally because of third party pairings).

THE COMMUNICATION OF A MANAGER'S PHILOSOPHY

Managers pair behavior patterns and stimuli that are reinforcing to them with reinforcers, and behavior patterns and stimuli that are aversive to them with aversive stimuli in the presence of their subordinates. Consider the illustration of a highly cautious, conservative sales manager whose only goal is to live out his few remaining years in the organization without some subordinate causing trouble and jeopardizing the manager's position and subsequent retirement. A new subordinate enters his office and the following exchange takes place:

Subordinate (in a quiet but excited tone): Hey, Jim, I just got an order for two hundred units from the Touhy Corporation.

Manager (in a quiet monotone): That's good. (Looks down at his desk and picks up a piece of paper, then speaks more loudly and with much more inflection): While you're here, John, there's some question about a difference in the expense report you turned in last Friday. I noticed you stayed in the same motel on Wednesday and Thursday nights but you charged almost twice as much for dinner on Thursday night. Someone upstairs is going to call me on it unless we give them a reasonable explanation. What happened?

The manager did not pair the sale with any strong reinforcers; he did, however, pair the behavior pattern of "inconsistencies on the expense account" with aversive stimuli. His reaction has decreased the probability that the subordinate will focus his attention on sales, while it has increased the probability that the subordinate will focus on avoiding discrepancies on his expense account.

Since people pair those things that are reinforcing to themselves with reinforcers, it is absolutely essential that the company product or service be reinforcing to its salesmen. When this is not true, sales calls can be destructive. To illustrate: New management had been brought into a large company and numerous firings and demotions in the sales force resulted. Sales fell badly. One demoted salesman, in a prospective customer's office, introduced himself by saying, "I'm Jim Smith from Micro-Data Company. As you may know, we've had a lot of personnel changes at our company, but hopefully things will settle down soon." Another demoted salesman replied to a complaining customer, "Well, our people always seem to have trouble maintaining the quality of that line." These men were pairing their company with aversive stimuli, a procedure not likely to elicit sales.

The frequency with which salesmen engage in these types of pairings would probably astound many managers. It is the manager's responsibility to make certain the company and its product or service are reinforcing to his salesmen. The alternative is, at best, a salesman who will discuss baseball, fishing, or family with his customers—anything, in fact, but his company and its product, since aversive stimuli are avoided.

VERBAL STIMULUS TRANSFERS TO ACTUAL STIMULUS

Classical learning allows an individual to build in a reaction to a given stimulus on the part of another individual even when the stimulus is not present. (Hartman, 1965; Razran, 1961) Consider the consulting psychologist, Sanders, whose job it is to interview and evaluate management people. People can be influenced to react differently to Sanders by pairing the word "Sanders" with either a reinforcer or an aversive stimulus. The comment, "I understand Sanders is responsible for getting you promoted" (reinforcer), will elicit quite a different response pattern from a manufacturing manager when he actually meets with Sanders again from that elicited by the comment, "I understand Sanders is out to get you fired." The important point here is that a verbal stimulus, given in the absence of the physical stimulus to which it refers, is capable of changing the behavior of another person when he is subsequently in the presence of the physical stimulus.

One of the most disruptive pairings of this sort occurs when a manager, in his subordinate's presence, pairs his own immediate superior with aversive stimuli. Suppose, for example, a new young manager (Randall) is hired to head up a plant operation. In the presence of the foreman, the old-line plant superintendent pairs his boss, the new plant manager, with aversive stimuli by means of remarks such as, "That guy Randall doesn't know how to open a door, let alone run a plant," and "That Randall is going to get us all fired with his screwball ideas." The new plant manager will soon find the foreman implementing his policies in a halfhearted, uncooperative manner; communication between the manager and the foreman will be superficial at best; productivity in the plant will slide downhill.

These situations occur quite frequently in life. If a close friend becomes hostile for no apparent reason, it is almost certain that a third party has been providing the friend with "other people–aversive stimuli" pairings.

Actions do not speak louder than words. Words are actions and their impact on behavior is just as strong. That is to say, an actual event and verbal interactions concerning the event are separate and discrete experiences. Both, however, impact a person in terms of the same behavioral principles. Actually saving an individual's life may well pair you with a strong reinforcer to him; *telling* other people you saved his life may well pair you with aversive stimuli to him. Indeed, telling other people frequently and in detail how you saved his life may lead him to wish you had not. A husband may be surprised to hear his wife complain about his frugality when, in reality, he has given her a good deal of money to spend; her complaints are a reaction to his frequent aversive *comments* about her spending habits. A husband may pair himself with the reinforcer of actually taking his wife to Europe; that she dislikes him may be the result of his *telling* her ten times prior to the trip that she would not be able to go. The wife's animosity is based on ten aversive pairings while the husband's is based on the wife's "unreasonable" negative feelings since he actually took her to Europe.

EMOTIONAL INVOLVEMENT AND CLASSICAL LEARNING

Emotional involvement represents a major difficulty in implementing the principles of classical learning. Consider this interaction between a father and his 7-year-old daughter. The young girl is socially inhibited and sweet; she would never hurt anyone. Her father loves her deeply and finds anything that hurts her intensely aversive. She has refused to go outside and play for three days. Finally, the father questions her reasons for staying in. She responds, "Mrs. Sampson [a next-door neighbor] said I kicked her child. She said I was a mean girl for doing it and she doesn't want me around her children."

The child has just paired Mrs. Sampson with what to the father are intense aversive stimuli. His natural reaction is to have a "talk" with Mrs. Sampson or, at least, turn to his wife and say, "Who the hell does Mrs. Sampson think she is?" The fact is, however, his daughter will not go outside because Mrs. Sampson is an aversive stimulus to her. The father's natural reaction will increase his daughter's withdrawal because he is also pairing Mrs. Sampson with aversive stimuli.

If the father's goal is to have his daughter go outside, he must pair Mrs. Sampson with stimuli reinforcing to the girl. He must make comments like, "Mrs. Sampson is really a very nice person. I know Mrs. Sampson likes you very much. If you go outside, you will see that Mrs. Sampson is happy to see you." The father was able, in this instance, to make these comments with successful results.

It is asking a great deal of an individual, however, to expect him to engage in this type of behavior under such emotional circumstances. The manager says to his subordinates, "I think the record will show that I have done a very effective job since taking over this division. I have increased sales 30 percent and I've cut our overhead costs 18 percent. I think everyone will agree that things are going much better since I came here." Because of his intense emotional need to impress people, the manager is pairing himself with reinforcers. But reinforcers to whom? To himself! To everyone else, he is probably pairing himself with aversive stimuli; thus the emotional difficulty of saying the right thing at the right time.

This is the reason the reader should *not* be concerned with these principles every waking moment of his life. When an individual encounters stimuli that are intensely aversive or reinforcing to him, he should usually respond naturally to them. Any other approach is often doomed to failure. In many managerial interactions, however, stimuli are not intensely emotional. Nor is the manager being paid "to do his own thing." He is being paid to elicit the most effective behavior patterns possible from his subordinates as judged by a profit criterion. Those who cry for the "open and honest" expression of feelings had better be certain that "open and honest" managerial goals are profit-oriented and not destructive to an organization and people in it.

SUMMARY

We have seen that any stimulus can become a reinforcer if it is paired with reinforcers and any stimulus can become aversive if it is paired with aversive stimuli. These pairings go on constantly throughout our lives and account, in large measure, for our attitudes and opinions about people, events, ideas, and situations.

The manager, primarily through his verbal responses, is a potent source of these pairings. Whether or not he is an effective source depends on a host of factors, including his ability to determine stimuli that are reinforcing or aversive to himself and to his subordinates. His effectiveness is also dependent upon his emotional stability and his ability to look at his own behavior objectively.

Unless the manager grasps the consequences of his behavior, which is to say, the consequences concerning the impact he is having on his subordinates, he will always be walking a treadmill. He will always be wondering why his subordinates do not achieve practical results and continually engage in noneffective behavior.

The manager may not like the thought that he has so much influence over the behavior of his subordinates, but ignoring the fact does not decrease his impact; it merely makes that impact less effective.

CLASSROOM EXERCISES

1. Let each student attempt to influence the opinions of another student about a third student. What pairings were used? What does the speaker really feel is reinforcing and aversive to the listener?
2. Present a logical, rational argument in favor of some behavior (e.g., abstaining from alcohol or drugs). Are pairings being made? Are reinforcers and aversive stimuli being used? Are they effective reinforcers and aversive stimuli?
3. Analyze the effect on the listener of the following comment: I love you.
4. What pairings would an effective manager engage in when interacting with his subordinates?
5. Determine two positive things about another student. Incorporate them in a series of you-reinforcer pairings. Examine the feelings of the speaker and the listener.
6. A manager is not being paid to "do his own thing." He is being paid to engage in effective, profit-oriented behavior. Discuss this concept.
7. Change the impact of the question, "Where did you go yesterday?" by changing only the tone of voice (inflect a different word each time) and facial-body gestures.
8. Say, "I really like you" in as many different ways as possible, changing only your emotional expressiveness.
9. Have two students pair themselves with reinforcers and aversive stimuli separately to the instructor. Ask the instructor his feelings about their grades.
10. Have four males pair themselves with reinforcers to a blindfolded female, asking her to pick one to date. Why did she pick that one?
11. The instructor should pick out the best student in the class. Extol the student's virtues to the class. At the end, examine everyone's feelings.

SUGGESTED READINGS

Beecroft, R. S.: Classical conditioning, Goleta, Calif., 1966, Psychonomic Press.
  A thorough treatment of the subject.
Kimble, G. A., editor: Foundations of conditioning and

learning, New York, 1967, Appleton-Century-Crofts.
Includes sections covering the history, method, theory basic phenomena, and other topics in both classical and operant conditioning.

Marrow, A. J., Bowers, D. G., and Seashore, S. E.: Management by participation, New York, 1967, Harper & Row, Publishers.
A study of two merged companies and how the attitudes and philosophy of one were integrated into the other.

Pavlov, D. P.: Conditioned reflexes, London, 1927, Clarendon Press.
One of the basic books in classical learning.

CHAPTER 3

Changing attitudes, beliefs, and behavior

CLASSICAL LEARNING II

I am not now that which I have been.
BYRON
Childe Harold's Pilgrimage

Up to this point, we have been discussing people as they are and what has made them that way. Now we will turn to the area of changing behavior.

A word of warning. There is a strong trend in our society to pair "independent" behavior with reinforcers and "dependent" behavior with aversive stimuli. The fact is that in a civilized society, no one is independent; we all depend on each other. We depend on the pilot to land our plane safely; we depend on people driving their cars not to run into us; we depend on people in positions in the government to keep us out of war and to run an efficient operation. Sometimes our dependent expectations are not met; then many people suffer.

The above examples, however, reflect an almost physical dependency. There is also a psychological dependency. The attitudes and feelings of people with whom we interact frequently are affected by our behavior.

It cannot be otherwise. Our influence is intrinsic to the interaction. It does little good, therefore, to ask ourselves whether or not we should be audacious enough to change others. We will and we do. We can, on the other hand, study the process of change openly or we can ignore it; but we can never avoid influencing others in some way if we interact with them.

This is especially true in private industry. Everyone in a private industrial company depends on the behavior of the chief executive officer. Poor decisions at this level can hurt many people in the organization, monetarily, physically, and psychologically. So too does the behavior of managers. Managers have a strong impact on the behavior of their subordinates. Our job is to analyze that impact and how it occurs.

We can do this by examining four classical learning principles through which a manager can and does influence the behavior of his subordinates.

PRINCIPLE I
To decrease the probability of a response controlled by a reinforcer, pair the reinforcer with aversive stimuli (Estes and Skinner, 1941)

The phrase "to decrease the probability" is used to indicate that one or two pairings are not going to change behavior dramatically. We are dealing with people who have adopted certain attitudes after years of experience; we will not change them during a two-minute interchange (we shall see later that this quick change in behavior is quite possible, but dangerous). On the other hand, we can, with concentrated effort, alleviate the intensity of a given reinforcer or aversive stimulus quite effectively over a two- or three-week period.

The word "response" signifies overt (observable) behavior. Although behavior also encompasses such unobservable elements as thoughts, feelings, attitudes, opinions, and ideas, all anyone can know about a person is his overt behavior.

The phrase "controlled by a reinforcer" (much of our behavior is not) means that the behavior is being influenced by a rewarding stimulus immediately following it (see Chapter 4). As indicated in the previous chapter, determining this reinforcer can be a difficult proposition. Nevertheless, the manager must always make his best guess as to what is reinforcing and what is aversive to his subordinates. He must "know his people," and he does not know them until he has made this determination. He should always remember, however, that the most powerful reinforcers and aversive stimuli usually stem from the behavior of other people. (Ullman & Krasner, 1969; Watson, 1966) What a person says to us has far more impact on our behavior than the same words in a written report.

The phrase "pair the reinforcer with aversive stimuli" means pairing the reinforcer controlling the behavior with a stimulus aversive to the subordinate, not to the manager. This can be done verbally, since, as we have seen, the verbal transfers to the actual stimulus.

In other words, our principle might read, "To decrease the likelihood of behavior that is being influenced or maintained by a reinforcer, associate the reinforcer with stimuli aversive to the listener."

Suppose, for example, that attention from other people is a strong reinforcer to a subordinate. Indeed, it is so reinforcing that he constantly interrupts people to tell them jokes; he disrupts meetings by giving long-winded speeches on irrelevant matters; and he is forever disagreeing with people so that they must look at him when discussing a point. Almost every statement by his manager in the following developmental session will pair "attention from others" with an aversive stimulus.

Manager (in a disparaging, but soft, concerned tone of voice): Jim, I feel attention is a little too important to you at times. How do you feel about it?

Subordinate: I suppose it is at times.

Manager: Why? Why do you think attention would be so important to you?

Subordinate: I really don't know.

Manager: I wonder if you would consider the idea that people live in their own world; when people are giving you attention they don't really care that much about you. Most people are mainly concerned about whether or not their car will start, what they will have for dinner tonight, who won the football game. So when people are looking at you, they're not usually that concerned about you. As a matter of fact, when people are looking at you, they are often doing it because you have made them angry, and when they're giving you attention they're really looking down on you.

The manager's remarks have decreased the probability that the subordinate will find attention as reinforcing as he did before the remarks were made. As a result, they have somewhat decreased the strength of the subordinate's attention-seeking behavior. The remarks have not, however, totally eliminated attention as a reinforcer to the subordinate; this is because attention has probably been paired with strong reinforcers quite frequently in the subordinate's past. Periodic comments (and other action) along these lines by the manager, however, will gradually lessen the frequency and intensity of attention-seeking behavior by the subordinate.

When a new manager assumes authority over subordinates he has not previously known, surprises are often in store for him. Stimuli he assumes are reinforcing to virtually everyone will have a negative impact on some. Most managers, for example, assume that money is a reinforcer to all employees. To many people, it is not. Some religions pair money with the "root of all evil." Some young people today pair the acquisition of money with "crass materialism" and "a gross distortion of values" (sometimes even causing their parents to feel guilty about their salary). The current

ecological trend often pairs money with waste, with the result that some wealthy people wear old clothes and drive run-down cars.

The first function of a manager in taking over a new department is to diagnose his subordinates as accurately as possible. Most managers extol the cliché, "Every subordinate is an individual and must be treated differently"; few actually practice it, however. To really know a person in the work setting one must be aware of his effective and ineffective behavior patterns and which types of stimuli are reinforcing and aversive to him. Lacking a reasonable approximation of this knowledge, the manager will make numerous mistakes.

A new sales manager may assume, for example, that one of his subordinates, who is 140 percent over quota, is quite happy with his quota and his own performance. The manager is surprised to find the salesman actually hostile toward his quota and generally displaying an I-don't-give-a-damn attitude. What the new manager does not know is that the previous manager had, for several months, been pairing the salesman's outstanding performance and his quota with aversive stimuli with such comments as:

"Jim, I just got your sales figures for last month. You're doing a helluva job. Do you think your quota is too soft?"

"Jim, you're really beating hell out of your quota. We'll have to raise your quota by 100% next year to keep you humping."

"Say, Jim, I was tickled to see that you're maintaining your sales way over your quota, but

I noticed that your expenses are starting to go up a bit."

The new manager, therefore, can make numerous mistakes by logically—and wrongly—assuming that the quota is reinforcing to a salesman who is far ahead of his peers in maintaining his quota.

"Rational" analyses of human behavior can lead to a distortion of reality. To say that profits are the primary goal of a chief executive officer is, as we have mentioned, often untrue and misleading. The admiration and respect of incompetent subordinates may take precedence over increased profits as a reinforcer for a company president.

The managerial diagnosis of subordinates, consequently, should focus less on rational factors and more on interpersonal reinforcers and aversive stimuli. One of the most debilitating reinforcers to an individual is a "need to be liked by others." Such a reinforcer often prevents a person from speaking up for his ideas in the face of opposition, from making decisions that might hurt others, and from carrying out responsibilities without explicit guidance. A strong desire to be liked or approved of is a difficult reinforcer for managers to deal with because the behavior stemming from it is often reinforcing to the manager himself. It is the outstanding manager who pairs this reinforcer with aversive stimuli by saying to the subordinate, for example, "Your need to be liked by people is a weakness on your part," and, "When people like you, they often do not respect you." Toning down this deadly reinforcer by pairing it

with aversive stimuli (weakness, no respect) helps an individual contribute his fullest to his company and to society. To so influence behavior is the manager's responsibility; if he doesn't do it, who will?

Rational discussions with people seldom do much good unless they include effective pairings. A psychologist was treating an alcoholic manager who, when dealing with close friends and relatives, was consistently late, hypercritical, and generally obnoxious. It was pointed out to him that seeing significant people in his life emotionally upset was reinforcing to him. He accepted this diagnosis as accurate. He was told not to criticize anyone during the following week. This directive focused specifically on his critical behavior patterns; it did not pair the reinforcer of seeing people upset with any aversive stimuli. At his next appointment, he stated that he had experienced one of the most rewarding moments of his life over the weekend. He had spent the day with his children and had "never criticized them all day." What was the rewarding moment? When he returned the children to his ex-wife's apartment, "They cried because I was leaving." The rational discussion on emotionally upsetting significant people had apparently had little impact on him, since his "most rewarding moment" consisted of seeing his children weep! The psychologist would have been more effective had he paired "people emotionally upset," rather than critical behavior, with aversive stimuli.

The manager's primary concern should be the frequent, repetitious behavior patterns of his subordinates. When that behavior is nonconstructive, it is the manager's responsibility to change it. One method of doing this is to determine what in the behavior of others is reinforcing the subordinate's nonconstructive behavior and then pairing those reinforcers with aversive stimuli. If the manager finds his subordinate won't delegate because the subordinate finds "people being dependent on him" reinforcing, it is up to the manager to change that ("Having people afraid to move without your approval makes your job ten times harder; when people feel they need you, you can bet they won't like you."). Again, if the manager doesn't accept responsibility for the change, who will?

PRINCIPLE II
To decrease the probability of a response controlled by an aversive stimulus, pair the aversive stimulus with reinforcers (Skinner, 1938)

To illustrate: Suppose two subordinates are not communicating; in fact, they are avoiding each other. The obvious diagnosis is that they are aversive to each other. If communication between the two is important, it is the manager's job to pair one subordinate with reinforcers to the other subordinate. If Jack Smith and Jim Rolin do not get along, the manager might go to Jack and ask him what he feels Jim Rolin's greatest asset is in the work setting. After Jack has finished complaining about Jim, he will usually admit to one or two positive elements in Jim. The manager can then convey these positive elements to Jim: "You know, Jack Smith feels you are one of the best report writers in our company." After Jim's incredulous reaction, the manager should repeat the pairing: "Really. I was talking to Jack last Thursday, and he feels you write excellent reports."

These pairings will increase the likelihood that Jim will be less aversive in his subsequent interactions with Jack. It is not being suggested that one or two pairings of this type will have the two subordinates embracing each other. The pairings are but an example of what the manager should be doing to establish a proper interpersonal climate. The manager, incidentally, is not being asked to lie. He must elicit positive statements from the one subordinate before he conveys them to the other subordinate. If they are not true, the manager's altered tone of voice and other subtle cues will be aversive rather than reinforcing. Sincerity is therefore necessary for pragmatic as well as moral reasons.

It is important to remember that the manager always pairs himself with what he uses, reinforcers or aversive stimuli. The manager will be liked by Jim when he tells him "Jack thinks you write excellent reports." He is pairing both Jack and himself with a reinforcer. On the other hand, he will not be liked by Jack if he says to Jack, "Jim is the best report writer in the company." He is pairing both Jim and himself with stimuli aversive to Jack.

Managers should watch closely the pairings their subordinates verbalize. They are often a quick and certain cue to present or impending trouble. Consider this interchange between a sales manager and one of his salesmen in the presence of the manager's immediate superior:

Salesman: Instead of making all the salesmen memorize this canned sales pitch, why don't we just list some basic points and let them present the points any way they want?

Sales manager: Because half of the salesmen don't know which side of our product is up or down, and the other half couldn't care less.

The sales manager has paired his own subordinates with aversive stimuli. His immediate superior must start to look for other negative indices. He must find out if this attitude is temporary or permanent (as determined by the frequency of these remarks). He must ask himself whether or not the sales manager finds increased sales reinforcing or aversive. He must find out how aversive the sales manager is to his subordinates. Pairings such as these are the precursor to a drop in sales and profits. Managers who do not focus on these precursors—who focus on profits only, rather than the controllable *causes* of profits—will always react too late.

In line with Principle II, it is now the job of the sales manager's superior to pair the aversive stimuli (the salesmen) with reinforcers to the sales manager. "You know, I was out to dinner with some of your salesmen the other night. They all think a good deal of you. They feel you back them up and will go to bat for them when they need you. They really feel quite positive toward you." These types of constructive comments are not that difficult to find if we really look for them. They help develop a positive relationship between a manager and his subordinates, a relationship that often enhances effectiveness and profits.

Nowhere in a corporation is the principle of pairing an aversive stimulus with a reinforcer more important than in the sales department. Sales people are constantly forced into customer interactions that are aversive. This liability is compounded when the sales manager finds customers aversive.

This is evidenced by the manager pairing customers with ridicule or outright animosity. The same managers then wonder why their salesmen avoid making sales calls or are easily dissuaded from pursuing an account. The manager who comments, "The people at AIC Corporation are the biggest jerks I've ever run into," decreases the probability that his salesman will call on AIC Corporation. This manager should instead be saying to his salesman, "The people at AIC Corporation think you're one of the most conscientious salesmen we have." By pairing AIC Corporation with a reinforcer, this statement increases the probability that the salesman will indeed call on AIC Corporation. Of course, the statement must be true. Again, there are ample opportunities for these realistic and true reinforcer pairings.

Self-destructive behavior by managers is all too common. Consider this not unusual comment by a manager to his subordinate at salary review time: "I want to give you the raise, but Jack says our profits are so low that nobody will get a raise." The manager is obviously attempting to pair himself with what to his subordinate is a reinforcer, and to pair "Jack" (the controller) with an aversive stimulus. Such a remark not only reflects excuse-making or avoidance of responsibility, it also indicates negative attitudes toward other managers. It is not merely a reflection of a *weak* manager; it is a reflection of a *destructive* manager.

Companies sometimes reverse Principle II and pair a realistic reinforcer with aversive stimuli—to the detriment of everyone. It is well known that few people are inspired by fringe benefits and that many organizations do a poor job of communicating these benefits to the employees. The simple statement, "Our company has a pension plan that is second to none," pairs both the company and the pension plan with a reinforcer. Consider the following, however:

Our company pension plan will pay you, at age 65, 60 percent of your highest salary averaged over five years, conditioned upon the five years being continuous with the company, or it will pay you 40 percent of your highest salary averaged over the previous five-year period, if employment was maintained in this organization for the five years, and the employee declares retirement at age 60.

The complexities involved in this statement are so aversive to most people that the pension plan, after these pairings, is hardly considered worthwhile. Worse yet is the following:

The pension plan does *not* cover nonexempt employees unless they have been with the company a minimum of ten years. Pension Plan participation is *not* available to employees with more than three reprimands in their personnel folder. The pension plan payments will be *decreased* by the amount of social security benefits the employee receives.

Each of these statements tells the reader what the pension plan will not do; that is, the statements pair the pension plan with aversive stimuli. (It would sometimes be more effective to have the marketing department, rather than lawyers, write up the brochures describing company benefits.)

Aversive pairings caused by emotional involvement

Managers often find effective pairings difficult to make because of their emotional involvement in a given situation. This emotional difficulty can prevent a manager from doing the right thing at the right time. It is sometimes to the best interest of everyone concerned, for example, for an individual to pair himself with what to the other person is a reinforcer, even though that same stimulus is aversive to the individual himself. To illustrate: A father and son were running their jointly owned company. The father was aversive to his son because of his frequent "interference"; the son was aversive to the father because of his "different and totally ineffective ideas." Their animosity and lack of constructive communication was pulling the company apart and hurting its seventy employees. It was suggested to the son that he pair himself with stimuli reinforcing to his father. The son was asked to say to his father, for example, "Dad, based on all your years of experience, what do you think I should be concentrating on to develop myself?" The son's reply to this request was, "No way could I ever say that! I would choke on it!" However, the son did eventually bring himself to admit mistakes to his father when he made them, to ask his father's advice, and to praise his father's strengths to others in front of his father. These statements, although emotionally difficult, were true.

The result was a far more positive relationship between the two which benefited everyone in the company. The son had effectively paired what was an aversive stimulus to the father, the son himself, with reinforcers.

The manager's task is not an easy one. He is being paid, however, to elicit the best efforts of his subordinates. Sometimes this may require him to make statements which, while true, are highly aversive to himself. It might be highly effective for the egocentric sales manager to say to a subordinate, "You did an outstanding job on that sales call. Frankly, you handled that fellow better than I could have." Few managers, however, have the confidence to engage in behavior they feel will be self-deprecating.

Many managers, on the other hand, inadvertently pair themselves needlessly with aversive stimuli in subtle ways. Consider the following managerial memo:

I have noticed a recent trend toward using the phone for personal calls; this is permissible only during emergencies.

The manager could have toned down the subtle impact of pairing himself with aversive stimuli by changing the memo slightly:

There has been a recent trend toward using the phone for personal calls; this is permissible only during emergencies.

Managerial responsibilities require managers to pair themselves with aversive stimuli; some thought can minimize the frequency and intensity of these pairings.

Principle II: A managerial interaction

Developing a subordinate by pairing aversive stimuli with reinforcers is a topic we will examine in greater detail in Chapter 8. For now, we might look at one example of this type of interaction. Suppose a manager is having a developmental session with a meek, passive subordinate. The manager in this instance is attempting to elicit more decisive behavior on the part of the subordinate. The manager knows that interpersonal interactions have a greater impact on people than do any other stimuli. He has, therefore, reasoned that this subordinate is indecisive because the subordinate fears he might encounter dissension or an argument if he commits himself to a judgment in front of other people. The manager, therefore, must pair "dissension and arguments with others" with reinforcers.

Manager: John, I feel at times you're not quite as decisive as you could be. How do you feel about it?

Subordinate: Well, I suppose you might be right.

Manager: Why do you think you're a bit indecisive at times?

Subordinate: I don't really know.

Manager: I wonder if it's because you think someone might argue with you if you committed yourself to a judgment.

Subordinate: That might be part of it.

Manager: I wonder if, when someone argues with you, he's really telling you that your views have had an impact on him. When someone says to you, "No, John, I disagree with you," he's really telling you he respects your views enough to try to sway you to his point of view. When someone gets angry with you and starts shouting, he's really saying that what you're telling him is important to him, that he cares about you and your views. You know, if someone just accepts my ideas, I don't have much respect for him. But when he comes at me hot-and-heavy and really argues vehemently with me, I know that what I have said is important to him and that I'm important to him."

Here the manager is attempting to pair the aversive stimulus (dissension) with reinforcers (they care about you). The manager is also judging which stimuli are actually aversive and which are actually reinforcing to the subordinate. A man is often the worst judge of himself, and to ask the subordinate to determine which stimuli he finds reinforcing and aversive can often lead one astray.

We have discussed two critical principles that can have an impact on an individual's behavior. While the principles are two sides of the same coin, choosing which one to use (that is, whether to pair a reinforcer with an aversive stimulus or vice versa) can be crucial in diagnosis and impact.

These pairing principles are not the only tools available to the manager in carrying out his function of influencing the behavior of his subordinates, but they are important ones, and we will refer to them frequently. Our next two principles are closely related to them, but are sufficiently important to merit separate treatment.

PRINCIPLE III

To increase the probability of a response, pair the verbal equivalent of the response with a reinforcer (Hartman, 1965; Razran, 1961)

The key phrase in this principle is "the verbal equivalent of a response." By this we mean the words used to describe a particular type of behavior. Consider this comment about a third party from a manager to his subordinate: "Jim sure is decisive. I like to see that in a man." Assuming that what his manager likes to see in a man is a reinforcer to the subordinate, this statement has increased the probability of decisiveness in the subordinate. It has paired the verbal equivalent of decisive behavior with a reinforcer.

Advice-giving

This principle is frequently reflected in advice-giving behavior. Its use is not always effective, however, because people generally use stimuli that are reinforcers or aversive to themselves rather than to their listener. This accounts, in large part, for the fact that much of what we say goes unheeded or has the opposite impact of that intended on the subsequent behavior of our listener.

A consultant hoped to tone down the aggressive, abrasive behavior of a plant manager who had lost rapport with his subordinates. To do this, the consultant attempted to pair the verbal equivalent of the plant manager's behavior with aversive stimuli. He commented, for example, "When you yell at your people, you scare them half to death. You're so abrasive in the plant that people are frightened of you. You come on so strong that your subordinates back away from you." Subsequent reports indicated the plant manager had become even more aggressive with people below him. "People being afraid" may have been aversive to the consultant, but it was a strong reinforcer to the plant manager, thus increasing the frequency and intensity of his abrasive behavior.

Dealing with more than one person

The same problem occurs when a "mass audience" approach is used, whether it be in a textbook on management, the Bible, or the writings of Confucius:

The meek shall inherit the earth.
Selecting good people is the first step on the road to increased profits.
Positive attitudes make for positive results.

The purpose of all these statements is, of course, to effect behavioral change in others by pairing the desired behavior with reinforcers. However, the same stimulus may be neutral, reinforcing, or aversive to different people. "Increased profits" may be quite reinforcing to a chief executive officer, of little concern (neutral) to many people in the company, and even aversive to some in the company. Employment ads stressing the idea that the employer is an "aggressive company" may turn away people who are truly competent, but in whose experience aggressiveness has been paired with aversive stimuli.

Managers must therefore be careful with their use of reinforcers and aversive stimuli in general meetings. It is all too easy for the manager to pair a desired response pattern with a stimulus reinforcing to one subordinate but aversive to many others. The manager might, for instance, say to a highly ambitious subordinate in a group meeting,

"Mary, you are always so well organized. Why don't you make the presentation of our report to the president next week." There is little doubt that Mary's efforts to organize her personal work habits will be increased in the future. To other ambitious people at the meeting, however, an organized approach has just been paired with the aversive stimulus of Mary making the presentation to the president. Some of these people may subsequently complain about the "undue emphasis placed on organization in this department." To less ambitious people at the meeting, Mary's opportunity to make a presentation to the president is a neutral stimulus; little change in their behavior can be expected.

It should again be emphasized that if a manager uses reinforcers to influence the behavior of others, he will become a reinforcer. If he uses aversive stimuli, he pairs himself with those stimuli and will become aversive. In the above example, the manager is now more reinforcing to Mary, more aversive to the other ambitious people, and unchanged to the less ambitious people.

Pairing the verbal equivalent of a response with reinforcers is an essential in sales:

If you try our product, I think you'll find it quite effective.
When someone buys our computer, we give them free installation service.
The people who use the services of our firm are usually more aggressive than the average person.

Again, it is essential that the salesman have a direct knowledge of what is reinforcing to the potential customer. Anything short of this knowledge can only lead to a canned "shotgun" approach with many more failures than successes.

PRINCIPLE IV
To decrease the probability of a response, pair the verbal equivalent of the response with an aversive stimulus
(Hartman, 1965; Razran, 1961)

This is, of course, the obverse of Principle III. It is, unfortunately, more important, since aversive stimuli are used much more frequently than reinforcers to influence behavior in our society.

Social pairings

Almost all rules, regulations, and laws are a pairing of the verbal equivalent of a response pattern with aversive stimuli:

Anyone smoking in this area will be subject to a three-day suspension.
Anyone not wearing safety goggles on the plant floor will be terminated immediately.
Failure to yield the right-of-way to a pedestrian is punishable by one to six months in prison.
The divulging of information marked "top secret" shall be punishable by five to ten years in prison and a fine of not more than $5,000 or both.

Three pairings are actually taking place here. First, the behavior specified in the rule, regulation, or law is being paired with the aversive stimuli used as potential punishment. Second, rules, regulations, and laws *in general* start to become aversive, since they are almost always being paired (enforced) with aversive stimuli. Third the organization issuing the rules, regulations, and laws is becoming aversive to its people because it is pairing itself with both the rules and regulations and the same aversive stimuli used to enforce its standards. The

company that uses many rules and regulations, therefore, is likely to be aversive to many of its employees.

Individual pairings and questions

At an individual level, managers constantly pair response patterns with aversive stimuli with comments like the following: "You know, Jim, if you keep talking with your hand in front of your mouth, no one will listen to you." "If you can't get that job done by Thursday, all hell is going to break loose here." "All that guy does all day long is play up to the boss; some day he'll catch his."

Likewise, managers' questions tend to pair response patterns with aversive stimuli because they often are followed by reprimands.

Manager: Did you write up that report?
Subordinate: No.
Manager: Why the hell not? I told you I needed it today. Don't you ever do anything I ask of you? I want to see you alone in my office at three today. (The question, "Did you write up that report?" asked on subsequent occasions, will now be aversive to this subordinate because of the pairings used here.)

Indeed, the questions a manager asks his subordinates can set the tone of his entire department because they are often paired or followed immediately with aversive stimuli if the "wrong" answer is given and reinforcers if the "right" answer is given. The sales manager who constantly questions his people about their sales calls will increase the probability that his salesmen will be outside selling. The sales manager who repeatedly questions expense account discrepancies will soon find his salesmen spending an inordinate amount of time poring over their expense reports.

A consultant was called into an unprofitable plant operation. He spent two hours walking around the plant with the plant manager watching the latter interact with the superintendents and foremen. He ventured the opinion that the rejection rate by the inspection department must be very low. The plant manager, surprised the consultant knew this, said it was near zero. Indeed, the plant's high reputation for quality was acknowledged by both customers and competition. The consultant then pointed out the fact that every question the plant manager had asked his subordinates during the previous two hours had centered on accuracy and quality. Mistakes revealed by the manager's questions ("Is that piece within tolerance limits?" "Are the corners there rounded off enough?" "Is that angle perpendicular to this side piece?") were punished with reprimands. As a result, the pace of the plant was slow and cautious but certain. Quality was very high; productivity was very low. The plant manager was asked not to hire more help, but to start asking productivity questions. ("When will this job be finished?" "How much longer do you have to go on this job? Can't we get it out sooner?") The initial reaction was negative. One worker stated that he could run the machine at a faster rpm rate, but complained that it put stress on a washer and the wash-

er would periodically break. The washer cost five cents, however, while the profit from an increased rpm rate was in the thousands of dollars. After six weeks, productivity had taken a marked upswing in the plant. After six months, productivity had increased over 40 percent without an appreciable drop in quality.

Questions by a manager tell a subordinate what is important to the manager. Since they are often paired with reinforcers or aversive stimuli, the questions themselves can become reinforcing or aversive. A manager's questions, followed by reinforcers and aversive stimuli, constitute a primary vehicle by which his attitudes and philosophies permeate his department.

Managers, when they dislike a response, frequently pair the verbal equivalent of the response with aversive stimuli. A manager was ostensibly attempting to tone down the emotional frustrations of a subordinate. He said, "You're the kind of guy who aggressively seeks change in an organization, and you have to realize that you're bound to have more failures than successes." The manager was not pairing emotional reactions with aversive stimuli, but rather, the response of aggressively seeking change. This particular manager was close to retirement and "seeking change" was aversive to him. It is difficult for people to avoid pairing response patterns that are aversive to them with aversive stimuli.

The double negative

Pairing the verbal equivalent of a response with aversive stimuli often fulfills two obligations of the manager. It allows him to carry out company policy and, at the same time, get his *true* message across.

Gentlemen, we are being required to hire more blacks because of the threat of arbitrary governmental action. We have to look more closely at minorities when openings occur; this comes right from the bureaucrats in Washington. I also want you all to look at the women in your department for possible promotions because of all the fuss they're causing.

The manager is now in a position to say he carried out company policy. That the policy will be carried out less than enthusiastically because of his pairings is another matter.

Most managers use aversive stimuli so frequently that the use of reinforcers has all but been forgotten. It must be remembered that each time one individual uses reinforcers to influence the behavior of another, he is pairing himself with those reinforcers to that person. Using aversive stimuli, on the other hand, makes an individual more aversive to those with whom he is interacting. It makes sense, therefore, to use reinforcers to influence behavior whenever possible. Unfortunately, the "double negative" approach is more typical, often because intimidating their subordinates is reinforcing to many managers. Suppose a manager is attempting to inspire his subordinates to give more feedback to their subordinates. He will probably make comments like the following:

"If anyone here has not given his subordinates their annual performance review by the end of next week, I want to know about it, and the reasons had better be good."

"Most managers shy away from giving feedback to subordinates because they are afraid to do so."

"If you don't give your people more feedback, maybe you should not be a manager."

The speaker, in this case, is becoming aversive to his audience because he is using aversive stimuli. He is also pairing what they should *not* do with aversive stimuli. As a result, he has not made "giving feedback" more reinforcing; he has made "not giving feedback" more aversive! Contrast that approach with the following:

"You know, if you give Jack some personal feedback on that issue, his work will improve dramatically and I think he'll respect you for it."

"I noticed you gave Jim some feedback yesterday. Beautiful! He'll probably become an excellent salesman because of your help."

"The manager who gives his people feedback always gets my admiration; giving feedback takes guts and confidence."

The speaker, in this case, is making both himself and "giving feedback" more reinforcing. He will reap many benefits from this approach. "If you have the report in by Thursday, I'll worship the ground you walk on," is far more constructive than, "If you don't have the report in by Thursday, I can guarantee that you will regret it."

Classical extinction

Suppose a mother always spanks her child after shouting the word "no!" The word "no" would soon become an aversive stimulus to the child. If, however, she continues shouting the word "no," but never again spanks her child, the word "no" will soon lose its effectiveness in influencing the child's behavior. *This is called classical extinction. It means that any reinforcer or aversive stimulus that is presented frequently, but is not periodically paired with another reinforcer or aversive stimulus, will soon lose its effectiveness.*

Consider the manager who, in a frantic desire to be liked by her subordinates, constantly praises them for everything they do ("That was a beautiful job." "That was excellent.") The mere frequency of these comments, spoken without periodic pairing with other reinforcers, leads them to be quickly extinguished as reinforcers. New subordinates love this manager initially, but soon label her a "phony." A manager can only tell a subordinate he will "soon get a raise" so many times; this reinforcer will become meaningless (extinction) if it is not periodically paired with an actual raise.

The same is true of aversive stimuli. The manager who continually shouts at his subordinates, but always gives them appropriate raises and promotions, soon finds subordinates are initially terrified of him but soon learn that "his bark is worse than his bite."

The newly married husband frequently tells his wife such things as, "I love you." "You are the most beautiful woman I have ever seen." Frequent repetition of these comments will soon leave his wife somewhat less emotional in her reactions to them. Pairings must be made. "I love you and I'd like to take you out to dinner tonight."

Extinction is a pervasive factor in our lives. Its influence is often subtle but, in the long run, almost overwhelming. A dramatic news story or social issue elicits widespread attention, but this attention soon falters and dies. The first sales call by the trainee, the first employment interview conducted by the new personnel assistant elicit intense emotional enthusiasm on their part. However, hundreds of sales calls and interviews often lead to a gradual lessening of enthusiasm, conscientiousness, and attention to detail through the process of extinction. The same reactions hold true of almost all occupations, including those of the pilot and the surgeon. It is the manager's job to blunt the effects of extinction through a creative pairing of the work activities with reinforcers (e.g., letting the salesman role-play sales calls in front of trainees; having the personnel assistant give lectures on interviewing to line managers).

The negative effects of extinction are a counterbalancing force to the positive effects of experience. Thus, ten years in the same position not only means one year's experience ten times over; it also means ten years of undergoing the deadening effects of extinction.

The negative effects of extinction are also relevant in the many situations in which "expectation is greater than realization." Expectations are built through verbal reinforcer pairings which may exceed the true reinforcers of the actual event. Verbally pairing a particular movie with frequent and intense reinforcers (enthusiasm) can lead to expectations so great that no movie could satisfy them. The actual movie, since it is less reinforcing than the verbal pairings, is more of a disappointment than would have been the case without the pairings. The person is actually undergoing extinction while watching the movie. Overselling a product or the benefits of joining a particular company can have the same deleterious results when the product is actually used or the person actually starts working for the company.

No pairings

Much of what we say to people has little impact on them. We have seen that one reason for this is our use of stimuli that are reinforcing or aversive to us, but not to the people we are trying to influence. Another reason for lack of impact is lack of using reinforcers or aversive stimuli at all.

Extinction was defined as presenting reinforcers or aversive stimuli without periodically pairing them with other reinforcers or aversive stimuli. In the present instance, we are discussing the presentation of *neutral* stimuli or *neutral* verbal equivalents of a response pattern without pairing them with a reinforcer or an aversive stimulus. This compromises our impact a good deal.

No pairing: I hope you'll buy our product.

Reinforcer pairing: I hope you'll buy our product; I think you'll be very happy.

No pairing: Why don't you sit down and talk it over with John.

Reinforcer pairing: Why don't you sit down and talk it over with John; I'm sure you'll clear the air and be friends again.

No pairing: Come with us to the show tonight.

Reinforcer pairing: Come with us to the show tonight and I'll take you shopping tomorrow.

No pairing: Don't play in the street.

Aversive pairing: If you play in the street you could get run over and killed.

No pairing: Let's not have a general meeting.

Aversive pairing: If we have a general meet-ing everyone is likely to gang up on you over that issue.

The people who are effective in influencing the behavior of others are not necessarily the people who have more facts or an incisive grasp of truth. They are the people who take a second breath and use it to pair their points of view with reinforcers or aversive stimuli. They are the salesmen, the advertisers, the statesmen who intuitively use pairings to great advantage to sway people one way or another. They are the Darrows who do not merely say "Don't find this man guilty," but rather, "If you find this man guilty you will doom yourself to a life of Hell!"

Backward pairings

Another reason for lack of impact on others is the use of backward pairings. *The stimulus (verbal equivalent of a response) we are attempting to change must come before the reinforcer or aversive stimulus we are using in the pairing.* (Kling & Riggs, 1971; Pavlov, 1927) If the reinforcer or aversive stimulus comes first, the impact is minimized. The reader may find this difficult to believe, but it has been proved time and again in experimental work. For example: If we want to make "Mike" aversive to our audience, we must not only pair "Mike" with aversive stimuli, but we must also place the word "Mike" first in the pairing. It is much more effective to say, "Mike has an abrasive quality that hurts other people," than to say, "There's an abrasive quality that hurts other people in Mike."

The stimulus that is changed, in other words, is the one that comes first. The comment, "You did a fine job in your presentation, but you missed the point of the meeting," has the effect of making compliments aversive. Conversely, the comment, "You missed the point of the meeting, but you did a fine job in your presentation," has the effect of making criticism more reinforcing.

Ineffective (backward): No one will listen to you if you keep mumbling.

Effective: If you keep mumbling, no one will listen to you.

Ineffective (backward): You'll make quota easily if you make eight sales calls a day.

Effective: If you make eight sales calls a day, you'll make quota easily.

Not only are backward pairings ineffective, they are often destructive as well. The manager, for example, who *continually* follows compliments with criticisms or criticisms with compliments (as in the above examples) sets up unrealistic reinforcers and aversive stimuli in his subordinates. A new manager is then bewildered by the "demotivating" impact his compliments have on his subordinates, to whom compliments now seem "phony." Likewise, many people find affection from persons close to them aversive; the parent who punishes his child by saying, "I love you, darling, but you've got to learn to be more responsible," is leading his child to develop this unrealistic attitude.

In some highly aggressive departments the members have frequent, frank, but highly critical, interchanges, yet everyone seems to like and respect everyone else and few people voluntarily leave the department. This is because hostile criticism has become a strong reinforcer. New members of the department may be appalled at the apparent "hostility," but they will never feel accepted until everyone starts openly criticizing them ("What the hell did you do that for?"). Compliments are rarely given in such a department and are sometimes even used as a punishing device. Anyone leaving the department will require an "adjustment" period until criticism again becomes aversive and compliments reinforcing. If the individual lacks patience during this period, he will either request a transfer back to his old department or leave the company.

SUMMARY

We have now examined the four principles of classical learning. They are simple principles in the abstract; they are complex in practical application. The manager should practice observing and diagnosing pairings before he attempts to use them. Printed material is a perfect vehicle because of its permanence. The manager should be sensitive to the pairings politicians use when they are quoted in the daily newspaper as saying, "We cannot divulge that material because it would compromise national security" or "Communists cannot be trusted." The reader should ask himself why the speaker has made the pairing, whether the reinforcer is really reinforcing (or aversive) to a large number of people, and whether the speaker has used backward pairings. After developing proficiency in this area, the manager should attempt quick analyses of verbal behavior while observing children, watching movies, attending meetings, and, most important, when analyzing the behavior of his subordinates.

Implementation is the next step. It requires, above all, accurate diagnosis (see Chapter 6). It requires objectivity and emotional maturity. It requires a flexible sensitivity and adaptation to the specific audience at the moment. Effective pairings of the company require different reinforcers when one is talking to customers than when one is talking to financial analysts. Goal-setting by management requires the pairing of company goals with different reinforcers to different employees or employee groups; any other approach is likely to be less effective.

These requirements are most important when a manager is dealing with his subordinates. He must be (and is in any case) a different person to different people. To be an effective manager, he must use different pairings with the subordinate who lacks sufficient confidence to make decisions from those used with the subordinate who is himself destructively pairing customers and clients with aversive stimuli.

The most important decision an organization makes is the selection of its chief executive officer. His attitudes and philosophy will permeate the organization, primarily because of the pairings he makes. If a cautious, conservative chief executive finds mistakes intensely aversive, he will frequently pair mistakes with his wrath (aversive stimuli) in the presence of his immediate subordinates, the vice presidents. This will quickly set up mistakes as an aversive stimulus to the vice presidents,

which they will in turn pair with aversive stimuli when dealing with their subordinates, and so on down the line. Promotions (reinforcers) will be paired with people whose behavior pattern reflects a lack of mistakes, that is, cautious, conservative people who take few risks. The entire atmosphere of the organization will eventually become aversive to more risk-oriented people and they will leave.

The pairings involved in human interactions can be effective tools in helping managers develop confidence and competence in subordinates. Consider the atmosphere created by a manager who pairs customers, peers, and superiors with reinforcers; who pairs "you" and a desire for excellence with reinforcers; who pairs competent behavior patterns, independence, confidence, and laughter with reinforcers in the work setting. It is a long and arduous task to develop expertise in this area, but the rewards are well worth the effort.

CLASSROOM EXERCISES

1. Pick the student who has spoken up most often in class and pair "attention from the class" with aversive stimuli.
2. Now pair the verbal equivalent of the response of speaking up in class with aversive stimuli.
3. Do the opposite with a student who rarely speaks up.
4. Ask two females, "Where did you get that blouse?" making the question reinforcing, then aversive by changing the tone of voice only.
5. Pick someone out in the classroom. "Sell"

him on doing a specific thing by pairing his doing it with reinforcers and not doing it with aversive stimuli.

6. Pair off the class. Assume your partner is too concerned with what other people think of him. Diminish that concern.

7. Now assume your partner does not allow people to get emotionally close to him. Make him more trusting of people.

8. Now assume your partner lacks sufficient confidence. Increase his confidence.

9. "Sell" the instructor on skipping a specific class session in the future.

10. "If you don't kiss me, I'll never talk to you again." Analyze the impact of this statement on the listener.

11. You are responsible for developing more positive attitudes in your partner toward this class. Carry out this responsibility.

12. Turn your instructor against another student in the room.

SUGGESTED READINGS

Drucker, P. F.: The effective executive, New York, 1967, Harper & Row, Publishers.
Has some insights into the characteristics of a "tough-minded" manager.

Kling, J. W., and Riggs, L. A.: Woodworth and Schlosberg's experimental psychology, ed. 3, New York, 1971, Holt, Rinehart, and Winston, Inc. chaps. 14-17.
A technical and thorough treatment of many topics in classical and operant conditioning. Many seminal experiments are referenced and described here.

Lieberman, D. A., editor: Learning and the control of behavior: some principles, theories, and applications of classical and operant conditioning, New York, 1974, Holt, Rinehart, & Winston, Inc.
A collection of basic articles in both classical and operant conditioning.

CHAPTER 4

Reinforcement and extinction

OPERANT LEARNING I

*The sick in mind, and, perhaps, in body, are rendered more darkly and hopelessly
so by the manifold reflection of their disease, mirrored back from all quarters
in the deportment of those about them; they are compelled to inhale
the poison of their own breath, in infinite repetition.*

NATHANIEL HAWTHORNE
The House of Seven Gables

Up to this point, we have discussed methods of influencing people without regard to their overt behavior at the moment. That is, the influence was dependent only on the behavior of the speaker and the pairings he initiated. In the following two chapters we will consider changing behavior directly, the moment it happens. To do this, we must examine four basic principles of operant learning.

The reader should heed two warnings. First, while the principles are deceptively simple, their actual application in the "real world" is enormously complex. No one can hope to accurately diagnose and perfectly implement these principles all the time; imperfect implementation some of the time is a reasonable goal. Second, we tend, in our interactions with other people, to focus on their behavior and its impact on us; we should really spend more time examining our own behavior and its impact on other

people. With these points in mind, let us turn to the first two principles of operant learning.

PRINCIPLE V: REINFORCEMENT
**Any response followed immediately by
a reinforcer has a greater probability of
recurring** (Skinner, 1938)
PRINCIPLE VI: EXTINCTION
**Any response not immediately followed by
a reinforcer has a lesser probability of
recurring** (Kling and Riggs, 1971)

It is important to note that *extinction always leads to hostility*. Thus, extinction not only decreases the likelihood of the behavior it follows, it increases the likelihood of irritation or anger, whether expressed or not.

Let us begin with an example showing the effects of both reinforcement and extinction. John Blake was promoted to Vice President of Operations at 10:00 one morning. At 2:00 that afternoon he walked into the apartment of his mistress.

John: I've just been promoted to Vice President of Operations.

Mistress (excitedly): Oh John, that's wonderful! Let's open a bottle of champagne and celebrate.

The reinforcing emotional reaction of John's mistress had three effects: (1) it increased the likelihood of John feeling good about his promotion; (2) it increased the likelihood John will tell his mistress good experiences of his in the future; and (3) John's mistress has classically paired herself with the reinforcer, thereby increasing John's love for her. At 6:00 that evening, John walked into his home and said to his wife:

John: I've just been promoted to Vice-President of Operations.

Wife (monotonely): That's good. By the way, Jimmy went to the dentist today and didn't have any cavities.

The monotone reaction (extinction) of John's wife had three effects: (1) it decreased the likelihood of John feeling good about his promotion; (2) it decreased the likelihood that John will tell his wife about good experiences of his in the future; and (3) it increased John's feelings of irritation.

Consider two examples of a subordinate speaking up in a meeting with his manager and six of his peers. In the first example, the manager's behavior will increase the probability of the subordinate speaking up in group meetings. In the second example, the manager's behavior will decrease the probability.

Manager: How do you feel about our treatment of the bad debt reserve, Joan?

Subordinate: I don't think we've allocated enough reserves here. We've averaged 25% more than this over the last three years.

Manager (with strong inflection): Excellent point! I think we had better discuss Joan's idea that our allocation is underestimated here. John, how do you feel about it?

(The manager has followed Joan's response with what we will assume is a reinforcer to Joan; he has thereby increased the probability of Joan speaking up in meetings.)

Manager: How do you feel about our treatment of the bad debt reserve, Joan?

Subordinate: I don't think we've allocated enough reserves here. We've averaged 25 percent more than this over the last three years.

Manager (in an uninterested monotone, meanwhile looking down at papers in front of him): All right. Let's turn now to the next item on our agenda; here we've got the figures on our current inventory. John, how do you feel about these figures?

(The manager has *not* followed Joan's response with a reinforcer; he has thereby decreased the probability of Joan speaking up in meetings.)

It is important to note, in the second example, that the manager has not merely *decreased* the probability of his subordinate speaking up about the bad debt reserve; he has also decreased the probability of the subordinate speaking up in meetings generally. In the first example, the manager *increased* the likelihood that his subordinate will speak up at subsequent meetings.

The manager's behavior, in a specific situation, will influence his subordinate's behavior in all situations that are *similar* to that specific situation (for example, meetings). This accounts for the fact that people behave differently in *different* situations. The subordinate who rarely says anything in group meetings may be quite talkative in one-to-one interactions because he has been extinguished in the former instance and reinforced in the latter.

Again, extinction *always* leads to anger. (Azrin, 1964; Ferster, Culbertson, and Boren, 1975) When a manager does not respond to a subordinate's comments directly and immediately, the subordinate will experience feelings of irritation. (This crucial point will be discussed in more detail later.)

Operant, unlike classical, learning is directed toward the immediate environmental consequences of behavior. By "environmental consequences" we mean, primarily, other people's behavior, especially the behavior of people in higher level positions. Few stimuli have as strong an impact on an individual's behavior as does the behavior of another person. This explains why staff personnel and consultants often weaken their impact on line managers and on an organization when, after completing their "objective" study, they submit a written report. Figures and graphs rarely have a strong impact on an individual, and such reports are likely to gather dust in someone's desk drawer. Were the consultants to take the time to interact at a personal level by successfully establishing rapport with top management, it is much less likely that their recommendations would be ignored. Likewise, sales are rarely achieved by written correspondence; they require face-to-face interactions—again, because virtually no stimulus is as potentially reinforcing or aversive to an individual as is another person's behavior.

REINFORCEMENT
Bad consequences from "good" management

It is important to be specific when analyzing manager-subordinate interactions. The details of a manager's behavior (minute gestures, subtle changes in tone of voice, choice of words) as well as its timing can have a crucial impact on a subordinate. General theories of manager-subordinate interactions can therefore lead to mistakes on the manager's part. For instance, a general philosophy of "concern" for one's subordinates may sound like "good" management, but it can have unfortunate results. Consider the following example: A subordinate was known to be self-deprecating. He frequently used such phrases as, "I sure couldn't do that as well as you can," or "I sure am bad when it comes to adding figures." The manager supposedly wanted to eliminate this behavior. One day, the subordinate was asked to role-play a performance review in the presence of a group of people which included his manager. When the review was finished, the following exchange took place:

Subordinate: "Well, I sure bombed that one."

Manager (showing "concern"): "No you didn't, John. That was a fine job! I thought that was handled very well!"

Why is the subordinate self-deprecating? *Because people, especially his manager, reinforce that type of behavior.* The manager has followed his subordinate's self-deprecating response with a stimulus reinforcing to the subordinate, thereby *increasing* the probability that the subordinate will engage in similar behavior in the future. Indeed, the manager has actually decreased the subordinate's confidence and increased his dependency on others. A more effective response in this situation would be silence, or merely ignoring the response and addressing oneself to another topic (extinction). This response, by failing to reinforce the unwanted behavior, would decrease the probability of its recurrence. The subordinate would soon stop making self-deprecating responses if the manager were to stop reassuring (reinforcing) him and simply change the subject.

"Showing concern" for a subordinate often results in lengthy discussions with the subordinate about his problems and complaints. This is another example of a "good" management theory that is too general to be effective. If a manager's attention is reinforcing to a subordinate (as it frequently is), and if the subordinate only elicits this managerial attention when he complains about the company, then he will complain about the company whenever he can. For example: A large Midwestern company was undergoing a complete revamping of its sales department. Numerous firings and demotions, as well as promotions, were occurring. Some of the man-

agers asked that further changes be delayed so that the "dust could settle" because "morale was falling to a low level." Investigation showed that a typical interchange between a manager and his subordinate went as follows:

Subordinate: What the hell is going on here? I just found out they fired John Smith in the Western region. Hell, he's been with this company twenty-five years.

Manager: Well, why don't we go into my office and talk about it? (Reinforcer)

Subordinate: All right, but I don't know what the hell there is to talk about. When a guy gives up twenty-five years of his life and then has the company put him out in the street, I don't know what you're supposed to expect next.

Manager: Well, I think things are settling down now. (Reinforcer) How do you feel about your own position?

Subordinate: How the hell should I feel about my position! I'm scared. Everybody's scared. You've got a blood bath going and nobody knows who the axe will fall on next.

Manager: Now, Jim, you don't have anything to worry about. You're doing an excellent job. I was at corporate headquarters and all of us were talking about you and how well you were doing. You're one of the best salesmen we have and nobody questions that. (Strong reinforcer)

By following the subordinate's complaining response with reinforcers, the manager has increased the probability of further complaining responses on the part of his subordinate; in fact, he has increased the probability of low morale in his department. The manager's attention, concern, and compliments were contingent upon his subordinate complaining. A better response on the manager's part would have been a perfunctory acknowledgement of his subordinate's point, quickly followed by a change of subject:

Manager (in a quiet monotone): Oh, I don't think things are quite that bad. (Then quickly and with much more inflection): Say, how did your sales call go yesterday at Preston Corporation?

A valid objection might be raised that people need reassurance and concern when their behavior indicates they are frightened, upset, or lacking in confidence. The crucial element is timing, however. The time to give the salesman reassurance and compliments is when he says a sales call went well, not when he is complaining. Likewise, if a manager shows concern only when his secretary pouts she will pout in the future. If he shows interest on the other hand, when she expresses positive attitudes, she will hold positive attitudes. The time to tell one's wife she is liked by many people is when she says she has had a good time at a party, not when she says nobody likes her.

In other words, it is not concern that is important, but rather, *when* the concern is shown. To follow self-deprecatory or complaining response patterns with a show of concern is to reinforce and increase the probability of these responses. In both instances the manager might instead have replied with a quick monotone, "Maybe so," followed by a more interested, "Say, how are you coming along with your sales call on Preston Corporation?" While this might have been irritating to the sub-

ordinate (extinction), it would have *decreased* the probability of his ineffective behavior, and *increased* the probability of his focusing on relevant matters (sales). The road to hell is indeed paved with good intentions! A manager can destroy a subordinate's confidence by giving him reassurance and concern when he is self-deprecating.

In fact, there are many situations in which managers give subordinates attention and reassurance at the worst possible time. If a salesman does not successfully make a sale, many managers rush to his side, explore the situation in depth, condemn the customer, and reassure the salesman that he has made the best effort possible; whereas if the salesman successfully completes a sale, he is given a perfunctory pat on the back and sent away (extinction). The time to rush to the salesman's side, explore the intricacies of the transaction, and provide enthusiastic reassurance is when he has been successful, not when he has failed. The time to reassure the director of computer services is not when he apologizes for his inability to get reports out on time; it is when he does get the reports out on time. His apologies for tardiness would probably be best met with silence.

That we are loved by others is an insignificant matter. *Why* we are loved by others is of utmost importance. It is a relatively simple task to gather about ourselves those who love us when we are crushed by misfortune, when we feel despair, when we fail an appointed task, when we accept our inferiority, when we express our fears and self-doubts. Far more difficult is the task of gathering about ourselves those rare people who love us when we successfully accomplish our goals, when we are confident about our ability to handle a given task, when we are happy and content about our life.

Range of reinforcers

We will discuss how to diagnose reinforcers and aversive stimuli in Chapter 6. For the moment it is important to reemphasize that unusual stimuli can be and often are reinforcing to an individual. (Premack, 1959, 1962) Suppose we turn our reinforcement principle around to read: Any stimulus that increases the probability of a response recurring when it immediately follows the response is a reinforcer. When a particular type of behavior by a subordinate continually recurs, the manager should note what he himself is doing immediately after the behavior; that managerial behavior may well be a reinforcer to the subordinate.

Consider the following: A general manager of operations is talking to his subordinate, a plant superintendent. The general manager has always wanted his plant superintendent to fire the plant foreman, Paul Ruda. The plant superintendent rejects this idea, partially because he is a personal friend of Paul Ruda. The following interchange takes place:

Manager: How's Paul Ruda doing?

Subordinate: Well, he's fallen off a bit in the last few weeks. He's gotten a little lackadaisical.

Manager: How come?

Subordinate: I think it might be a personal problem. I think he's been having some trouble with his wife.

Manager (grimaces and makes a series of mildly skeptical, challenging responses): Do you really think it's due to a personal problem?

Subordinate: Yeah, I think it is.

Manager: Oh, come on. I don't think his personal life would have that much impact on him down here at the plant.

Subordinate: Sure it could. I was over at his house several weeks ago, and I know the problem is serious.

Manager: It can't be that serious.

Subordinate: The hell it's not serious. It's very serious, and it's having a very bad effect on him.

This example would seem to contradict our basic principle, but only because we often make wrong assumptions about what constitutes a reinforcer. The manager has emitted a series of skeptical, challenging responses, which have actually solidified his subordinate's position. The subordinate started off "thinking" Ruda's behavior was a personal problem and ended up "knowing" it. If following a response with a reinforcer indeed increases its probability of recurring, then a skeptical, challenging response by the manager is a reinforcer to this particular subordinate. Being astute, the manager accepts this fact and, on a later occasion, uses it to good advantage.

Manager: Have you made up your budget for next year?

Subordinate: Well, I've got the preliminary figures, but I think I might come in with a budget that is 96 percent of this year's.

[Most of the general manager's plants are estimating a budget that exceeds the present year's. Hence he wants to reinforce this subordinate's response.]

Manager: Ninety-six percent of this year's budget? I don't see how you can do it.

Subordinate: It won't be the easiest thing in the world, but I think we can do it.

Manager: I think you're making a mistake. I can't see how you could possibly go under this year's budget.

Subordinate: We run a pretty tight ship here. I'm quite sure we can hit 96 percent of budget.

Manager: Well, I doubt that you're going to make it.

Subordinate: Well, my own guess is that we'll not only make 96 percent, we might even go below it.

Can a skeptical, challenging response by the manager be a reinforcer to the subordinate? Absolutely.

The point is that virtually any stimulus is a reinforcer to someone. Many managers err in not being able to see and accept the fact that a stimulus that is quite aversive to them is reinforcing to several of their subordinates. In this example the subordinate initially "thought he might come in with a 96 percent budget," but firmly committed himself by the end of the interchange. It would now be emotionally difficult for him to come in with a higher budget. (We are not concerned with the appropriateness of the budget here, only with behavioral changes.) The manager has thus "motivated" his subordinate, not with a trite "pat on the back," but rather, with an argumentative response that is reinforcing to this particular subordinate.

Influence of subordinates on managers

Since the behavior of others has more impact on us than any other stimulus, it stands to reason that a subordinate can influence the judgments and attitudes of his superior. Influence depends not only on position, but also on behavior. To illustrate: A subordinate has determined that self-deprecating behavior in others is indeed reinforcing to her manager. She therefore engages in such behavior when her manager compliments her:

Manager: Michelle, you did a fine job on the sales call.

Subordinate (apologetically): Gee, I don't know. I think I made a few mistakes I shouldn't have made.

The subordinate has increased the probability that the manager will make positive comments to her. Also, by pairing herself with a stimulus reinforcing to her manager (self-deprecating behavior), she has increased the likelihood that the manager will think highly of her in future assessment and promotional situations.

Any individual can influence the behavior or any other person as long as there exists an opportunity to interact with that person.

Many managers find two or more of their subordinates interacting in a mutually positive manner aversive. This is especially true of chief executive officers. The "loneliness of command" often leads chief executives to feel even more alone and left out if they see two vice presidents chatting amicably and without any apparent need for their superior's advice and direction. This in turn leads the chief executive to reinforce negative comments by one vice president about another while giving real accomplishments short shrift.

Vice president, sales (walking into president's office): Say, I thought you would like to know we just sold Ford our first order of sheet roll steel.

President (looks up momentarily): Oh, that's good. I've got to pull these damn figures together for the board. (Extinction)

Vice president, sales (starts to walk out, then stops): By the way, I don't know if Carol (vice president, operations) will be able to give you those production figures by Thursday as you'd asked her to. (Pairs vice president of operations with aversive stimuli)

President (looks up with much more interest): When did you hear that? (Reinforcer to listener)

Vice president, sales: I heard her telling the auditors she's behind on those figures.

President: She always seems to be behind on figures. I don't know what the hell goes on in her mind. (Again reinforces critical attitude of vice president of sales)

Vice president, sales: Well, I don't think she feels they are too important.

President: There seem to be a few things she feels aren't important. (Reinforcer)

Vice president, sales: I know. I tried to get her to go with me on an important sales call, and she said there just wasn't enough time.

President: When did that happen?

Attention from the president is a rein-forcer to the vice president of sales. What is this attention contingent upon? Obviously not sales, since the announcement of a new customer was met with a perfunctory response by the president. Condemnation of a colleague, on the other hand, was met with a high degree of attention, inquisitiveness, and concern.

Operations and sales are often aversive to each other. This animosity is not innate. It is the result of the chief executive reinforcing mutually negative attitudes, which then sweep through the two departments. Destructive internal competition is the inevitable result. This internal criticalness is not confined to chief executive officers. The behavior of many managers indicates that close cooperative interactions between subordinates is aversive and will be broken through the subtle reinforcement of negative attitudes toward peers.

A possible solution lies in the subordinate's influence on his manager. A vice president can pair his president's reinforcement of such behavior with aversive stimuli. A subordinate can extinguish his manager's reinforcing comments when criticism of others occurs. It is important to note in the above example that the subordinate is also reinforcing the manager with his critical remarks about a colleague; stopping this reinforcement would alter the president's behavior.

The power of managerial influence

Any response by a subordinate that continually recurs in the presence of his manager is being reinforced by the manager. This broad statement may have exceptions. Obviously the manager cannot be new, for example; he must have interacted with the subordinate over a period of time in order to influence strongly the subordinate's behavior. Yet it is a statement most managers should simply accept as true, since it requires them to examine their own behavior when questioning the causes of a subordinate's behavior.

Sales managers, for instance, often agree with their superiors that the attitudes of their salesmen toward operations people are bad and should be changed. Yet the following example of an interchange between a sales manager and one of his salesmen is too often typical:

Sales manager: Mike, you're really not getting the sales we need out of your territory. How come?

Salesman: Well, I don't know how you can expect me to get sales when those bloody people in the plant can't make the product and never get it out the door on time.

Sales manager: Yeah, I know your problem. The plant manager is not really tough enough on his people. Well, do the best you can.

The manager's agreement has reinforced his subordinate's negative attitudes toward operations people. Notice also that both the salesman and the manager have paired operations people with aversive stimuli—a response that is not likely to enhance positive attitudes. Yet this manager would be the first to agree with higher management that attitudes must be "cleaned up"; he would be sincere in both instances.

Not only are negative attitudes toward fellow employees too often reinforced, but also negative attitudes toward the one source of all money to the organization, its customers.

Sales manager: How did your call go on United Corporation?

Salesman: Not good.

Sales manager: How come?

Salesman: Those people run one of the most disorganized places I've ever seen.

Sales manager: I know. They really don't have much going for them.

Salesman: They kept me waiting for over a half hour.

Sales manager (sympathetically): That must have been frustrating.

Salesman: Then when I did get in to see them, they gave me all of ten minutes.

Sales manager: And they're so dumb over there, they probably didn't understand anything you said anyway.

Salesman: I don't think they know their butt from a hole in the ground.

Sales manager: I know. I had the same trouble when I used to call on them. It is irritating.

This type of all-too-common interaction has the effect of decreasing sales for the company. It would be highly unlikely that this salesman could make an effective sales call on this customer in the future. Indeed, subconsciously he would not want to since failure with the customer is being so amply reinforced by his manager.

Organizations rarely reinforce managers for managing the behavior of their subordinates properly. Promotions to management levels are too often based on a person's technical competence or experience, a policy that often leads to failure. An individual reinforced (promoted) for his technical abilities continues to focus on technical problems rather than on his subordinates and their behavior. He often ends up with weak, ineffective subordinates because he does all the work and will not delegate. Eventually, the work load becomes too great, and his department functions at minimally adequate levels. If the company grows, more work is shunted to his department until a collapse takes place.

This sequence of events is especially true in the case of entrepreneurs who, when they start a company, must do everything themselves. If the company grows, the response of doing everything oneself is being reinforced. When the company grows to the point at which delegation of authority and responsibility is absolutely essential, the entrepreneur is unable to delegate. Why should he? He has been reinforced for doing everything himself. Changes in his behavior will require forceful external influences.

Causes of behavior are external

The foregoing example raises an important point. The causes of an individual's behavior are external and often stem from the behavior of his manager and, to a lesser degree, that of other people around him. The quickest way to change behavior is to change the individual's environment, especially his interpersonal environment. An individual can be quite successful under one manager and cause serious problems under another, even though his position remains unchanged. (One of the quickest ways to change the behavior of everyone in an organization is to change the chief executive officer.)

It is often tempting, nevertheless, to say that behavior is internally caused (by factors within the individual himself). This allows us to avoid blame for another person's incompetence by criticizing his faults rather than our own. In other words, we pair failures with our subordinates rather than with ourselves. This approach leads us into a blind alley, however. Outside of performing a lobotomy, there is little anyone can do to change what goes on inside an individual; even the behavioral changes caused by psychotherapists come about, not because of the patient's new and brilliant insights, but because of his interaction with and the behavior of the therapist. It is our behavior, not internal factors, that leads others to behave the way they do in our presence. *The most effective way to change an individual's behavior in the work setting, therefore, is to change his manager's behavior.* Conversely, any changes effected in the individual, without corresponding changes in the manager, will usually be short-lived.

Shaping behavior

Following a desirable response with a reinforcer increases its probability of recurring; but suppose the desirable response never occurs in the first place. We may be ready to jump in with a strong reinforcer when a lovely young lady says, "I love you," but what if she never says it? How can we reinforce behavior that is not occurring at all?

The answer is that we must "shape" behavior by reinforcing successive approximations to the desired response. (Skinner, 1938) The instance in which the manager gave a skeptical, challenging (reinforcing) response to his plant manager's budget projection was an instance of shaping. The subordinate initially "thought" he could make a 96 percent budget. By successively reinforcing this response, the manager made it stronger and stronger until the subordinate "knew" he was going to make the budget, or better.

Consider the following example in which a salesman is attempting to elicit a "purchase response" from a prospective customer:

Customer: So our present supplier is taking care of our needs.

Salesman: I think you might be making a mistake relying on only one supplier.

Customer: Well, you may have a point there.

Salesman: I believe you're right. Having two suppliers can give you better service.

Customer: I suppose I could try you on a small order.

Salesman: I believe you would be quite happy you did. You would have the sense of security of having a second source if anything happened to your other one.

Customer: How would I go about placing an order if I wanted to?

Salesman: Your wish is my command. Just tell me what you'd like now and I'll make sure you get it.

Customer: I suppose I could give you a small order for six gross of .5 nuts and bolts and see how you do.

Salesman: Excellent! I think you're making an excellent decision. When would you like them?

The salesman has successfully shaped the customer into a purchase response. It is important, of course, to know what is reinforcing to a specific customer (sometimes violent arguments are). Notice also that each time the salesman uses a reinforcer, he is pairing himself with it; he is becoming a reinforcer to the customer and

increasing the probability that the customer will see him on subsequent visits.

The point of shaping is to reinforce the listener's slightest tendency toward the desired response. Had the salesman settled for nothing but a large order, it is doubtful that he would have gotten any order at all. By aiming only for the big order, he would not have reinforced small, tentative responses on the customer's part that leaned in the direction of making a purchase—and by not reinforcing the responses, he would have extinguished them! Indeed, it is surprising how few salesmen even reinforce a customer who says, "I'll place the order with you." Most salesmen merely pick up their order books and start writing; then they wonder why their relationship with customers is so tentative.

Rational vs. reinforcement shaping

Behavior is not necessarily a rational, objective process. Consider the case of a somewhat contentious person who finds arguments with his manager reinforcing (probably because arguments have been paired with an emotional response on the manager's part).

Manager: Well, the consensus of opinion seems to be that we start shipping our goods by rail instead of trucking them. Dick, we haven't heard from you about it. How do you feel?

Subordinate: Well, I'm not as certain as apparently everyone else is that we should do it that way. You know, we really don't have solid figures on what it will cost us to ship by rail.

Manager: Yes, but the estimates given us by

the railroad people are substantially below our trucking costs.

Subordinate: Maybe, but we don't know if those estimates will hold water.

Manager: We don't know that they won't hold water.

Subordinate: I've got a friend who started to use rail and found out the estimates of cost were underestimated by 50 percent.

Manager: That doesn't mean this railroad is underestimating our cost.

Subordinate: Maybe not, but you know the railroad people never have pinned down their costs too well.

Manager: I think the service they have given us in the past when we did use them was pretty accurate.

Subordinate: Well, I think we're making a mistake. We know what the shipping costs are when we use trucks, and we are moving into an area where we don't know what's going to hit us. I think we should stay with trucking for our own good.

Unrealistic though it sounds, the subordinate's final determined option for trucking is not the result of rational, logical analysis; it is, rather, the result of reinforced shaping by the manager. The subordinate's response has been shaped from one of tentative choice (favoring trucking) to the point at which there is little doubt in his mind that trucking is the most effective alternative. Had the manager, instead of engaging in a debate, greeted his subordinate's initial tentative response with mild acceptance, he would have decreased the probability of the subordinate's firm, dissenting opinion.

Feelings are the fathers of thoughts. Virtually all management decisions involve subjective judgments. An individual's perceptions of an issue can result from his feelings toward the people holding a given position on the issue as much as from rational analysis. In the above example, had the consensus favored trucking, that particular subordinate might well have opted for shipping by rail—and would have supplied excellent reasons for using the railroad, because there are two sides to any management issue. Which one a person chooses often depends on his feelings toward the other people involved in the decision rather than on his feelings about the issue itself. Any expressed idea has to come from (be paired with) a person. If that person is an aversive stimulus to an individual, the probability is increased that the individual will disagree with the idea.

This is a much more common phenomenon than most people believe. In the example just mentioned, the manager—and possibly the group as a whole—constituted aversive stimuli to the subordinate, hence his oppositional response. Suppose, however, a manager has just given such a subordinate a large, unexpected raise. By pairing himself with this strong reinforcer, the manager has increased the probability that the subordinate will agree with any position the manager takes on a given matter. Both would probably be shocked if the subordinate were to oppose the manager in a meeting taking place a day after the raise was given. An individual assumes the position that is paired with the strongest reinforcers for him. This explains why management is for management, labor is for labor, and neither stands up for a rational, just analysis of the issues.

Shaping is an important concept for the manager. Wisely used, it can overcome a subordinate's resistance to the manager's views. Lest the manager fear developing a group of subordinates in his own image, however, he must remember that he should also reinforce reasonable dissension. Determining what is reasonable and what is not is the manager's responsibility and, in making this decision, the *frequency* of the behavior is his best criterion. (For example, repetitious contrariness by a subordinate is not reasonable.) Complaints should be given minimal attention when they come from a subordinate who *frequently* complains; they should be thoroughly explored when they come from a subordinate who rarely complains. Overly positive assessments of problem situations by a subordinate should be given short shrift when such assessments are frequent and unrealistic; they should be amply reinforced, however, when given by a constantly complaining subordinate.

Shaping someone's behavior requires tolerance and patience. It is surprising how tolerant and patient we are in shaping a child's behavior, but not an adult's. In helping a child make the "th" sound, for example, most people will reinforce reasonable approximations by the child with such phrases as, "That's good, honey. Now try it again. Beautiful! Try it one more time. Oh, that's very good!" When it comes to adults, however, our criteria are very stringent indeed; we demand precisely what we want or no reinforcement! This is a mistake and usually ensures our getting nothing. The girl may not say "I love you," but she may say, "You have a nice tie on." The man who responds with, "Actually I bought it because it matched the color of your eyes" is the man to whom she eventually will say "I love you." The man who finds her comment irrelevant will extinguish it *and* the possibility of more meaningful comments in the future.

Giving the person the benefit of the doubt is an important principle of life. It means that tentative gestures in the appropriate direction will be reinforced, thus increasing the likelihood of correctly shaping the person's behavior. Reacting with suspicion and distrust to tentative gestures, however, ensures extinction of those gestures, thus precluding the possibility of more intense and frequent behavior along the same lines.

EXTINCTION
Extinction after constant vs. periodic reinforcement

We have stated (Principle VI) that any response not immediately followed by a reinforcer has a lesser probability of recurring. This is called extinction. Unfortunately, the situation is not quite as simple as it first appears. It is true that when a particular response has been reinforced *every time* it has occurred, if the reinforcement is suddenly stopped, the response will quickly cease to occur. (Ferster and Skinner, 1957) Every time we drop something and look down for it (response), it is always there (reinforcement) because of the force of gravity. This does not hold true in outer space, however, and astronauts have easily adapted to looking around and up rather than down for dropped objects; the response of looking down has quickly extinguished because it had been reinforced every time in the men's past experiences.

Suppose, however, we don't follow every response with a reinforcer; rather, we reinforce every tenth response, on an average. That is, we might reinforce the eighth response of a given behavior, then the twenty-second response, the thirty-first response, and so on. We reinforce the response at a rate which averages every tenth occurrence of the behavior, but the reinforcement is given randomly. Extinction in this case takes much longer. *A response will have to be emitted many more times during extinction before it stops occurring if it has previously had periodic rather than constant reinforcement.* (Ferster and Skinner, 1957) Gambling behavior illustrates this situation. If a gambler who places bets on horses wins every time, he will soon stop wagering on horses if he suddenly begins losing every time. If he wins *periodically*, however, he will have to lose consistently many more times before he stops gambling completely. Such consistent losing is unlikely, which accounts for the tenacity and persistence of gamblers.

Not only is the manager not expected to reinforce every instance of constructive behavior, but also it would be inappropriate to do so. To maintain a high level of "prospecting" by a salesman, the manager should *periodically* go over his new sales calls and reinforce him for making them. This reinforcement should be given more

frequently initially. This periodic reinforcement will help maintain high levels of "prospecting" and make this important behavior more resistant to extinction.

Fixed time reinforcement

In some instances, an individual is reinforced on a time schedule. If we reinforce an individual for a particular response every half hour, we will elicit virtually no responding immediately after the half hour (reinforcement), followed by very little response for 15 to 20 minutes and then a gradual build-up preceding the time of reinforcement (the half hour). (Hilgard and Bower, 1975; Hilgard and Marquis, 1940) Suppose a report card is reinforcing to a child and he receives it every five weeks. He will normally devote minimal time and energy to homework for two or three weeks after he has received the report card. After three weeks, his attention starts slowly to drift back to his homework. After four weeks, he is spending still more time on his homework. After four and a half weeks have elapsed he will again be devoting much time and energy to his homework until he receives his next report card, at which time the cycle will repeat itself.

In industry, a subordinate's performance reviews are normally arranged on a similar schedule. If a performance review is given every six months, it will normally have its greatest impact for the few days prior to the review. It will have little impact during the long interim periods. The same is true of such regularly scheduled reinforcers as pay schedules and sales and expenditure reports. To the extent that a monthly sales performance report is a reinforcer to an employee, it will affect his behavior immediately prior to its issuance; it will have little impact during the long interim periods. To be effective, therefore, performance reviews, reports, compensation, and other reinforcers should be given at random intervals as much as possible, rather than on a rigid time-contingency schedule with long interim periods. This is, incidentally, one of the reasons a manager's behavior is so important in the work setting. Only the manager's behavior has the flexibility to be effectively used at the appropriate time.

Doing nothing does something

The effects of extinction are, therefore, contingent upon the prior history of reinforcement. Given the difference of constant and periodic reinforcement, however, the longer the history of reinforcement, the more resistant to extinction is the response.

As mentioned previously, there is one notable exception to our rule that not following a response with a reinforcer decreases its probability of recurring. This exception occurs when the response being extinguished is a hostile, aggressive response. It occurs because experiencing extinction is a frustrating situation that leads to anger and a desire to attack someone or something. We often engage in behavior because it has been followed by something we like; having the same behavior suddenly followed by nothing is irritating.

Consider the following interchange. The manager in this case is normally a cheerful, emotionally expressive person who readily compliments his subordinates.

Subordinate: We just got the figures in on our plant efficiency for last month. We ran the plant at 98.7 percent efficiency, our best record yet.

Manager (in a monotone): How did the figures on quality control come out?

This is a frustrating experience for the subordinate. It has decreased both the likelihood of his feeling good about constructive results and his desire to tell his manager about them. It has also, however, increased the probability of irritation on his part. He is likely to wonder why his manager "is in such a lousy mood." If this irritation shows itself, it, too, will have to be extinguished.

Aggressive behavior can be extinguished, but it shows an initial increase in intensity during the process. (Reynolds, 1975) Again, the manager must always be alert to what is really reinforcing or aversive to his subordinates. Suppose an indecisive manager is an aversive stimulus to his faster-paced subordinate. Seeing his manager uncomfortable or uneasy may then be a reinforcer to the subordinate. Consider the following interaction between manager and subordinate in a group meeting:

Manager: Is there anything else we should be discussing here?

Subordinate: Yeah. When are we going to get an answer on whether or not we bring in that new 707 computer?

Manager (feeling uneasy): Well, we're going to be discussing that in the finance committee next Friday.

Subordinate: Well, that decision's been hanging in the air for over two months now. Don't you think management has had enough time?

Manager (shifts in chair and tries to avoid

eye contact with anyone): Well, you know it's a complex issue and it takes time to pin everything down.

Subordinate: Good grief, it doesn't take that much time. Are we going to get a definite answer out of the finance committee Friday?

Manager (quite uncomfortable now): Well, I should probably have some news for you by then.

Subordinate: I certainly hope so. We can't go anywhere without decisions around here.

In this example, the manager has *reinforced* his subordinate's aggressive responses by exhibiting uncomfortable feelings in the presence of others. Suppose we now tell the manager to "toughen up" and extinguish those responses by his subordinate. The manager can accomplish this by responding in a relaxed manner to the subordinate's questions. This will at first increase the probability and intensity of the subordinate's aggressive responses because the manager will no longer be reinforcing them; the subordinate will find his manager's nonchalance frustrating. However, extinction will eventually occur.

Problems of new managers

Extinction often plays a role in the animosity new managers encounter in their subordinates. All managers reinforce various behavior patterns they enjoy in different subordinates. Hence, Manager A may reinforce (with his laughter) a good sense of humor in one subordinate and (with his admiration) impulsive action in another subordinate. After six months under Manager A, the two subordinates "know what to expect"; their behavior has been shaped, and they engage in it with subconscious satisfaction because it is periodically reinforced by their manager. After five years under Manager A, their behavior is quite stable. Now, however, Manager B arrives to assume A's position. He will almost always reinforce different types of behavior in the two subordinates from his predecessor. More important, he will *not* reinforce behavior that was previously reinforced by Manager A. Manager B, for example, may find the one subordinate's sense of humor a "time waster" and the other subordinate's impulsivity a cause of too many mistakes. Even if Manager B does not reprimand these types of behavior, he will certainly not reinforce them. The extinction that results almost invariably leads to animosity toward the new manager.

Extinction, in fact, is unavoidable when a manager assumes a new position, because he will always extinguish some behaviors previously reinforced, and, until full shaping has taken place, this will be a frustrating experience for his new subordinates.

The problem is intensified because most managers "pull back" from responding when they are given authority and responsibility in new and unfamiliar areas. Their immediate goal is to find out what is happening and get their feet on firm ground before giving guidance, direction, praise, and reprimands. If their predecessor was quite liberal in reinforcing his subordinates, there will be a sudden drop in the frequency of reinforcement. This partly explains the behind-the-back, hostile remarks subordinates often direct at new managers. If, however, the previous manager was an aversive stimulus to the subordinates and rarely gave out reinforcers, "extinction anger" will be minimized when the new manager takes over. (Of course, other factors may be involved as well. The new manager, for example, may use too many aversive stimuli, thus contributing to his subordinates' feelings of anger.)

Managerial failures caused by extinction

If the typical manager could be justly accused of any one failing, it would be that he misses far too many opportunities to reinforce subordinates. This may result from his uneasiness at having authority over others, his lack of emotional expressiveness, or the fact that he does not like to see subordinates enjoy their work. Whatever the reason, extinction is not only an all too common phenomenon in manager-subordinate interactions, but is probably *the* most common phenomenon in manager-subordinate interactions.

Extinction also accounts, in large part, for the frequent lack of communication and understanding that occurs between a manager and the people below him, as the following example illustrates:

Subordinate: (enthusiastically): I think the merger possibilities are excellent, and I think we ought to take this company over; I know a lot of people here don't feel that way, but I think our profits per share would eventually increase 30 percent if we bought this company.

Manager (looking at his watch): I've got to get into a management committee meeting in a few minutes. Maybe we can discuss this some other time.

The subordinate will leave this meeting not knowing where he stands, what his manager is thinking, what is expected of him. As a result, he may not diligently pursue his analysis of the merger. At a subsequent meeting, however, the manager may reprimand him for this neglect of duty; the manager may want the merger desperately, but he has failed to communicate his feelings. The manager may reasonably state that he did indeed have a meeting to attend and was preoccupied with it, hence the inadvertent extinction of his subordinate's enthusiasm. Had the manager assumed responsibility for his subordinate's behavior, however, he would have taken the three seconds necessary to say, "It sounds great to me" in their initial meeting on the topic. This is the reason the emotionally expressive person has an advantage over others managerially; his emotional expressiveness tells people where they stand and what is expected of them.

Managerial guidance is a vital reinforcer. If a subordinate states, "We just got AIC as a customer, but we lost DOT," the manager should at least quietly mutter "Excellent" in the middle of the statement and frown at the end of it. The subordinate will then be more likely to focus on getting customers than he will if the manager remains silent. Even trite exchanges have a subtle influence. Managers frequently ask their subordinates, "How's it going?" before going on to the topic they want to discuss. This often elicits a positive response, "Good," reflecting a positive attitude. The manager should quickly reinforce this attitude ("Excellent" or "I'm glad to hear that") before moving to his target topic. Most managers instead fire back another question ("How are the sales figures?"). Subordinates soon stop responding with "Good." The manager has extinguished the response, and, more important, he has missed an opportunity to reinforce constructive behavior and pair himself with a mild reinforcer in the process.

Extinction is a difficult experience. Most people know a married couple in which the husband is a negative, complaining person who is not above making critical remarks about his wife in front of others. Yet his wife is a sweet, quiet, unassuming person who would not hurt anyone. Most men dream of how pleasant their lives would be married to someone as nice as that woman. What is not seen is the terrible frustration and resulting hostility the husband experiences when he desperately, but vainly, tries to elicit an emotional reaction from his quiet, unassuming wife. The result of his efforts is extinction; and the result of extinction is his complaining, critical behavior.

The effects of extinction are pervasive and frequently invade long-term relationships. Consider the following interchange by a newly married couple after their first meal in their new apartment:

Husband: That was a wonderful dinner, darling.

Wife: Thank you, sweetheart.

Husband: I love you very much.

Wife: I love you too.

This is indeed love-mutual reinforcement. (The more cynical reader must remember that these are newlyweds.) Since this interchange must end sometime, we must ask, what happens to the last response in the interaction? It starts to undergo extinction. If we return to our couple three months later, we would hear words to the effect:

Husband: That was a wonderful dinner, darling.

Wife: Thank you, sweetheart.

Husband: I love you very much.

Wife: (smiles weakly and clears the table)

Three months later:

Husband: That was a wonderful dinner, darling.

Wife: Thank you, sweetheart. (clears the table)

Three months later:

Husband: That was a wonderful dinner, darling. (gets up to read the paper)

Three months later:

It is difficult in any long-term relationship to override the effects of extinction. In the work setting, the manager who uses extinction frequently and has managed the same people for a long time will usually be found to have a lethargic, slow-paced department that resembles a cemetery.

Constructive use of extinction

It is important to note that extinction can be used in a positive sense. Allowing a subordinate to air his negative views or holding group gripe or crisis intervention sessions are of little consequence in and of themselves. The important factor is whether the negative views or gripes are reinforced or extinguished. Indeed, such sessions can be destructive if the manager or others in the group start reinforcing complaining behavior, since complaints can easily grow beyond the bounds of reality. In such instances extinction must be relied upon to stop the destructive behavior.

Yet the effect of managerial extinction is paradoxically dependent upon the manager's history of reinforcing his subordinates. If he has rarely reinforced his subordinates, withholding reinforcement at an appropriate time will have minimal impact. The superior who has never told his subordinate he is doing an excellent job will have little influence on his subordinate's gripes by *not* telling the subordinate he is doing an excellent job when his subordinate is complaining. A primary reason managers should use reinforcers frequently, therefore, is that it gives the manager the added tool of extinction as a means of influencing behavior. Using reinforcers infrequently blunts the impact of deliberate use of extinction since the manager is always extinguishing behavior anyway. The parent who rarely gives his child love has minimal impact if he withholds his love deliberately when his child is behaving badly. Again, the manager who rarely reinforces his subordinates will eventually end up with a lethargic or frustrated department and any attempted constructive use of extinction will have minimal impact.

The constructive use of extinction is especially important in personnel counselling. Too many personnel departments reinforce complaining behavior by management and labor employees with their concern and sympathy. This reaps them two benefits. First, it increases conflicts in the company, thus increasing the importance and necessity of their jobs. Second, by giving concern and sympathy, they pair themselves with reinforcers, thus leading people to like them more and turn to them in times of trouble. Sensitivity group leaders also fall into the trap, at times, of extinguishing positive attitudes and reinforcing, with their emotional support, depression, fear, anger, and other deleterious emotions. This ensures the need for more sensitivity group sessions. Does a therapist find dependence or independence reinforcing in a patient? Does a divorce attorney find cooperation or animosity toward a spouse reinforcing in his client? Does a police department find high or low crime rate statistics reinforcing? Reinforcement and extinction, like most potent tools, can be used constructively or destructively.

SUMMARY

Managers are required to pair themselves with aversive stimuli. They have to say "no" periodically, to reprimand, to demote, and to fire. They should therefore take every opportunity to pair themselves with reinforcers by reinforcing constructive behavior. This will increase their subordinates' effectiveness and motivation, minimize misunderstandings, and enormously enhance the cooperative manager-subordinate relationship.

Extinction is probably the most frequently used tool of managers. It creates a deadly atmosphere and accounts for much of the unhappiness found in private industry. For this reason, *one of the primary responsibilities of upper-level managers is to reinforce their subordinates for reinforcing their subordinates.*

Manager: What did you do when you found out Jim did such a good job?

Subordinate: I told him we were sending a memo up to the president on it and I promised him lunch at any restaurant he picked.

Manager: Beautiful! That's why you're so damned effective. You're really a helluva manager, Bob.

The atmosphere created by this type of interchange will permeate this department just as the atmosphere created in a home will be most positive when each spouse reinforces the other spouse for reinforcing the children.

The effective manager also reinforces positive attitudes by subordinates toward customers, peers, and superiors; he reinforces confidence, competence; he reinforces laughter and fun in the work setting; he reinforces warm, close cooperation between subordinates; he reinforces *behavior* that he feels will lead to constructive results rather than waiting for the results themselves. The effective manager realizes he has to use extinction on occasion, when negative attitudes are unrealistically frequent, when negative emotional reactions are too intense. He also realizes, however, that he must counterbalance the inherent tendency toward extinction with a creative thrust toward reinforcement.

The effective manager (and person) develops a greater determination to seek out the good in others, a greater perceptiveness in seeing the good when it appears and, above all, the wisdom to emotionally express appreciation for the good he does see.

CLASSROOM EXERCISES

1. Have several students give a two-minute talk to the class on any topic. Have one side of the class watch the lecturer and the other side never look at him. Which side does he end up talking to? What are his feelings?

2. Ask your partner a question. When the answer has been fully given, ask a question on an entirely different topic (extinction). Repeat several times. Examine the feelings of the person giving the answers.

3. Ask three people a question. After the first has answered, emotionally reinforce him. After the second has answered, say nothing, look down at your watch, and then ask the third person the question.

4. Try to shape another person to agree to go somewhere with you.

5. Your partner engages in self-deprecation. Elicit the self-deprecation (e.g., How did you do on the exam?), extinguish it, and try to shape more positive self-attitudes.

6. Your partner is emotionally upset and complaining about the unfairness of the instructor. Calm him down.

7. Someone tells you they said nice things about you to a mutual friend. They are obviously lying. What should you say to them while they are telling you these lies.

8. Ask your partner what he thinks your grade should be in this class. Try to shape him to a higher grade.

9. Your partner is bragging about an "A" he just received. React to his comments.

10. Your partner is socially withdrawn. Shape a more outgoing, friendly approach toward people.

11. Pick two people who have opposing views on a topic. Using pairings, reinforcement, and extinction, see if they can change each other's viewpoint.

12. Have two people each give a two-minute talk on any topic. Applaud the first speaker, remain silent after the second speaker is

finished. Examine the feelings of the two speakers.

13. Have your partner tell you about the most exciting experience of his life. Show no interest. Then ask him if he wants to hear about your most exciting experience.

SUGGESTED READINGS

Catonia, C. A., editor: Contemporary research in operant behavior, Glenview, Ill., 1968, Scott, Foresman and Co.

Includes papers on important topics in operant conditioning, such as the nature of reinforcement, schedules of reinforcement, stimulus control, aversive control, and others. Also includes a very good glossary of terms with thorough definitions.

McGregor, D.: Leadership and motivation, Cambridge, Mass., 1968, The M.I.T. Press.

A summary of the concepts of one of the foremost organizational behaviorists of our time.

Reynolds, G. S.: A primer of operant conditioning, Glenview, Ill., 1975, Scott, Foresman and Co.

An excellent review of the principles of operant conditioning. Highly recommended for laymen.

CHAPTER 5

Changing behavior by changing consequences

punishment and avoidance learning
OPERANT LEARNING II

There is so much good in the worst of us,
And so much bad in the best of us,
That it ill behooves any of us
To find fault with the rest of us.
ANONYMOUS

We have seen how a stimulus becomes a reinforcer or an aversive stimulus. We have also noted the effects of following a response with a reinforcer and extinguishing the response by not following it with a reinforcer. Let us now look at the effects that aversive stimuli have on our behavior.

PRINCIPLE VII: PUNISHMENT
Any response immediately followed by an aversive stimulus has a lesser probability of recurring (Estes & Skinner, 1941; Estes, 1944)

Following a response with an aversive stimulus is known as punishment. (Hilgard & Bower, 1975; Kling & Riggs, 1971) Again, the principle is quite simple; how-

ever, there are two considerations one must always bear in mind. One is the intensity of the aversive stimulus. If the stimulus is intensely aversive, it will lower the probability of the response quickly and to a very low level. (Camp, Raymond and Church, 1967; Estes, 1944; Karsh, 1962) If the stimulus is only mildly aversive, however, the response may recur, although at a weaker level. (Azrin, 1960; Estes, 1944; Karsh, 1962) The other consideration is the history of the response. If it has a long history of reinforcement, following it with an aversive stimulus has special effects, which we will discuss later in the chapter.

Responses followed by intense aversive stimuli

Following a response with a stimulus intensely aversive to the other person can potentially stop the response from ever recurring. For example: A spontaneous, aggressive line manager was complaining that a highly competent but somewhat sensitive staff man was not taking the initiative in communicating with him any more. A meeting was held consisting of both men and a psychologist:

Psychologist (to staff man): Jim, how do you feel about Mike here? Is there anything about him that might bother you a little bit?

Staff man (somewhat hesitatingly): Well . . . I sometimes think Mike says things he doesn't really feel, I think . . .

Line manager (interrupting staff man and pounding hand on desk): Oh, not true! Dammit, that's just not true!

Psychologist (to staff man after quieting Mike down): Are there any other feelings you have toward Mike that you would like to explore?

Staff man: No . . . no, I think that about covers it.

Two things have occurred here. First, the line manager has obviously followed the staff man's attempts to communicate with him with a stimulus intensely aversive to the staff man. The line manager's behavior has, consequently, decreased the probability of the staff man communicating with him. This is not an atypical situation in industry. Managers often complain about the "lack of something" in a subordinate's behavior, yet closer examination reveals that when that "something" did occur, the manager followed it with a

response that was aversive to the subordinate. Managers, for example, often complain about the lack of people who will "*really* tell me what they think"; when a subordinate does just that, however, he often finds himself meeting a barrage of criticism or an emotional self-justification (aversive stimuli) from the manager.

The second occurrence in the above example is that the line manager has also paired *himself* with stimuli intensely aversive to the staff man. He will therefore become a more aversive stimulus to the staff man, and this will further decrease the probability of the staff man communicating with him. Aversive stimuli, as we shall see, are avoided. The critical point to remember here is that the use of aversive stimuli pairs the user with those aversive stimuli (Chapter 2); to that extent, the user will himself become an aversive stimulus.

Let us look at a slightly more constructive use of aversive stimuli to knock out a response. A general sales manager has been having difficulty getting one of his regional sales managers to give feedback to the regional manager's subordinates. The general manager knows that "interference by people over him" is an intense aversive stimulus to the regional manager.

General manager: How's Dick [a salesman] coming along?

Regional manager: He's doing all right.

General manager: Is he taking more initiative in getting out to see his customers?

Regional manager: Frankly, I haven't seen much change in him.

General manager: Have you talked to him about it recently?

Regional manager: Well, I've been at meetings for the last two or three weeks and I've been working with Jack a good deal of the time on those financial reports. I haven't really had a chance to talk to Dick.

General manager (grimaces): Well, why don't I talk to him about it while I'm here. (Aversive stimulus, interference)

Regional manager (quickly and spontaneously): No, that's all right, I'll set up a meeting to see him tomorrow morning and make sure we go over it.

General manager: Excellent! (Reinforcer)

This manager has decreased the probability of his regional manager avoiding a discussion of Dick's lack of initiative with Dick himself. By using aversive stimuli, however, the manager has taken two risks. First, he has paired himself with an aversive stimulus. Second, by following an "admission of guilt" with an aversive stimulus, the general manager has decreased the probability that the regional manager will again tell him about things he has *not* done.

This second factor is frequently a cause of the "breakdown in communications" so often discussed in industry. The subordinate does not want to "admit" his mistakes to his manager for fear of encountering aversive stimuli from the manager. His reluctance is usually justified, since telling his immediate superior about something he did that he should not have done (or vice versa) does indeed elicit anger (aversive stimuli). If the aversive stimuli are intense enough, the subordinate will be reluctant to pass on any bad news to his manager, even news concerning matters for which the subordinate has no responsibility. This situation is not uncommon in departments headed up by hypercritical managers who go into a tirade at the slightest opportunity.

These shortcomings can be somewhat minimized if the manager pairs himself with reinforcers whenever possible. He should also use only mild aversive stimuli. This will not have as dramatic an impact on the behavior of his subordinates as will the use of intense aversive stimuli, but, as we shall see, certain undesirable side effects will not occur. (Of course, if the manager's interactions with his subordinates consist *only* of mild aversive stimuli but no reinforcers, he will become an aversive stimulus to his subordinates.)

It must be remembered that what constitutes an intense aversive stimulus to an individual is a highly personal matter, contingent upon his past experiences. It does not necessarily involve shouting and screaming. For example, a sensitive young man had recently been evaluated and reviewed by a management psychologist. The psychologist had told him to be less subservient with authority figures, to speak up for his ideas more forcefully, and to be less awed by people in high positions. (The young man was four levels below the president.) Several days after the review, the young man ran into the president and told him some of the things he had discussed with the psychologist. He concluded by saying, "And frankly, I'm not going to treat you like Jesus Christ any more," to which the president quietly, but indignantly, responded, "Well, I am the president after all."

The president's quiet remark virtually eliminated any gains the psychologist had made in this area. It was an intense aversive stimulus to the young man, an aversive stimulus that immediately followed the response of "speaking up more forcefully to authority figures." A competent person can probably change almost any behavior in an individual, but only the manager can maintain the changes. And if the manager does not like the changes, he can eliminate them in short order, as the above example indicates.

Punishment as a destructive tool

Just as managers reinforce destructive behavior (e.g., showing interest when one subordinate downgrades another), so too can they punish constructive behavior. The salesman who exceeds his quota by a wide margin is "rewarded" by having his quota increased an inordinate amount the next year. Hourly workers who exceed their piece-rate suddenly find the rate increased. If such changes must be made, they should be made gradually and paired with effective incentives (reinforcers).

Intensely competitive managers often lock themselves into direct competition with their own subordinates. As a consequence, the subordinates' practical achievements (which increase profits) are punished by their managers. Consider the following examples:

Salesman: I just sold ten carloads of tires to BIM Corporation.

Sales manager (who should have reinforced): That's good, but you still haven't gotten into Tad Corporation; when are we going to get an order from them? (Punishment)

Manager: Jim, how come you never call on Lod Company?

Subordinate: I do. I called on them last week.

Manager (who should have reinforced): What happened? (Extinction)

Subordinate: I'm supposed to get together with them on Friday. They said they would place a small order with me in order to try out our product.

Manager: (who should have reinforced): God, don't blow it! (Punishment)

Clearly, another person's achievements are not necessarily reinforcing to the manager. A company that promotes its best salesman into a managerial position simply because he excels in sales often runs into this difficulty. The individual is the best salesman because he is so competitive. He is a poor manager for precisely the same reason; he is so competitive that he punishes success in others, even his own subordinates. Thus, performance is not the best criterion for promotions.

Punishment often destroys self-confidence. Certainly, confidence in one's own abilities helps one to function effectively in the industrial or business setting. Yet many managers seem intent on destroying their subordinates' confidence. Every manager should ask himself, "Is confidence in a subordinate really reinforcing to me?" In the following examples, the answer apparently is "No."

Subordinate: I think the management committee is really going to be impressed with this report on inventory. I think we did a good job.

Manager: Don't be too optimistic. There are a couple of guys on that management committee whom you can never please. (Punishment)

Salesman (in the middle of a defensive argument with the manager): I'm a good salesman.

Manager: Yeah, but you've got a lot to learn. I used to think I was good at your age too, but you'll find there's a lot going on you don't know about. (Punishment; also, the manager's last sentence paired the verbal equivalent of confidence with an aversive stimulus.)

When we speak of confidence, we are not speaking of arrogance or conceit. The truly confident individual treats other people with respect and consideration. He is realistic enough to know that everyone does something better than he does or knows something he does not know. The person who is arrogant and conceited, on the other hand, actually lacks confidence. He acts superior because he feels inferior; if he were truly confident, he would have no need to impress others with his confidence through his arrogance.

Being other-oriented

The effective use of management psychology requires, in one sense, the most selfless, altruistic orientation possible; one must focus entirely on what is reinforcing or aversive to the other person, not to oneself. This is a very difficult orientation for most people to achieve. All too often we assume that what is reinforcing to us is reinforcing to others—and then we wonder why we are failing to have an impact on others. If someone is having an argument with his wife, for example, his irritation is a reinforcer to her; his anger at her pouting does not allow him to see that he could punish her by being happy. Or, consider the following:

Subordinate: Jim is just not doing his job; I've got to let him go.

Manager: I think a lot of people are going to be upset if we let Jim go.

Subordinate: I don't think so. I think many of the competent people will be happy.

In the above example, the weak manager has attempted to block the firing by punishing his subordinate's response. The punishing vehicle (other people getting upset) may be aversive to the manager, but it is not to the subordinate. We know this because the strength of his response pattern has not diminished; he is still fighting to fire the man.

As previously mentioned, questions readily become aversive stimuli because of their frequent pairing with other aversive stimuli. Denials to the contrary, questions are often used to punish unwanted behavior on others. A manager may bemoan the fact that Paul Smith is indecisive to everyone except Paul Smith; however, he punishes actual decisions by Paul Smith with harsh questioning. Married people may relate to more homespun examples:

Wife: Darling, we'll go to dinner anywhere you'd like.

Husband: Well, why don't we go to Chasen's.
Wife: Why would you want to go there?

Husband: I may not be home Saturday morning; I told Joe I'd play golf with him.
Wife: Why didn't you tell me sooner?

In both instances, the wife would certainly contend that she was merely seeking more information. Being sensitive to the impact our behavior is having on others, however, would diminish the likelihood of such questions if this contention were indeed true.

In any event, the presentation of an aversive stimulus decreases the likelihood of the response it follows. The aversive stimulus can come in the obvious form of an insult or a reprimand, or it can come in the less obvious, but just as effective, form of a question or quiet grimace.

AVOIDANCE LEARNING

Avoidance learning is a quick and certain way of changing behavior. It also accounts for many problems people experience when dealing with each other. It is subtle and frequently difficult to diagnose while it is happening, which is often in the business setting. Let us take a look at the principle and attempt to break it down into recognizable parts.

PRINCIPLE VIII: AVOIDANCE BEHAVIOR
Following a response with the cessation of an aversive stimulus increases the probability of the response recurring (Keller & Schoenfeld, 1950; Skinner, 1938)

Implicit in the principle is the idea that aversive stimuli are avoided. The proverbial breakdown in communications in an organization is usually the result of managers pairing themselves with aversive stimuli; hence, the managers are avoided, and people "just don't get around" to telling them what they should.

In many situations, however, an aversive stimulus suddenly arises while two people are interacting. It can come in the form of a request, a question, an order, a directive, a suggestion. It is at this moment that avoidance learning takes place. Any response that stops the aversive stimulus, that shuts it off, will have a much greater probability of recurring. Consider the salesman to whom making out sales call reports is aversive; he avoids the task merely by not doing it.

Manager: Bob, I didn't get your sales call report last Friday. Do you have it?
Salesman: Gee, I just haven't had time to get around to it.
Manager (angry): Oh, for God's sake! I want that sales report in here and I want it on time! Maybe we should start looking at whether or not you need a company car since we don't know if you're making sales calls! (Punishment)

The manager has paired a question on sales call reports with aversive stimuli. He has followed his subordinate's response with a strong aversive stimulus and decreased its probability of recurring. Hence, on subsequent occasions, the salesman is unlikely to use the excuse of "not having enough time." Notice that the manager has not done anything to decrease the aversiveness of making out a sales call report. The probability of the salesman not making out his report, therefore, remains as high as it ever was.

Two weeks later the following conversation takes place:

Manager (angrily): Bob, where the hell is your sales call report? (Aversive stimulus)

Subordinate: Remember you wanted me to work with Ed on that sales call to Ram Corporation? Well, Ed really wasn't prepared for the call, and I had to spend a lot of time working with him on it. I'm awfully sorry, but I thought helping Ed on this call was more important. (Avoidance behavior)

Manager (much more gently): Well, see if you can get it in as quickly as possible, will you? Why wasn't Ed prepared? (Avoidance behavior successfully stopped aversive stimuli.)

This subtle interaction occurs quite frequently in private industry. *Excuse-making, rationalization, and placing blame on other people, as well as absences, illnesses, and other more dramatic and deleterious forms of behavior, are often the result of such responses having been followed by the successful stopping or cessation of aversive stimuli, most of which emanate from the manager.* In the above example, the salesman successfully stopped the aversive stimuli from his manager by placing blame on another person. Since "blaming others" was followed by the cessation of an aversive stimulus, the salesman will be much more likely to blame others when he again encounters aversive stimuli, especially from his manager.

This is not to say that the salesman is doing this consciously; he is not. It is to say that his behavior is following certain principles. The principle here, from a manager's point of view, is this: Once I have started an aversive stimulus, I will eventually have to stop it; whatever the person is doing when I stop it will increase a good deal in its likelihood of recurring. *Once a manager has started an aversive stimulus, therefore, he should never stop it until the other person is engaging in constructive behavior.*

Consider the following example: An aggressive personnel manager is attempting to get a management development program started in his organization through his training director. The training director is a meek, passive person who finds it aversive to talk to various vice presidents and attempt to sell them the training program.

Manager: How's the training program coming? (Aversive stimulus)

Subordinate: Well, all right.

Manager: Have you held any management development sessions yet? (Aversive stimulus still "on")

Subordinate: No, not yet.

Manager (his anger starting to show): Why not? (Aversive stimulus still "on")

Subordinate: Well, we don't really have the budget to bring in the speakers we want to bring in.

Manager: Oh, for God's sake! I don't ever want to hear that excuse used again. If you need the money, I'll get it for you! I've told you and everyone else on my staff that before! (The manager has just knocked "budgeting-excuse-making" out of his subordinate's repertoire by punishing the response severely. The aversive stimulus is still "on" and the subordinate tries again to stop it.)

Subordinate: Well, I've tried to get to the V.P.'s of operations and sales, but they're always out of town. And when they are in town, their secretaries tell me they're all tied up.

Manager (anger subsiding somewhat as his attention is shifted to the V.P.'s): How many times have you tried to get them?

Subordinate: At least three times. I don't think they feel this management training program is very important. (The subordinate has paired the vice presidents of operations and sales with what to the personnel manager is an aversive stimulus—their resistance to management development.)

Manager: Well, we'll see whether they want management development or not. Let me give them a call and we'll both go up and talk to them. (The subordinate succeeded in stopping the aversive stimulus by blaming others.)

Again, blaming other people has been followed by the cessation of aversive stimuli (the manager's anger). This interaction has increased the probability that the training director will blame others when faced with aversive stimuli. At the same time, it has diminished the likelihood that the training director will blame the budget, because this response did not stop his superior's harsh manner.

Because of its pervasiveness in industry, it is important that the manager grasp the principle of avoidance learning. Once the manager starts an aversive stimulus when dealing with a subordinate, *he must not stop the aversive stimulus until the subordinate has made a constructive response.*

Consider the following ineffective and effective examples:

Manager: Why didn't you get that order completed and shipped out yesterday?

Subordinate: I wasn't feeling too well yesterday.

Manager (sympathetically): Why? What was wrong? (The manager stopped the aversive stimulus after the subordinate made an "excuse.")

Manager: Why didn't you get that order completed and shipped out yesterday?

Subordinate: I wasn't feeling too well yesterday.

Manager: Why didn't you tell one of your people to get it out? (The manager appropriately keeps the aversive stimulus going; hence he is unlikely to encounter more excuse-making in subsequent dealings with his subordinate.)

Subordinate: I'll check with John now to see why it didn't go out. (Constructive response)

Manager: Good. Are you feeling all right now? (Appropriately "turns off" the aversive stimulus)

In some cases the individual must make a direct effort to elicit a constructive response lest the aversive interaction go on too long. This is often best effected by a direct question.

Father (angry): Were you out playing in the street?

Son: Yes.

Father: I told you I never wanted you out in the street!

Son: The other kids were . . .

Father: I don't care what the other kids were doing!

Son is silent.

Father (still in angry tone): Are you ever going to play out there again?

Son (weakly): No.

Father (much more softly): Good. (Turns and walks away)

It is important that the direct effort (question) to elicit the constructive response still maintains an aversive tone. After the manager has punished his subordinate with numerous aversive questions ("Why was it late?"), it is time to stop the aversive interaction by eliciting a constructive response. One last aversive question is then asked, "When will you do it?"

Liabilities of using aversive stimuli

There are three major liabilities a manager encounters when he uses aversive stimuli to influence the behavior of his subordinates. First, he pairs himself with the aversive stimuli he uses and, to that extent, becomes aversive to his subordinates. Second, while he eliminates (punishes) some ineffective response patterns, he does nothing to increase the probability of any effective behavior. Third, by following a subordinate's deleterious responses with the cessation of aversive stimuli, he often increases the probability of behavior (such as lying and blaming others) more harmful than that which he is trying to eliminate. (A fourth liability will be discussed later in this chapter.)

The complications and side effects involved in the use of aversive stimuli should make the manager quite hesitant to employ them. When they must be used, they should be kept at a mild level. The only area in which mild aversive stimuli are probably not used frequently enough is sales calls on potential customers. Most salesmen go to such lengths to pair themselves with reinforcers and not antagonize a potential customer that they inadvertently reinforce rejection responses by the customer. The customer who says, "I don't think I'll try an order at this time" often encounters much acquiescence, even in good salesmen. Highly competent salesmen, however, mildly punish such a response by saying, for example, "I think you're making a mistake."

Some common avoidance behaviors

Sales and operations are inextricably linked to profits. If profits drop, sales blames operations and operations blames sales. The president reinforces both for blaming each other so no one will blame him. Within a short time, the vice president of sales and the vice president of operations are intensely aversive to each other. Anyone who pairs the one vice president with aversive stimuli to the other vice president will be reinforced. The subordinates of both vice presidents soon learn this and use the knowledge to good advantage:

Vice president, sales: Why the hell aren't we getting any sales out of your region? (Aversive stimulus)

Regional sales manager: Well, it's pretty difficult to get sales when the operations people make such shoddy stuff and ship it late on top of that.

Vice president, sales: You've got a point,

and I know you've been hurt more than the other regions. Considering the circumstances, you're doing pretty well.

Not only did the regional manager successfully stop the aversive stimuli by blaming the operations people; he was reinforced as well. We can be certain he will subsequently be trying, through his subordinates, to find as many operations mistakes as possible. After all, this is the behavior for which he is reinforced. The vice president of sales should have said, "If we made a perfect product and always got it out on time, what the hell would we need you for?"

One of the most aversive situations for both manager and subordinate is the performance review. Each contributes his share toward making the situation less aversive and less productive. The manager tones down his criticisms, and the subordinate placidly agrees with all of them. That way no one gets hurt and both successfully avoid aversive stimuli (although no one becomes more adept, either).

One of the most self-destructive avoidance patterns occurs with the meek, highly sensitive subordinate who exists only to say "yes" to anything his superior suggests. The most abrasive, demanding manager has his limits; few managers want to destroy anyone. As a result, most "tough" managers become quite gentle when dealing with the meek and sensitive subordinate—and that is exactly why the subordinate remains meek and sensitive. He has frequently seen his manager "chew out" a confident subordinate, and he successfully avoids this aversive stimulus by remaining subservient. Indeed, the common denominator of the aggressive person

and the passive person is that both successfully stop aversive stimuli; the difference is that the aggressive person does it by attacking, the passive person by withdrawing.

A more subtle avoidance pattern occurs when both the salesman and his customer are aversive to each other. The following phone conversation might then take place:

Salesman: I'll be in your area Wednesday, and I was wondering if I could see you.

Customer (hesitant): Well, I have a meeting with the management committee at ten in the morning.

Salesman: That will probably tie you up for a good part of the day. Why don't I try to catch you on my next trip?

Customer: I wish you would.

Salesman: Good. I will.

We might call this avoidance of aversive stimuli through mutual reinforcement. Note that, if asked, the salesman will tell his manager quite sincerely that he has been trying to get to this company, but they are always busy.

Discriminative stimuli

Earlier we discussed three disadvantages managers encounter in using intense aversive stimuli; let us now consider a fourth disadvantage. If a response pattern has been reinforced in the past, then punishing it with severe aversive stimuli will stop the response immediately, *but only in the presence of the punishing agent.* (Azrin, 1956; Dinsmoor, 1952) Suppose a 4-year-old boy has played in the street and enjoyed it (reinforcement) for several days. On this particular day, however, the boy is seen in the street by his father and severely spanked. The boy will not play in the street any more—when his father is around; he will when his father is absent, however. The street has been paired with reinforcers for several days; one aversive pairing will not overcome that. Also, it is the father, not the street, who is being paired with aversive stimuli. The father becomes a *discriminative stimulus* in the presence of which the undesirable response is not made, in the absence of which it is made. Finally, the father never really reinforced the boy for *not* playing in the street.

By using severe aversive stimuli, the manager may stop an undesirable response pattern immediately, but only in his own presence, when the response has previously been followed by reinforcement. For example: Imagine a young man joining an encyclopedia company as a salesman. The young man is "highly independent" (doing things his own way has been reinforced in the past), and he dislikes being told how to reach his goals. After a short training program, his systematic, methodical manager gives him a "canned sales pitch" and orders him to memorize it word for word and use it on his sales calls. Because of his independence, this procedure is aversive to the young salesman, and he does not memorize the talk. A week later, both the salesman and his manager go out on their first sales call together. The salesman does not use the "canned" approach. The manager and his salesman leave the house and the following interaction takes place:

Manager (angrily): I thought I told you to memorize that sales speech I gave you.
Salesman: I didn't feel it fit my personality.
Manager (in a low, quiet voice, very angrily): I told you to memorize that sales pitch. I don't care about you or your personality. I'm going out with you on a sales call next week and if you don't present it word for word, I'll have you out of this company so quick you won't know what hit you.

One week later both the manager and the salesman go out on their next sales call. Lo and behold, the salesman presents the canned sales pitch, word for word. And he continues to do so as long as he remains with the company—but only when his sales manager is with him! The sales manager has become a discriminative stimulus in the presence of which the canned sales pitch is made; in the absence of the sales manager, however, the salesman reverts to his old style of doing things his own way.

Few response patterns change overnight. If an individual suddenly engages in behavior that is virtually incompatible with his particular personality, it is almost invariably the result of severe aversive learning that has led to the establishment of a discriminative stimulus. Consider the case of a large Midwestern steel company. The previous chief executive officer had found it aversive to delegate authority and responsibility to other people. As a result, he had surrounded himself with cheerful but highly dependent personalities who were adept at following orders and doing little else. The predictable drop in profits had occurred. The board of directors then brought in a highly aggressive, hypercritical president from outside the industry. In his first meeting with his vice presidents, the president turned to the first man on his left and asked what problems he saw in the company. The vice president, as he had for the past five years, cheerfully responded, "I think we're doing pretty well." The new president quietly said, "This company's profits have dropped 40% in the past three years. If you don't see anything wrong, maybe you don't belong in this company." Almost overnight, a number of weak personalities began engaging in highly critical, aggressive behavior patterns—but only in the presence of the president.

It has previously been noted that many salesmen do not use mild aversive stimuli frequently enough when a potential customer is rejecting the idea of placing an order. The opposite extreme is also quite possible. If a customer agrees to an order in the salesman's presence and then cancels the order by telephone several days later, the salesman may have been using overly intense aversive stimuli to get the order. If customer cancellations are a frequent occurrence with a specific salesman, this is almost certainly the case; hence customers "buy" in his presence, but cancel in his absence.

This type of behavior is best described as "sham behavior"; it generally occurs when a new manager joins a company and starts to follow his subordinates' undesirable response patterns with strong aversive stimuli. This is a difficult and dangerous technique for a manager to use because it requires him to perceive that a subordinate's behavior is quite different in his presence from that in his absence. It changes behavior very quickly, but the negative side effects almost always outweigh the advantages. If a manager sees quick, dramatic changes in a subordinate when the subordinate is in the manager's presence, he can be almost sure that he has punished the subordinate's previous responses too strongly.

Extinction of avoidance behavior

To extinguish a response that occurs because it has been followed by a reinforcer is relatively simple: merely remove the reinforcer. (Skinner, 1938) *Behavior that is controlled by reinforcers is adaptable.* A young man may have been reinforced in his school years for his athletic abilities. Despite some initial problems, he can usually make a good adjustment in his vocational life when entirely different behavior patterns are reinforced and his athletic abilities undergo extinction.

Behavior that is learned because of avoidance contingencies, on the other hand, is extremely stable; indeed, it is rigid. (Solomon, Kamin, & Wynne, 1953) Hence, avoidance behavior is nonadaptable. There is generally no stimulus to remove to extinguish the behavior; in fact, it continually recurs precisely because nothing follows it. Take, for example, the case of Terry Smith. Terry was raised by hypercritical parents, including an obsessive-compulsive mother who criticized everything Terry did that was not up to her criteria of perfection. Terry, as a result, developed into a cautious, conservative thinker whose basic goal in life was to avoid mistakes, which had become an intensive aversive stimulus to him because they had been paired with, and punished by, severe parental criticism. Terry is now 58 years old and he has spent his entire vocational life desperately avoiding mistakes. Because he has succeeded in this, nothing harmful has happened to him. He will never know that taking a few risks and making some mistakes would also lead to nothing really harmful happening to him (his parents died thirty years ago), because he will never engage in such behavior. He has, in other words, always successfully avoided aversive stimuli. He will never know that aversive stimuli would not have occurred had he adopted a different set of behavior patterns.

John Landon, now 43 years old, gave two speeches in high school. In both instances, his peers ridiculed him. He may now be an excellent speaker—but no one will ever know it. He assiduously avoids making presentations in front of groups. Because he successfully avoids group presentations, he successfully avoids aversive stimuli. He will never know that his speeches would be met with ovations, because he so successfully avoids them. Since he avoids groups, there is no way to extinguish his negative reactions to them.

Susan, 38 years old, is compulsively, rigidly on time for appointments. As a young girl she was severely punished by her father for being late. She will never know that being late now will not result in any punishment, because she compulsively, rigidly avoids being late.

There is a way out of this circular trap, but it requires a perceptive manager who is willing to take a risk. We have seen that an aversive stimulus that is not periodically paired with other aversive stimuli will extinguish in effectiveness. (Reynolds, 1975) If the manager can determine what stimuli his subordinate is avoiding and can verbalize these stimuli to him, the manager will start the extinction process. The statement, "You know, you seem to be afraid of people disliking you," is a case in point. Some people have spent their lives successfully avoiding the dislike of others. Because they were successful in avoiding this stimulus, they have never learned that the dislike of others is not always harmful and thereby extinguished their negative reaction to it. It is one of those unspoken fears which, if spoken by someone, becomes less aversive. Sex is another good example. Most of use have experienced sexual–aversive stimulus pairings. When explicit sexual scenes are shown openly and not paired with the aversive stimuli of threatened legal or moral judgments, some of our inhibitions break down.

Had someone said to Terry Smith concerning his avoidance of mistakes, "You seem to be too frightened of criticism from people in positions of authority," he would have started to extinguish a stimulus Terry feared (and always would fear because he avoided the stimulus). It would have been better still to pair the aversive stimulus with reinforcers, for example, "When people in high positions of authority criticize you, it's because they feel what you think is important." The manager should not hesitate to take chances in this area. If the manager fails to act in such cases, his subordinate will spend his life engaging in self-destructive behavior patterns because of "irrational fears."

Frequency is the criterion

Managers must be careful when using aversive stimuli with subordinates. As we have seen, the critical point occurs not only when the manager initiates an aversive stimulus (punishment), but also when he stops it (avoidance learning). The key question is, "What behavior on the subordinate's part immediately preceded the cessation of the manager's aversive stimulus?" Let us apply it in the following example:

Manager: When do you think you'll have that report finished? (Aversive stimulus)

Subordinate: In about two weeks.

Manager: Oh, come on. You can get it in by next Wednesday, can't you? (Maintains the aversive stimulus)

Subordinate: Well, I hate to make promises I can't keep. You know, my wife hasn't been feeling too well lately, and I've been helping out around the house. (Critical point: excuse-making response)

Manager: Oh, I didn't know that. Well, two weeks will be all right. (Cessation of aversive stimuli)

As cold and inhuman as it sounds, this manager may be seriously harming his subordinate. By stopping the aversive stimulus, he has increased the probability of the subordinate's excuse-making behavior. At the least, he should have explored the extent of the wife's illness. He should probably have also used a mild aversive stimulus after the subordinate's plea for sympathy, "Well, you know we do have to get this work out."

When should the manager punish ineffective responses? When their frequency indicates they have gone beyond the bounds of reality. This decision is the manager's responsibility; no one else will or can make it. If more managers punished meek, passive behavior and reinforced confident, adventuresome behavior, we would have far fewer meek, frightened people in private industry.

Frequent, repetitious behavior patterns are the criterion by which a person should be judged and the criterion by which a manager should gauge his own intervention. In the above example, the "wife-illness" excuse should be punished only if this type of excuse-making is deemed frequent and repetitious by the manager. If it is not, the manager's response of stopping the aversive stimulus would be somewhat appropriate, although it still increases the likelihood of excuse-making in the future.

Many people compound problems by responding to, rather than ignoring, atypical behavior that is neither frequent nor repetitious. Suppose a wife tells her husband she loves him twenty-four times over a three-month period, but tells him she hates him on one occasion. If he responds angrily to the one occasion, he will eventually find her saying she hates him twenty-four times and loves him once. This is because his anger is a reinforcer to her when she initially told him she hated him; thus his angry emotional reaction reinforced her. *Infrequent* absenteeism or tardiness or complaining or ineptness is best ignored. The alternative is too often an increase in the frequency of such behavior.

Long-term consequences of using aversive stimuli

Many organizations have paid a heavy price for the overuse of aversive stimuli and the minimal use of reinforcers to control their employees' behavior. Avoidance learning and aversive pairings are probably the quickest ways to influence behavior. Firing a few people who are not producing can have an immediate, dramatic impact on the remaining employees. To avoid being fired, they work harder. This quick change is short-lived, however, for two reasons. First management has done nothing to make the work itself more reinforcing. As a result, new forms of avoidance behavior will arise. (These might include anything from employee agreements to "cover for one another" to subtle sabotage of plant equipment to leaving the company.) Second, by using aversive stimuli to control behavior, management is constantly pairing itself with these stimuli and quickly becomes an aversive stimulus itself. Likewise, the goals of management, since they are now paired with the new aversive stimulus (management), soon become aversive stimuli to the employees—stimuli to be avoided or stopped.

Many people (employees) have, consequently, learned successfully to stop aversive stimuli by adopting overly aggressive, almost hostile behavior patterns. Consider the following:

Manager: Jim, I'd like you to stay late tonight and help Ed with the night shift.

Subordinate: Why the hell am I always being picked. I stayed late twice last month.

Manager: Well, let me see if I can find someone else.

The manager who initiates a demand (aversive stimulus) and then backs down (stops it) in the face of hostile opposition is clearly headed for trouble. He increases the likelihood of hostile behavior by stopping the aversive stimulus at the wrong time. Nevertheless, these hostile, noncooperative reactions may never have occurred in the first place if top management had not made itself so aversive to other employees.

The trend toward less aversive stimuli

Forty years ago, one of the most intense aversive situations was being out of work. Because of enormously increased job mobility and a rapidly expanding economy, leaving or being laid off by a company is far less aversive today. As a result, there has been a sharp swing away from the managerial use of aversive stimuli to influence the behavior of employees. This is especially true in times of a tight labor supply. To avoid the aversive stimuli of a company, a subordinate can simply resign. His resignation is an aversive stimulus the company will try to avoid.

The current situation has led to a sudden increase in theories of worker motivation that oppose the managerial use of aversive stimuli as a controlling device. These theories suggest that the use of such external controls is nonconstructive and even unnatural. They favor instead a new emphasis on self-control and self-direction. (It is not surprising that the impact on industry of these theories of management generally drops dramatically in periods of high unemployment.)

Before one allows "self-control" to assume dominance as a management tool, however, one had better be certain that organizational goals are reinforcers to the individual. (The employee to whom "seeing people in positions of power hurt" is a reinforcer could prove disastrous to a company when left to "self-control.") This is not to say that such concepts are not useful and effective. It is to say, however, that management has a critical task before it, that of pairing organizational goals with stimuli that are reinforcing to the individual employee.

There is a further complication in using self-control as a management tool. As we have seen, people are largely controlled (influenced) by the people around them (managers, peers, subordinates). This control is implicit in interpersonal interactions; an individual could achieve total self-control only if he were to function in a vacuum. Too often, therefore, is the concept of self-control used as a convenient abdication of the manager's responsibility for the impact he has on the behavior of his subordinates.

STIMULUS GENERALIZATION

Stimulus generalization refers to the fact that the more similar one stimulus is to another, the more likely it is to evoke a similar response. (Mednick & Freedman, 1960; Razran, 1949; Reynolds, 1975) The more intense the original reinforcer or aversive stimulus, the more inclusive is the generalized response. (Margolius, 1955; Mednick & Freedman, 1960; Spiker, 1956) Many male homosexuals, for example, have had women paired with intense aversive stimuli (frequently their hypercritical mothers) in their previous experiences. The aversiveness has been so intense that

it has generalized to include all women.

Generalizations will only take place in situations that involve reinforcers or aversive stimuli to the individual. Suppose a new chief executive officer joins a company. If he fires and retires a number of employees and also brings in a number of new men, cliques will normally form. These cliques will consist of people who consider themselves pre–new-president employees on the one hand and post–new-president employees on the other.

Stimulus generalization accounts for the fact that a specific stimulus does not have to be repeated precisely the same way to be a reinforcer. (Mednick and Freedman, 1960; Razran, 1939, 1961) The words, "You did a fine job and you're going to get a bonus for it," set up the phrase, "You did a fine job," as a reinforcer. Similar complimentary phrases will also be reinforcers because of stimulus generalization. The more similar a phrase is to the original phrase, the more reinforcing it will be. (Razran, 1961)

The authority problem

One of the most important generalizations in private industry is the "authority problem." The individual with an authority problem has experienced numerous, often intense, aversive stimuli paired with authority figures, the first of which is normally the individual's father. These aversive pairings have been so severe that they generalize to include all authorities, including policemen, government officials, people in high positions of authority within an organization, and especially the individual's immediate superior. Uncomfortable feelings in authority figures are reinforcing to such persons, and they are frequently quite aggressive and hostile in order to elicit these feelings. They often quite openly pair authority figures with aversive stimuli.

These hostile response patterns are often misinterpreted. Such individuals are frequently hired because their supposed "aggressive" behavior appears to reflect an ability to get the job done. To the dismay of the organization that hires them, however, these people are far more intent on hurting authority figures than on getting the job done; indeed, their presence in an organization can be quite disruptive. The authority figure syndrome seems to be increasingly prevalent in our society. This may well be, at least in part, because government officials have paired themselves with aversive stimuli such as the Viet Nam war, scandals, and high taxes.

SUMMARY

The use of aversive stimuli involves far more complexities and ramifications than does the use of reinforcers. Yet the use of both is intrinsic to managerial responsibilities. To suppose that a manager can function effectively using only one or the other is unrealistic. In the present industrial environment, however, too much behavioral impact is gained through the use of aversive stimuli and too little through the use of reinforcers.

Using aversive stimuli is a quick and effective way to influence behavioral change. The negative long-term complications, however, are often not readily apparent to the manager. Excessive intensity in behavior is one such complication. A superior may chafe because one of his subordinates is too dependent. If the manager were to reinforce and shape independent behavior patterns, he would gradually develop an effective, adjusted employee. By instead severely punishing dependent behavior, he will quickly develop an *overly* independent subordinate, one who is intent on *proving* his independence. He will not develop a subordinate who loves independence, but rather one who hates being seen as dependent. This avoidance drive almost always leads to excessive behavioral intensity. ("Methinks he doth protest too much.")

Reinforced behavior is flexible, realistic, and appropriate. Avoidance behavior resulting from experiencing aversive stimuli is rigid, nonrealistic, and inappropriately strong. These are the criteria for judging this distinction in a given individual. "Macho" behavior that is natural, relaxed, and appropriate is usually the result of masculine behavior patterns having been reinforced. "Macho" behavior that is overly intense, overly frequent, and inappropriate is usually the result of "nonmasculine" behavior having been punished (ridiculed by peers). Reinforced behavior goes to something; hence, it often leads to happiness. Avoidance behavior goes away from something; hence, it often leads to nothing.

In operant learning, the use of reinforcers involves only one basic question for the manager: What behavior was my subordinate engaged in when I used that reinforcer? The use of aversive stimuli involves two basic questions at once: (1) What behavior was my subordinate engaged in when I *started* the aversive stimulus? (Punishment) (2) What behavior was my subordinate engaged in when I *stopped* the aversive stimulus? (Avoidance learning)

The answers to these questions are critical if a manager is to gain insight into the impact he is having on his subordinates—into his managerial style. Yet it is difficult to engage in behavior and, at the same time, objectively observe and analyze that behavior. The answers, therefore, must come from others, and the most important source is the manager's manager.

CLASSROOM EXERCISES

1. Ask someone his views on an issue (e.g., Vietnam War). When he's finished say, "That's baloney." Keep the aversive stimuli going (without any factual arguments) until his views start to weaken.
2. Have three speakers make a presentation. At the conclusion of each, reinforce the first, extinguish the second, and punish the third. Examine the feelings of each.
3. Your partner has negative attitudes about the class. Using only punishment and avoidance principles, change his attitudes.
4. Your partner just came from the best date of his life and goes into detail on the wonderful experience. Make him feel sad.
5. Despite the classical pairings involved, operantly make someone express a liking for you through the use of punishment and avoidance principles.

6. Break into small groups. Appoint one person manager. Everyone else in the group express negative attitudes about the company. It is the manager's job to stop those negative expressions.
7. Appoint someone else manager. Have this manager *increase* the negative attitudes of the group toward the company.
8. Appoint someone else manager. One of the group always turns in his reports late. Elicit a commitment from him to do them on time.
9. Appoint someone else manager. One person is always bad-mouthing others in the group. Stop him.
10. Appoint someone else manager. Have him tell the group they can ask him any question they would like. Then have him cut off all questioning by punishing those who do question him.

SUGGESTED READINGS

Campbell, J. P., Dunnette, M. D., Lawler, E. E., and Weick, K. E.: Managerial behavior, performance and effectiveness, New York, 1970, McGraw-Hill Book Co.
Comprehensive review of theory, research, and trends in organizational behavior.
Honig, W. K., editor: Operant behavior. Areas of research and application, New York, 1966, Appleton-Century-Crofts.
A compendium of knowledge on the subject.
Skinner, B. F.: The behavior of organisms: An experimental analysis, New York, 1938, Appleton-Century-Crofts.
The foundation of operant learning.

CHAPTER 6

Diagnosis and an overall view

The emergence of management may be the pivotal event of our time, far more important than all the events that make the headlines . . . It is the success story of this century . . . It has provided economic goods and services to an extent that would have been unimaginable to the generation of 1900. And it has performed despite world wars, depressions, and dictatorships.

PETER DRUCKER
The Practice of Management

Diagnosing the behavior of another person is an extremely complex task. Behavior occurs very quickly. The stimuli that are reinforcing or aversive are often subtle and difficult to determine when a mass of stimuli are present. Our own emotional involvement sometimes precludes us from analyzing a situation objectively. Indeed, an objective analysis of another person's behavior can be a depressing, even frightening, experience. For example, it is difficult to accept the fact that someone who "loves us very much" is really reinforcing dependent attitudes and feelings on our part.

Yet behavior can be diagnosed with a surprising degree of accuracy. Objectively observed, it provides us with clear and useful insights about other people. And, while some diagnoses may lead to depressing

conclusions, the principles we have learned allow us to change the behavior of another person. We need not focus only on behavior as it is, but also on behavior as it could be.

In diagnosing behavior, the reader should always remember that the other person's behavior is contingent upon his own. In a real sense, we should be held accountable, not for our own behavior, but for the behavior of those with whom we interact frequently. This standard requires us to focus our attention on the manner in which we influence others; it can quickly lead to changes in our own behavior. If a man determines that his wife has been punishing his decisiveness, he should not react by "hurting" her. If his decisiveness is aversive to her, it is probably because he made it so, possibly by making arbitrary (aversive) decisions involving his wife. In any case, he can make his decisiveness reinforcing to her by constructively changing his own behavior. A wife cannot change her own pouting behavior as quickly and effectively as can her husband. Retaliation is not an effective, constructive change vehicle.

Let us now consider several diagnostic principles and tools. Another procedure used in diagnosis, interviewing, will be considered in Chapter VII.

OPERANT DIAGNOSTIC PRINCIPLES
Reinforcement of reinforcers

An individual generally reinforces behavior in others that is reinforcing to himself. Hence the reader must dispassionately observe the individual in his interactions with other people and note which behavior in others the individual is immediately following with reinforcers.

Subordinate: You know, I'm really nervous over making this presentation to the management committee.

Manager: I'm sure everything will go very well. Your nervousness will probably result in your doing a better job.

Is "lack of confidence" in this subordinate reinforcing to the manager? Despite our protests that the manager is merely reassuring his subordinate, the answer is probably yes! Not only has the manager followed the subordinate's statement of fear with a reinforcer, he has also paired the verbal equivalent of fear with a reinforcer ("your nervousness—your doing a better job"). We are reminded again that logic and rationality are not strong determinants of behavior. We often attack the person who speaks ill of us to other people; yet it

is the other people, those who listen to gossip and subtly reinforce the speaker, who should be punished.

Punishment of aversive stimuli

An individual generally punishes behavior (follows the behavior with an aversive stimulus) in others that is aversive to himself. If it is difficult to believe that "lack of confidence" is reinforcing to the manager in the above example, consider the following interchange between the same manager and another subordinate:

Subordinate (excited): The purchasing agent for PDI Corporation just called in an order. I knew it! I knew I sold them!

Manager: Don't be so sure you sold them. It's a small order and they may have called it in only because their regular source couldn't handle it. We may never hear from them again.

The manager now punishes the subordinate, hence he does not like success and confidence in others. Before the reader rebels at this diagnosis, he should ask himself how many people really find confidence and success in others reinforcing. The man who inherits a large sum of money is not usually looked upon with favor by his neighbors; indeed, he is often subjected to a good deal of subtle criticism.

If a diagnosis reached through the above two principles conflicts with our sense of reality or appropriateness, it is most likely the principles that come closest to the truth, and not our own prejudices about what should or should not be true as opposed to what is or is not true.

Consider this more personal example: A mother is well known to "love" her 5-year-old daughter; she would do anything for her child's happiness. The girl is frightened by interactions with strangers. She is about to be driven by her mother to a birthday party at a playmate's house.

Daughter: I don't want to go.

Mother (concerned): Why, honey?

Daughter: I don't know the other children. I'm afraid.

Mother: Everything will be fine. You'll enjoy it. You'll have a good time.

The mother has reinforced her child's "fear with strangers" response. Two hours later, the mother picks the child up from the party:

Daughter: Oh, Mommy, I had such a good time. We played games and I won prizes. I had so much fun.

Mother: See! Didn't I tell you it was silly to carry on so about going to the party? Aren't you sorry you didn't want to go?

The mother has now punished her daughter for "having fun with strangers." No one doubts the fact that the mother "loves" her child, but "love" involves very complex behavior. Is the child's happiness really a reinforcer to the mother? More specifically, is the child's happiness with others when the mother is absent a reinforcer to the mother?

Let us consider the impact on the little girl if the mother had virtually reversed her own behavior in the two instances.

Daughter: I don't want to go.

Mother: Why?

Daughter: I don't know the other children. I'm afraid.

Mother: Isn't that a little silly?

After the party:

Daughter: Oh, Mommy, I had such a good time. We played games and I won prizes.

Mother (emotionally): Oh, I'm glad everything was fine and you had such a good time.

Let us consider the previous managerial examples from a more effective frame of reference:

Subordinate: You know, I'm really nervous over making this presentation to the management committee.

Manager: I think that's a bit foolish. Being nervous can only hurt you in your presentation. (Punishment)

Subordinate (excited): The purchasing agent for PDI Corporation just called in an order. I knew it! I knew I sold them.

Manager (emotionally): Beautiful! I must admit I didn't think we'd get them. You must have done a hellava job out there. Hey, Ed, did you hear Jim got PDI Corporation? (Reinforcement)

Lack of confidence in subordinates is aversive to this manager; practical achievements by subordinates, on the other hand, are reinforcing to him. The behavior, feelings, and attitudes of his subordinates will soon reflect this fact.

Extinction of aversive and neutral stimuli

People generally extinguish the behavior of others they find aversive or neutral.

Husband: My boss said he is sending my report to the president because it was so well done.

Wife: That's good. Did you want peas or corn for dinner tonight? (Extinction)

Subordinate: I just sold eight carloads of steel to DTO Corporation.
Manager: Fine, Say, we're going to have a sales meeting Thursday. You'll be able to make it, won't you? (Extinction)

Subordinate: I finished the financial analysis. I think I've put in some pretty good ideas.
Manager: Good, Say, I heard you flew in from New York with the president yesterday. What did you talk about? (Extinction)

This type of extinction can be quite harmful. Not only does it decrease the probability of effective behavior in many instances, it also can lead to frustration and aggressive behavior. The manager (or spouse) who uses extinction frequently will normally elicit much negative emotional behavior that may itself be the reinforcer following and increasing the extinction responses of the manager (or spouse). For example, although a wife may find that her husband's emotional reactions over work-related situations are aversive, she may at the same time find that his emotional reactions related to her are reinforcing. She increases the probability of her husband's emotional reactions toward herself if she extinguishes his emotional reactions to situations that do not involve her (a double benefit).

Self-development

It is my conviction that an individual cannot change himself. Many would disagree. Few would disagree, however, with the idea that the behavior of others has a strong influence on one's own thoughts and feelings. If a person cannot change himself, he can change his environment; more specifically, he can change the people with whom he interacts.

How does one diagnose a person with whom he should or should not interact? He does it by engaging in behavior he would like to develop in himself in the presence of the other person and noting whether the other person reinforces, punishes, or extinguishes the behavior. Suppose we wanted to develop greater self-confidence. We might then make the following comment to three individuals on separate occasions: "You know, I think I did a pretty good job on that report." We then note their reaction, including their emotional expressions:

First person: I believe it! You almost always do good reports. (Reinforces)
Second person: Don't be too sure of that. I don't want you to be disappointed if the boss doesn't like it. (Punishes)
Third person: Good. Say, are we going to play tennis tonight? (Extinguishes)

Clearly, we should seek out the first person and interact with him frequently. His behavior will have a beneficial impact on our behavior. We should avoid the second and third persons; they will destroy our confidence.

To verify our diagnosis, it might then be helpful to make a self-deprecatory statement and note the same people's reactions: "You know, I'm not sure I can do what the boss wants me to do."

First person: Oh, hell, that's stupid. (Punishes) Say, are we going to play golf Saturday? (Extinguishes)

Second person: Well, I'd be happy to help you with it. I think we'll be able to do it together. (Reinforces)

Third person: You'll do a fine job. Anyway, it's not that important a project. (Reinforces)

Again, we should seek out the first person and avoid the other two. We must recognize that many people find self-destructive behavior in others reinforcing. This should not be surprising in a society that censors sex and love-making in the mass media and allows violence to go unchecked. The highly sympathetic person who gushes with emotion when we complain about our mistreatment at the hands of others is not a good person to be around. We may relish his emotional sympathy but we will soon find ourselves getting more and more sensitive to mistreatment by others, since we are being reinforced so adequately for doing so.

This can be compounded by the dearth of reinforcement in our lives. It represents one of the most dangerous situations an individual can encounter in life. Suppose an individual's "interpersonal world" consists of about thirty people with whom he interacts frequently (parents, spouse, children, manager, friends, etc.). Of these thirty people, only Joe really reinforces the individual. Since Joe is the only one classically pairing himself with reinforcers, the individual will naturally seek Joe out most often. But suppose Joe makes his reinforcers operantly contingent upon the individual expressing a dislike of others or

feeling depressed or being self-deprecating. The individual will be trapped. He will always seek out the only reinforcing person in his life, Joe, but he will also be constantly feeling a dislike of others or depressed or self-deprecating.

In the preceding example, our insecure response ("I'm not sure I can do what the boss wants me to do.") was reinforced by the second and third persons ("I'll help you," and "You'll do a fine job."). These reinforcers lead us to like these two people more (they classically paired themselves with reinforcers) *despite the fact that our insecurity is increased* (they operantly reinforced insecurity on our part). Repetitious experiences like this will lead us to like them a great deal and, at the same time, lead us to doubt our own ability. *It is not enough to seek out people who reinforce us; we must also determine what it is about ourselves that leads them to reinforce us.*

Thoreau has said that "What a man thinks of himself, that it is which will determine his fate." What a man thinks of himself (and most other things in this world) will be determined, to a large extent, by the behavior of the people he deals with most frequently. Choosing these people well will have more impact on a person's life than all other factors combined. That a person reinforces us is not enough. The critical question is: Does he reinforce us when we are confident or fearful, happy or sad, dominant or subservient, enthusiastic or complaining?

Evaluating changes in ourselves

Of course, it is very difficult to respond to situations and people, and at the same time, analyze our own responses. How, then, does an individual know he is growing and changing? By noting changes in the people around him. *The best criterion of change in an individual is a change in the behavior of people with whom he interacts frequently.*

If confidence in others has become a reinforcer to an individual, people around him will become more confident, because he will be punishing and extinguishing lack of confidence and reinforcing confident behavior. Just as a parent is frequently judged by the behavior of his child, so too should a friend be judged by the behavior of his friends, a spouse by the behavior of his spouse, and a manager by the behavior of his subordinates. This is not to say other people do not influence the individual. It is to say, however, that the behavioral influence on the individual from people with whom he interacts frequently is enormous, especially in the presence of those people.

CLASSICAL DIAGNOSTIC PRINCIPLES
Pairing reinforcers with reinforcers

Another diagnostic tool consists of noting which stimuli (including the verbal equivalent of response patterns) the individual pairs with reinforcers in his behavior patterns. *People generally pair those things they find reinforcing with other reinforcers.* The key diagnostic element is found in the fact that it is usually the stimulus that comes *first* that is the most reinforcing to the speaker.

The individual who says, "People are basically good," is usually outgoing and comfortable with others. People are generally reinforcing to him, and his behavior

will reflect this fact. The diagnostic approach is to first determine that the individual is using a reinforcer ("are basically good"). To find what is truly reinforcing to him, we must then determine what he is pairing with the reinforcer (in this case, "people").

Likewise, the comment, "His sense of humor sure breaks me up," indicates that humor is reinforcing to the speaker, while "His ability to fire incompetent people quickly has probably increased profits threefold" is a comment we would expect from a tough line manager. It is difficult, if not impossible, for people to avoid pairing stimuli they find reinforcing with reinforcers. Moreover, the mere fact that they can use reinforcers is to their credit; many people cannot.

Pairing aversive stimuli with aversive stimuli

Pairing aversive stimuli with aversive stimuli is far more common than is pairing reinforcers with reinforcers. How often do we hear statements like the following: "This company sure is cheap when it comes to giving raises." "Mike's impulsiveness is going to get him in trouble one of these days."

In order to diagnose behavior properly, one must focus not on the obvious aversive stimulus used, but rather on the stimuli being paired with it. *Oddly enough, the stimuli being paired with the supposed aversive stimulus are the ones which are truly aversive to the individual.* This is a critical point. Many analyses are incorrect because the listener focuses on the aversive stimulus used rather than on the stimuli being paired with it. In the above statements, for example, greater insight is gained when one realizes it is the company that is aversive to the person, not its cheapness. It is Mike's impulsiveness (and Mike himself) that is aversive to the speaker, not Mike's getting into trouble. Yet most listeners would respond with, "Cheap in what way?" or "What kind of trouble?"

It is absolutely critical that the diagnoses be made on the basis of actual, observed pairings. "Logical inferences" that go beyond the actual pairings usually lead one astray. Consider the following statements of a husband to his wife: "You never give any thought to anyone but yourself. You live in your own little world. You never ask me about my work and never appreciate what I do for you. You never give me any attention or affection. You live only for yourself. You are the most self-involved, egocentric person I've ever met." Do these statements indicate that his wife's attention and affection are reinforcers to this person? Not necessarily. They indicate that, at that moment, the man's wife *is an aversive stimulus to him* (he is pairing her with aversive stimuli), and the reinforcement he is probably working toward is that of seeing his wife "hurt" or "upset." In order to elicit hurt feelings from his wife, he pairs her subconsciously with what he feels are aversive stimuli to *her,* not necessarily to himself. If his wife were sensitive about being accused of spending money foolishly, he would instead pair her with these stimuli at that moment. ("You spend money like it grows on trees. You have no conception of how hard I work for money.") The diagnosis, based on observed pairings only, is the same in both instances, the wife is aversive to the husband; no further diagnoses (about attention or money) can be made.

People may deny that the stimuli they are pairing with aversive stimuli are really aversive to them, but such denials must be accepted with great caution. The man who calls his company "cheap" may protest that he loves his company; that is doubtful. Likewise, the individual who pairs his wife with aversive stimuli may protest that he loves her; that too is doubtful. The women's liberation movement leader may protest the idea that she dislikes men. Such protests are doubtful if she makes comments such as "Men have abused women for generations" and "Men should realize they may not like what happens to them if they continue trying to dominate us."

Opposites are not necessarily opposite

The opposite of a reinforcing stimulus is not necessarily an aversive stimulus and vice versa. The women's liberationist may find men aversive, but may not find women reinforcing. If she did, she would be more inclined toward pairing women with reinforcers than toward pairing men with aversive stimuli. The authoritarian manager frequently finds authority exercised over himself quite aversive.

Again, we can go no further in our diagnoses than the actual observed pairing. It is in this area especially that "logical" inferences lead to mistakes.

A black activist says: "Whitey is a honkey." The correct diagnosis is that whites are aversive to him. Do we now know how he feels about blacks? Not at all. And the same black could make either of the two following comments: "Black is beautiful," or "Most blacks are Uncle Toms." We know how he feels about blacks based *only* on his statements about blacks, not based on his comments about whites.

Making logical inferences leads to both improper diagnoses and ineffective remedial action. Some people find "lack of attention" or "being insignificant to others" quite aversive. This can lead to behavior that involves anything from intense emotional reactions to oppositional argumentativeness. To infer that receiving attention and being significant to others are reinforcing to such people is often incorrect. Indeed, when they do elicit a good deal of attention and become significant to someone, they often lose interest in that person. Pairing attention with aversive stimuli, therefore, has little impact on their behavior. Pairing lack of attention and being insignificant to others with reinforcers, on the other hand, can lead to constructive behavior change. In short, attention is not reinforcing to the person, lack of attention is aversive; being significant to someone is not reinforcing, being insignificant is aversive.

Many social activist groups pair injustice with aversive stimuli; this does not mean they love justice. The liberal pairs the rich with aversive stimuli ("Profits are a rip-off of the American people" or "Large corporations show a total lack of social concern"). Does this mean the liberal loves the poor? Sometimes, yes, sometimes no (sometimes he loves no one). Hating what is evil does not necessarily mean loving what is good. Many young people today find unjust people quite aversive; they do not necessarily find just people reinforcing. They may be reinforced by hurting unjust people but not by complimenting just people. If they loved good, in the loving, they would be good. But they hate evil and, in the hating, they are evil.

Everything can be aversive

That opposite stimuli are not necessarily reinforcing and aversive is an important and frequent phenomenon. Since aversive stimuli are so often used in our society, opposites and alternatives may all have been paired with aversive stimuli and be aversive themselves. This is called an avoidance-avoidance conflict, and its effects are devastating, despite its frequency of occurrence.

The mother may punish independent behavior one day ("If you ever do something like that again without asking my permission, you'll regret it") and punish dependent behavior a day later ("Why do you always bother me with such questions? You're old enough to take care of yourself"). The married person may dislike living with his wife and living alone. The employee may find staying with his company aversive, joining a new and unfamiliar company aversive, and being without a job aversive. The highly independent salesman may find his manager's statement, "I will help you," aversive; but he may also find his manager's statement, "All right, I won't help you," aversive.

Repetitious response patterns

The final method of diagnosing behavior is first to note which of an individual's response patterns occur frequently and then to observe what immediately precedes and follows these responses. The most important stimuli to observe preceding or following the responses are those involving the behavior of other people, including oneself if possible. This is because the most reinforcing or aversive stimuli to an individual are usually to be found in the behavior of other people.

In the case of avoidance behavior, the stimuli to notice are those involving the behavior of others immediately preceding the response; that behavior is aversive to the individual. If the individual repetitiously makes excuses, for example, we must determine what type of stimulus immediately precedes his excuse-making behavior.

Manager: I want you to break that machine down and put in the replacement parts this afternoon.

Subordinate: I was going to ask you if I could have this afternoon off. I've been getting pains in my chest and I wanted to see a doctor about them.

It is important to note that we are talking about repetitive behavior. One "excuse" response by a subordinate does not tell you much. If the subordinate in the above example engages in this behavior frequently, and we determine that it is usually a reaction to the type of stimulus presented above by his manager, we can conclude that having work demands placed on him by others is aversive to him.

In the case of reinforced behavior, one must determine what immediately follows the response. Suppose we noted frequent complaining in an individual. We would then look for reinforcing stimuli in the behavior of others to whom he complains:

Subordinate: You know, I think we're headed for a lot of trouble.

Manager: How's that?

Subordinate: People are upset with this company.

Manager: In what way?

Subordinate: They feel the salaries are too low.

Here we might determine that the manager's interest and concern as reflected in his questions are reinforcing to the subordinate. Indeed, few managers realize how reinforcing their attention is to subordinates. This manager has unfortunately made his attention and concern contingent upon the subordinate's complaining. Here, again, we are discussing repetitive behavior. Obviously, if a subordinate rarely complains, the manager should explore the reasons when he does.

Diagnosis by means of repetitive behavior is not easy. Does an individual constantly ridicule other people in front of a group because he finds the group's laughter reinforcing or because he finds the ridiculed person's discomfort reinforcing? This is a difficult question to answer, and sometimes trial-and-error methods must be used to change the ineffective behavior.

The distinction between behavior controlled by a reinforcer and that controlled by an aversive stimulus is often a difficult one to make. Does the obsessive-compulsive housewife continually wash her floors because a clean floor is reinforcing to her or because the dirty floor is aversive to her? Is the cautious, detail-oriented person bogging down in details because "being right" is reinforcing to him or because "being wrong" is aversive to him? There are some clues to look for: If a response recurs repeatedly and nothing follows it, the best guess is that it is avoidance behavior, and the stimulus preceding the response is aversive to the individual. If behavior is stable, intense, and of long duration, it is probably avoidance behavior controlled by aversive stimuli. If, on the other hand, the behavior is flexible and adaptable and consistently leads to similar reactions on the part of others, it is probably reinforced behavior.

All behavior is repetitious and fairly stable for two reasons. First, most people's interpersonal environment is fairly stable. We see and interact frequently with essentially the same people over long periods of time. Second, the people we seek out as reinforcing and avoid as aversive are usually compatible with our present likes and dislikes; this ensures a stable interpersonal environment (and a lack of growth and change). The meek, quiet person often seeks out other quiet people and avoids outgoing, emotionally expressive people. The depressed person often seeks out sad people and avoids happy, cheerful people. Thus, our potential growth is blunted by our own lack of initiative.

Behavior is complex, but this should not discourage us from analyzing it. This analysis can be legitimately based on "gut feel" because of the complexity of behavior. The following comment, imbedded in an ongoing speech, would be difficult to intellectually analyze:

Historians teach us that the primary function of people in government is the protection of the citizen; history teaches us that people in government are the primary thing the citizen should be protected from.

If the listener "feels" the speaker dislikes people in government, he is correct; being intellectually unable to justify the interpretation is reasonable because of complexity.

The rewards of analyzing behavior can be worth the effort when the analysis results in more constructive, effective behavior by ourselves and those with whom we interact. Indeed, the analysis of the behavior of ourselves and others probably offers us one of the most potent tools available for developing social growth and human potential.

• • •

We have now covered the basic principles of classical and operant learning, and we can begin to consider how to put them to use.

CLASSICAL LEARNING PRINCIPLES
Principle I

To decrease the probability of a response controlled by a reinforcer, pair the reinforcer with aversive stimuli.

Principle II

To decrease the probability of a response controlled by an aversive stimulus, pair the aversive stimulus with reinforcers.

Principle III

To increase the probability of a response, pair the verbal equivalent of the response with a reinforcer.

Principle IV

To decrease the probability of a response, pair the verbal equivalent of the response with an aversive stimulus.

OPERANT LEARNING PRINCIPLES
Principle V: Reinforcement

Any response followed immediately by a reinforcer has a greater probability of recurring.

Principle VI: Extinction

Any response not immediately followed by a reinforcer has a lesser probability of recurring.

Principle VII: Punishment

Any response immediately followed by an aversive stimulus has a lesser probability of recurring.

Principle VIII: Avoidance behavior

Following a response with the cessation of an aversive stimulus increases the probability of the response recurring.

We know that these principles are not as simple as they seem. If the reader is overwhelmed by their complexity, however, he should remember that he is not expected at this point to recall all of their many facets. It is enough if he has grasped some major ideas—the general consequences of ex- tinction, for example, or of using aversive stimuli.

Some words of advice: Using the principles successfully takes practice, and mistakes are bound to be made. This is not an alarming prospect, however; we can learn from our mistakes and avoid repeating them.

Remember, too, that the principles should not be applied in every situation. Many interpersonal interactions are too emotional (too reinforcing or aversive) for an individual to apply to them a set of technological principles. If a manager is able to use the principles 5 or 10 percent of the time, it will be more than adequate, as his own behavior will show. As he sees behavioral changes occurring in others, he will be reinforced for using the principles, and this will shape his own behavior so that, consciously or not, he will use them more and more.

Another point to remember is that it is always helpful to have a "partner" (a secretary, for example) who is also familiar with management psychology and who is frequently nearby. This person can evaluate the manager's impact on others and provide invaluable feedback.

Finally, it is best to begin by practicing just two principles. This narrow focus avoids confusion, since any real-life situation always involves two, three, or four of the principles, as we can see from the following example:

Subordinate: I would like to hold off on that decision just now.

Manager: You always want to hold off on a decision and, frankly, I'm fed up with it!

The manager, by his angry statement, has paired both his subordinate and himself with aversive stimuli (Principle I), has paired the verbal equivalent of a response (delayed decision) with aversive stimuli (Principle IV), and has punished the subordinate's response (Principle VII). One statement thus reflects three principles. (Indeed, Principle VIII is also involved, since the manager now has an aversive stimulus "going," which he must stop sooner or later.)

CLASSICAL VS. OPERANT

Which principles one chooses to use and practice should be contingent upon one's own behavior patterns. Most managers start off with Principles V and VI. These principles can be very difficult to implement, however, if the manager is a highly critical person. He is then attempting to change not only others, but also himself, a difficult proposition at best.

Although many managers choose the operant principles, there are advantages to beginning with the classical ones. *Operant principles require an immediate reaction to a response on the other person's part.* The manager must therefore be able to think rapidly when using them. Classical principles, on the other hand, can be preplanned and deliberately thought out. It is true that operant techniques can give the manager quick feedback, since behavioral changes can be seen immediately after his response. *But classical principles allow much more certainty, because their use is not contingent upon the behavior of someone else at the time of implementation.*

Both sets of principles require an intimate knowledge of the individual to whom they are being applied. They require not only an analysis of typical response pat-terns, but also, and more important, a knowledge of what is really reinforcing and aversive to the individual. Some managers attempt to list "typical" or "common" reinforcers and aversive stimuli applicable to many people. This leads to mistakes, because typical reinforcers and aversive stimuli do not exist. Some people love attention, others hate it. Some people love compliments, others hate them. Some people love being touched, others hate it. Some people enjoy responsibility, others are frightened by it; a promotion in the latter case can be an intense aversive stimulus.

We might summarize the principles as follows: Classical principles merely require the speaker to pair a stimulus or the verbal equivalent of a response with stimuli reinforcing or aversive to the listener. Operant principles require the speaker to respond to another person's behavior. This is because changes in the person's behavior during operant learning occur only as a result of what happens immediately after the behavior, consequences that usually involve the behavior of other people.

A CASE STUDY

It might be helpful now to apply all eight principles to one simple "target" response. Since firing incompetent subordinates seems to be the most emotionally difficult response a manager has to make, let us take the case of a manager whose goal is to increase the probability that his subordinate, John, will perform this necessary task.

The manager must first determine what

reinforcers and aversive stimuli are precluding John from firing incompetent people. His observations indicate that John has a "strong need to be liked" and a "strong need to avoid being disliked" by his subordinates. (Most responses are controlled by more than one reinforcer and one aversive stimulus, but our example should be a simple one.)

Principle I. Since "being liked by people" is too strong a reinforcer to John, the manager must pair it with an aversive stimulus.

Manager: John, you seem to go out of your way to be liked by people below you. When subordinates like you, many times they don't respect you. They may be saying they like you to your face and laughing at you behind your back. So a need to be liked by subordinates can be a self-destructive thing.

The manager has three times paired "being liked by subordinates" with aversive stimuli. He has increased the probability of John firing incompetent subordinates.

Principle II. Since "being disliked by subordinates" is too strong an aversive stimulus to John, the manager must pair it with stimuli reinforcing to John. (The conversations throughout this sample would, of course, take place days apart.)

Manager: John, you seem to be going to some lengths to avoid subordinates disliking you. I think you might be making a mistake. When they express a dislike of you, it sometimes means they trust you enough to be open and honest with you. So if someone seems to dislike you, I hope you'll see it as a sign that he has

confidence in you. When people below you indicate they dislike you, they often are indicating they trust you.

The manager has paired "being disliked" with reinforcers. He has decreased the probability that John will get upset if someone indicates a dislike of him and increased the probability that John will fire incompetent people.

Principle III. Here the manager must pair the verbal equivalent of the response pattern (firing incompetent people) with reinforcers.

Manager: You know, John, I think the manager who fires incompetent people is a rare commodity these days. The manager who does fire incompetent people is worth his weight in gold to a company. Firing incompetent people is the real mark of a truly professional manager.

The manager has again increased the probability that John will fire people.

Principle IV. Here the manager must pair the verbal equivalent of the undesirable behavior (not firing people) with aversive stimuli.

Manager: I was talking to Jim the other day, John, about how the inability to fire incompetent people probably leads to more business failures than all other factors combined. As a matter of fact, not firing incompetent people can really make competent people quite angry toward their manager. By not firing incompetent people, a manager probably gets more people upset with him than for any other reason.

These, then, are possible classical responses the manager could make to increase desirable behavior in his subordinate. They did not require any response from the subordinate. They could be planned deliberately in a calm, analytical manner. They are not the result of a manager "playing God," but rather of a manager assuming his responsibility for the behavior of others, of a manager doing what he is paid to do. The problem with being a manager is that from time to time one must act like a manager.

Now let us consider operant procedures, which require a response on the part of the subordinate. Here we will use a dialogue between manager and subordinate which reflects the four operant principles.

Manager: John, I feel you aren't firing incompetent subordinates you should be firing. How do you feel about it? (Aversive stimulus)

Subordinate: Well, there may be some weak people below me, but firing them could upset the others. We'd be in real trouble if everyone walked off the job. (Attempts to stop the aversive stimuli by pairing "firing people" with aversive stimuli)

Manager: Oh, come on, John. Nobody is going to walk off the job and you know it. That's just an excuse for not doing your job. (Punishment; aversive stimuli still "on")

Subordinate: Well, maybe. But I don't have any replacements for people I'd fire. (Still attempts to stop the aversive stimuli)

Manager: We'd be a helluva lot better off with no one in those positions than some of the people you've got there. My God, we've been living with some of them for three years! (Punishment; the manager did not stop the aversive stimuli when John tried the excuse of no replacements.)

Subordinate: Well, I suppose I could call the Personnel Department and ask them to help get me some replacements.

Manager: I think that would be an excellent idea. (Shaping; stops the aversive stimulus and reinforces a constructive plan of action)

Subordinate: Do you really think I'd be better off without the people though? We're under a tight schedule.

Manager: Not tight enough to carry incompetent people on the payroll. (Mild punishment)

Subordinate: I suppose not. I suppose I could let Jack go. He's certainly been goofing off more than anyone, but . . .

Manager: John, if you let Jack go, I think everyone around here would have a good deal of respect for you. I know I would. (Interrupts to reinforce)

Subordinate: O.K., I'll do it, but . . .

Manager: Excellent! (Reinforcement)

Subordinate: But it's going to be difficult.

Manager: Say, how are those two machines we got in Wednesday working? (Extinction)

The manager has successfully shaped the desired behavior in his subordinate. Clearly, operant learning requires a quick response to ongoing behavior. However, the immediate result—the changed behavior—is there for the manager to see and provides his own necessary reinforcement.

Conversations of this type are usually unpleasant, because they involve stimuli aversive to both people. For this reason, managers often allow themselves to get sidetracked by a subordinate onto irrelevant issues. These side issues often involve a discussion of third parties, because most people enjoy talking about others in their absence. In the operant dialogue, for example, the subordinate might easily have swung the conversation off himself as follows:

Subordinate: Who do you feel I should fire?

Manager: That's up to you, John.

Subordinate: Well, Jack's been having trouble lately.

Manager: In what way?

Subordinate: I think he's got problems with his wife.

Manager: What kind of problems?

Soon both people are talking about what to them is a reinforcing topic, Jack's problems with his wife. They not only waste time doing it but also avoid getting back to the real issue. The reason is that the real issue is aversive to both.

No one can change the behavior of anyone who is not present at the time, since only stimuli that have an impact on an individual's sensory organs can influence his behavior. As mentioned previously, conversations between managers and subordinates about absent third parties should be held *only* if the manager is planning or attempting to change the behavior of his *listener* in relation to the absent third party. Rarely is there any other justification for talking about anyone not present. For too many managers gossip is a reinforcing and useful device to avoid aversive stimuli.

SYMPTOM TREATMENT

Both operant and classical experiences cause behavior. Problems may occur in changing behavior when a classical experience causes the behavior and an operant technique is used to try to change it, and vice versa. This ineffective approach causes some people to regard reinforcement principles merely as a form of "symptom treatment." In the former case, for example, a sudden loud noise may frighten a child; thunder and lightning are paired with sudden loud noises (classical experience): hence a storm frightens the child. The child's crying response can be effectively eliminated by punishing the crying behavior (operant technique) but other symptoms will probably develop. The child still fears storms. The "cause" can be eliminated by pairing the storm with reinforcers, for example, "Look how beautiful that lightning makes the sky. Gee, I like storms; they make the air so clean. Storms make the trees grow so beautifully" (classical technique).

Conversely, operant experiences are not truly remedied by classical procedures. If a subordinate finds his manager's approval reinforcing and the manager makes his approval dependent on the subordinate saying derogatory things about another person (operant technique), the subordinate will increasingly say derogatory things about the person. Pairing the third party with reinforcers (classical technique) will not stop the subordinate from saying derogatory things about him in his manager's presence as long as the manager continues to reinforce the response.

Socially pervasive operant procedures can result in widespread response patterns. While the American flag may have little reinforcing value to a child, failure to stand and "pledge allegiance" in school will often lead to aversive stimuli (punishment). The Protestant ethic leads to the reinforcement of work behavior and, more importantly, the punishment of nonwork behavior. Consequently, many people experience guilt feelings when they are not engaged in productive activities. This behavior cannot be changed by classical techniques. As a result, many lives are spent striving for goals which, when attained, are soon found to be wanting (extinguished). This may well eliminate the goal, but rarely the striving.

Most failures in this area, however, occur when operant procedures are used on responses classically caused. More specifically, punishment is often used by organizations to stop behavior that is occurring because a particular stimulus has become quite reinforcing to the individual. Seeing people hurt, for example, may be a strong reinforcer to a child. Rather than classically pairing this stimulus with aversive stimuli, a parent operantly punishes direct expressions of hostility. The child then turns to subtle, often devious means to achieve the goal of seeing people hurt.

Many subordinates find the attention of their manager quite reinforcing. Consequently, they may prolong meetings with their manager. Punishing the subordinate for prolonging or disrupting a meeting does little good if the manager's attention remains an overly strong reinforcer to the subordinate. He will merely get it in other ways. The effective manager will make the attention contingent upon constructive, results-oriented behavior or classically pair attention with aversive stimuli.

An individual may express strong belief in an idea because the idea was classically paired with reinforcers or aversive stimuli ("capitalists create false needs"). The manager can eliminate these *expressions* of belief merely by punishing them when they occur. Few people would argue the fact that the beliefs are still held, however. "You have not converted a man because you have silenced him."

Most organizations, and especially people in government positions, use aversive stimuli to control the behavior of people. In industry, no one is reinforced for wearing safety goggles, but anyone who does not is quickly punished. In government, one is rarely reinforced for pleasing and being loyal to his immediate superior, but anyone who is not is quickly punished, sometimes severely. In an effort to have more people use mass transit, government officials do virtually nothing to improve mass transit, but they increase the taxes on cars parked in the downtown area, place a limit on parking places, and stop building highways. They do nothing to make mass transit more reinforcing, but they make private auto driving more aversive. As we have seen, the use of aversive stimuli can have deleterious results.

The accusation of symptom treatment, therefore, merely reflects the inappropriate application of the principles—more specifically, the application of classical principles to operant-induced behavior and vice versa. Other common reasons for failing to influence people have already been discussed. They include backward pairings, no pairings at all, misdiagnosis of reinforcers and aversive stimuli, and the emotional difficulty of saying the right thing at the right time.

SUMMARY

Some managers fear that if everyone knows these principles their implementation can be compromised. This is simply not true. If compliments are reinforcing to an individual, sincerely telling him he did an outstanding job will have a reinforcing impact on him, whereas insincerely telling him he did an outstanding job will have an aversive impact on him; in both cases the impact will take place whether or not the individual knows the principles of reinforcement theory.

Reinforcement theory will be used most effectively in groups of people, all of whom are aware of the principles and all of whom give each other feedback about the effect of their behavior on others. This feedback should be factual; it should not reflect the emotional approach of many so-called sensitivity groups that give love and concern to depressed, self-deprecating souls and short shrift to confident, effective individuals. Quietly telling a manager he has just paired his own subordinates with aversive stimuli can have a beneficial influence on all concerned. Thanking someone for his expressed reinforcement of one's own achievements or pointing out a manager's subtle punishment of new ideas can be quite reinforcing and punishing comments in their own right.

Behavioral impact is contingent upon the effective utilization of reinforcement principles in face-to-face interactions. It is not contingent upon positions of authority. Just as managers grossly underestimate their influence on subordinates, so too do subordinates grossly underestimate their influence on their superiors. Many subordinates complain about the lack of feedback from their managers, but few will pair giving feedback with reinforcers in discussions with their managers. Fewer still will reinforce the manager when he attempts to give feedback. Indeed, few people realize how many managers leave their positions because of the emotional difficulties involved in managing people, difficulties that emanate from subordinates and that become too aversive for the manager to withstand.

The diagnosis of another person is a difficult, but essential, aspect of human relations. It should be based on intellectual analysis and, because of the rapid bombardment of complex stimuli, it should also be based on "gut feel." Analysis must always involve insight into the external causes of behavior. We know that John does not like Mary, yet he continues to date her. He does so because the response of not dating her would be more severely punished by his having to be alone. His dating of Mary is an avoidance behavior pattern rather than one controlled by the reinforcement of Mary (a fact which should stop social pressures to get married). An appropriate analysis of behavior, therefore, should look not only at alternative modes of behavior, but also at the external consequences of that behavior.

Influencing behavior through classical principles is emotionally difficult because behavioral changes are not spontaneously observable in the other person. Thus, using classical pairings is often extinguished. Yet classical pairings are one of the most precise and powerful tools of influence.

Using operant principles is intellectually difficult because the immediate behavior of another person is often too difficult to analyze and respond to. If there is one secret, it might be this: *Always be of good cheer.* This rather banal advice has two important operant consequences. First, if you are interacting with someone who is being *constructive* toward you, your good cheer will almost always be a reinforcer to him, thus you will increase the likelihood of constructive behavior on his part toward you. If someone is behaving *destructively* toward you, your good cheer will almost always be an aversive stimulus to him, thus you will decrease the likelihood of destructive behavior on his part in the future.

CLASSROOM EXERCISES

1. Jim is dating a young widow whose deceased husband, Bob, was not known by Jim. She makes one of the following comments to Jim:

   You would have liked Bob.

   or

   Bob would have liked you.

   On the basis of which comment should Jim marry her and which comment indicates trouble ahead? Why?

2. **Mary:** Why do I always have to go out and do what you want to do?

   Joe: I'm proud of you. I like to show you off to my friends.

   Mary: I feel I'm just a thing to you.

   Joe: That's not true.

   Mary: I'm just too subservient with you.

   Joe: Hey, not true. I love you more than anything in the world.

   Mary: I don't think you do. I let you get away with too much.

   What is reinforcing to Joe? Will Mary always love Joe? Why? What is Joe's impact on Mary?

3. **Sales manager:** Why didn't we get the Dow order?

   Salesman: They said, and it's true, that our shipments are late and there are too many defects in our steel.

   Sales manager: Look, what the hell would we need you for if we made a perfect product and always shipped on time?

   Is this an effective managerial response? Why?

4. You offer to take your spouse to Chasen's for dinner. She (he) makes one of the following two comments:

   Chasen's has lousy food and worse service.

   or

   Why would you pick a lousy restaurant like Chasen's?

   Which comment indicates an impending divorce and which tells you to just pick a different restaurant? Why?

5. Diagnose the speaker and analyze the impact on the listener of the following comment:

   Your subordinates get frustrated when you're indecisive.

6. Diagnose the manager and subordinate involved in the following interchange:

   Manager: You did a beautiful job on that report.

   Subordinate: I really felt I wasn't as concise as I should have been.

   Manager: I thought it was an excellent job. All of us are proud of you.

7. Diagnose the speaker and the effect on the listener of the following comment:

   I sure do enjoy being around you.

8. Someone has paired you with aversive stimuli to your best friend who now avoids you.

What should you do to get your best friend back?

a. Pair the other person with aversive stimuli to your friend.

b. Operantly punish your best friend's "poor" opinion of you.

c. Pair yourself with reinforcers to your best friend.

d. Try to elicit positive comments about you from your best friend and operantly reinforce them.

9. One of the best ways to get someone to like you is to pair yourself with reinforcers to that person's friends. True or false? Why?

10. Two of your subordinates despise each other. What concrete steps would you take as their manager?

SUGGESTED READINGS

Gellerman, S. W.: Motivation and productivity, New York, 1963, American Management Association.
One of the more widely read books in the management field.

Hilgard, E. B., and Bower, G. H.: Theories in learning, ed. 4, Englewood Cliffs, N.J., 1975, Prentice-Hall, Inc.
Readable reviews of classical, operant and many other learning theories.

Hulse, S. H., Deese, J., and Egeth, H.: The psychology of learning, ed. 4, New York, 1975, McGraw-Hill Book Co., chaps. 1-5
A detailed review of both operant and classical theories and research.

McGregor, D.: The professional manager. New York, 1967, McGraw-Hill Book Co.
A follow-up to *The Human Side of Enterprise*.

CHAPTER 7

Interviewing

eliciting and interpreting behavior

Speech is the index of the mind.
SENECA

There are two general reasons for including a chapter on interviewing in a book on management. First, good interviewing techniques are good management techniques. A large part of a manager's job is to ascertain the thoughts and attitudes of his subordinates on a day-to-day basis. This not only provides the manager with useful information in the form of helpful suggestions for getting the job done, it also allows him to understand better his subordinates' behavior and its causes. Through good interviewing techniques he can monitor not only the work activities of subordinates but also their attitudes about various facets of their responsibilities—both of which will have a strong impact on how well those responsibilities are, and will be, carried out.

Effective interviewing is also a strong motivating force; it tells a subordinate someone else in the world is concerned about what he is doing. Finally, interviewing helps a manager to spot trouble areas before they reach unmanageable proportions. It allows the perceptive manager to spot the subtle clues that tell him results are going to be disappointing and action is

required, rather than waiting for the results themselves to tell him there are problems. The techniques of good interviewing should be used by the manager *daily* in his interactions with subordinates.

The second reason for discussing interviewing is that selection-promotion decisions are the most important decisions a manager will ever make. At the highest level, the board of directors' selection of the chief executive officer will determine the fate of the organization for years to come.

Some might say that interviewing is not necessary in a promotion decision, since the employee's performance is already a matter of record. There are three reasons, however, why promotions should not be based on a person's performance in his present position. First, performance is difficult to interpret objectively; there are no objective objectives in this world. Second, performance is the result of numerous variables, many of which the individual cannot control. Third, promotion means moving a person into a new environment, where, as we have seen, he will confront new reinforcement contingencies, new personalities, new duties, and responsibilities; in short, an entirely different set of interactions. For example, consider the following case:

A large Eastern company took over a small family-owned Midwestern company. The large organization tried to show its faith in the small company by promoting the vice president of purchasing for the small company to the corporate vice presidency of purchasing for the entire corporation. Despite the fact that the two functions were essentially similar in that they both dealt with the same product lines, the man became an alcoholic within six months. This was because he had moved from a friendly, "calling-the-president-by-his-first-name" atmosphere into a cold, aggressive, hypercritical atmosphere in which "survival of the fittest" was the dominant theme.

Clearly, the criterion for promotion decisions is not our analysis of past performance. It is, rather, our best estimate or prediction of how a person will respond in a new situation. We will base our inferences, of course, on the only data we have available, those concerning the present *behavior* of the person, rather than solely on his present performance. One of the most effective situations in which to elicit and analyze behavior is the interview.

THE INTERVIEW
Preparation

A good interview requires preparation in two areas. We must know the job responsibilities the interviewee will assume and the personalities of the people with whom he will interact, especially the personality of his potential immediate superior. Lacking this information, we are merely sending a man into a vacuum. The fact that one superior is a precise, thorough, detail-oriented person, whereas another is an impulsive, fast-paced, aggressive person, is critical when we attempt to estimate the success of any given individual under these managers. Even if the job duties are quite similar under the two managers, the same person could find himself a stunning success under the one and a miserable failure under the other. Like it or not, success in a given position is determined, to a large extent, by what the manager of that position says it is.

The subject of job descriptions needs further explanation. A job description is normally a series of physical facts that are of little help in predicting performance. To be useful, these physical facts must be translated into behavioral terms. The position of plant controller, for example, may list as one of its responsibilities the coordination of materials inventory. This tells us little. If, however, we know that the inventory consists of small parts that are rapidly moving in and out of the plant, we can infer some of the psychological characteristics necessary for the position. In this instance, for example, responsibility for the inventory may require that the applicant be detail-oriented, capable of handling a number of variables at one time, well-organized, and able to make quick decisions. These are behavioral characteristics we can determine from an interview. They will tell us more than we can learn by simply asking a person if he is capable of handling inventory or relying on supposed past experience. If job descriptions are translated into behavioral terms, the behavioral description of a given applicant can then be compared with the required behavior traits of the position.

It might be helpful to list some basic behavioral terms that could be relevant for some positions. The reader should not approach these as a cookbook, but as a stimulant; the evaluator should always attempt to describe the uniqueness of the person.

APPROACH TO PROBLEMS

Detail orientation	Quickness
Thoroughness	Efficiency
Follow through	Judgment
(finishes tasks)	Risk orientation
Organization	Factual
Creative	

APPROACH TO RESPONSIBILITIES

Emotional stability and	Initiative
expressiveness	Conscientiousness
Attitudes (toward	Aggressiveness
authority)	Cooperativeness
Decisiveness	Pace
Independence	Determination

APPROACH TO PEOPLE

Persuasiveness	Reaction to
Tactfulness	criticism
Forcefulness	Humor
Openness	Listening skills
Sincerity	Responsiveness
Friendliness	

APPROACH TO MANAGERIAL RESPONSIBILITIES

This will not be elaborated since this is the primary thrust of the entire book. Suffice it to say: What is the candidate's be-

havioral impact on subordinates; what does he find reinforcing and aversive in the behavior of others?

In this connection we should note that three of the most overrated criteria on which selection-promotion decisions are based *at the managerial level* are intelligence, experience, and technical knowledge. The basic problems of an organization do not require an Einstein (indeed, Einstein might well have been a poor manager); their solutions are usually found in the reinforcement and aversive contingencies discussed earlier. The problems of most managers are more emotional than intellectual. Experience in handling a function tells us little about a manager's ability to handle it well and nothing about the crucial aspects of his job (whom does he select, can he fire incompetent subordinates, does he communicate with subordinates, are practical results more reinforcing to him than merely getting along with others, does he develop subordinates). Technical knowledge becomes more important as one *descends* the managerial ladder. The steel mill foreman had better know what is happening at a technical level. The steel company president, however, needs little technical knowledge; most of his contributions will be reflected in his impact on the behavior of other people in the organization.

It is unfortunate that a good two- or three-hour interview generally tells a manager more about an individual than does managing him for two or three years. This is not only because of the manager's prejudices, but also because the vast majority of managers focus only on the results of behavior, rather than on the behavior itself and what causes it. If three subordinates submit the same report with the same error, most managers focus on the report and the error. Effective managers go one step further. They analyze their subordinates' behavior and conclude that the same error is the result of a repetitious authority problem in subordinate A, a lack of detail orientation in subordinate B, and indecisiveness in subordinate C. By dealing directly with these behavioral characteristics, the manager gets at causes and eliminates the need to put out the fires constantly caused by these characteristics.

After engaging in a thorough behavioral analysis of the job and the personalities it involves, we are ready to begin the interview. The type of interview we will describe here is called a conversational interview. It has no tricks or gimmicks. Its purpose is to elicit a sample of behavior in order to determine the interviewee's most probable responses and which stimuli are reinforcing and aversive to him. In other words, the interview should help the manager to predict frequent behavior and should give him information that will allow him to influence this behavior effectively in subsequent interactions.

Let us now consider twelve principles which, if implemented, should help the manager to conduct a better interview. While this chapter is written in terms of a selection-promotion interview, it is worth noting again that these principles are also applicable in day-to-day interactions with subordinates who have been with the company for years.

PRINCIPLES OF ELICITING BEHAVIOR
The interviewer must always be nonjudgmental in his responses

The difference between a good interview and normal conversation is that the effective interviewer does not selectively reinforce or punish the behavior of the other person. This is what is meant by being nonjudgmental. Suppose we ask an individual what traits he likes to see in other people. If we respond to his answer nonjudgmentally, his subsequent behavior is likely to reflect his true attitudes. However, if we respond, "I'm surprised you think those traits are important; I think they're kind of superficial," we are not likely to subsequently elicit his true attitudes.

Most interviewees are quite alert and perceptive during the interview; after all, important decisions are going to be made about them. The basic goal of the interviewee during the interview is to please the interviewer. In other words, he will attempt to pair himself with stimuli reinforcing to the interviewer. Therefore, any indication the interviewer gives suggesting what he finds reinforcing or aversive will color the entire interview. If, for example, the interviewer pairs the phrase, "We have a good aggressive management team here," with an enthusiastic tone of voice, he has increased enormously the possibility that the interviewee will pair himself with aggressive traits in his own behavior, whether he is truly aggressive or not. For this reason, interviewing is one of the most emotionally difficult functions many managers have to perform. It requires the interviewer to subjugate his entire personality to that of the interviewee. The interviewer cannot afford to have overt attitudes and opinions during the interview.

Many organizations make the mistake of attempting to sell the interviewee on joining their organization before they interview him. In selling their organization to the interviewee, they indicate what is reinforcing and what is aversive to them. The interviewee quickly pairs himself with these reinforcers in the subsequent interview and is highly recommended as a result. However, his behavior during the interview may be nothing like his behavior on the job. A high rate of turnover is the result. An interview should *precede* any other step in the selection-promotion process. Indeed, convincing the interviewee to join the company is much easier after the interview, since the manager should now know what is reinforcing and aversive to the applicant.

Ask general, ambiguous questions

One might best conceive of a human being as a pool of potential responses. Every human being, given the right circumstances, is capable of emitting any human response, from patting a man on the back to shooting someone. Different personalities are the result of the different probabilities of responses that have been established by an individual's past experience with the contingencies of reinforcers and aversive stimuli. A decisive person is likely to have decisive response patterns because they have frequently been reinforced in his experience; an indecisive person is far less likely to have such response patterns because in his experience they have been followed by aversive stimuli. To describe a person as decisive does not mean he is *always* decisive; again, frequent behavior is what we want.

The goal of the interview, then, is to elicit an individual's most probable response patterns. This is accomplished by asking general, ambiguous questions, such as "Could you tell me a little about your business background?" or "How was the company?" or "What was the atmosphere of the company at that time?" or "Was the atmosphere of that company different from the other one you worked for?" Asking specific questions such as, "Could you tell me how they organized their paper flow in the purchasing department?" may well elicit a response pattern the interviewee is not likely to emit in the general work setting. It also indicates to the interviewee what is reinforcing to the interviewer (in this case, organizing material).

General, ambiguous questions serve two purposes. First, they make most interviewees feel comfortable because there are no right or wrong answers. Second, general, ambiguous questions elicit different behavior patterns from different people. They allow the individual to project himself as he really is into his response, rather than confining him to a narrow range of behavior. It is this projection of himself under ambiguous conditions that reflects his most probable (frequent) behavior patterns.

Ask value judgment, not factual, questions

The interview is not a fact-finding mission. Attempting to determine whether a man left a position in May or June of 1962 tells us little about the man. Also, interpretations cannot be based on the factual material the interviewee presents during an interview. We do not know that a man has good initiative merely because he says he worked full time while attending college at night; the interviewer cannot be sure of such facts without doing reference checks, and this is far too time-consuming.

We will elicit much more meaningful material if we ask the interviewee for value judgments. Asking an individual what he liked and disliked about his former company or former superior tells us much more about the person than whether he left a position in May or June. Likewise, the *fact* that the interviewee was in a management training program in 1953 tells us little; asking him how good he felt the training program was can tell us a good deal. His assessments rather than his enumeration of past experiences can tell us, for example, whether or not he is decisive, hypercritical, or too detail-oriented. They can tell us which situations and types of behavior in others he finds reinforcing and aversive. (Never ask an individual anything about anyone in the company for which he is presently working, however; the interviewee does not know how you will use that material, and it can be a strong aversive stimulus to him.)

Ask questions on subjects external to the interviewee

One of the major goals of the interview is to create a spontaneous, conversational atmosphere. Questions such as "I haven't

heard of that company—what do they do?" are the sort one would ask another person at a party. If this type of question is asked sincerely, the interviewee will feel the interviewer has "left the interview" and is genuinely interested in what that particular company does. Such questions will elicit more spontaneity from the interviewee. As a result, his responses will be similar to those likely to occur in the work setting; they will not simply reflect the interview setting.

This is a subtle point. The word "you" should be dropped from questions whenever possible. A less effective question is more likely to put the person on guard: "How did you find the people in Kansas City?" More effective would be: "How were the people in Kansas City?" The focus of the latter question is on the people in Kansas City, not on the interviewee. The response of the interviewee, however, will tell us more about the interviewee than about people in Kansas City.

Ask simple, basic questions in the interviewee's field of expertise

Good interviewers have sufficient confidence in themselves to adopt a naive, somewhat subservient manner. They are not afraid to ask basic questions which might reflect a lack of knowledge, for example, "What is a steel ingot?" "How do you drill for oil?" or "What is a preferred stock?" These basic questions in the interviewee's field of expertise put him in a dominant position; they also encourage him to be relaxed and spontaneous. Many interviewers are so intent upon impressing the interviewee that they shy away from topics that would reveal their ignorance. This is a critical mistake. The effective interviewer makes the interviewee feel more expert, more knowledgeable, than anyone else in the room.

Maintain an interested, conversational tone of voice with appropriate inflection

No variable is more important in eliciting spontaneous behavior from an interviewee than is the interviewer's tone of voice. Unfortunately, no variable is more difficult to master. Since they often determine whether or not the interviewee gets a job, most interviewers are in a position of power. This power is often reflected in their tone of voice, which is likely to be flat and authoritative. The best interviewing tone, however, is soft and inflected. Its softness connotes respect for the interviewee, if only for the pragmatic reason that a commanding tone will elicit only the response patterns evoked by an authority figure, whereas the goal of the interview is to elicit the interviewee's most probable behavior in all situations. The interviewer's inflection connotes a respectful interest in what the interviewee is saying. This is likely to be quite reinforcing to the interviewee and will increase the probability of his responding during the interview. Any interviewer who cannot elicit two hours of useful responses is not using the proper tone of voice. A commanding or uninterested tone can be a severe aversive stimulus, which decreases the probability that the interviewee will respond.

The reinforcing interest of the interviewer is, of course, a response to everything and anything the interviewee says. If it occurs only when an interviewee says certain things, shaping will take place, and the interviewee will soon be focusing his attention on those certain things. The interviewer who communicates interest only when the interviewee talks about the technical areas of his previous responsibilities will quickly find the interviewee discussing only technical matters, even if his on-the-job orientation is much more toward people. The reinforcing concern of the interviewer, therefore, must be a constant, pervasive stimulus that is contingent upon whatever the interviewee says; providing reinforcement periodically and contingent upon specific content areas of the interview will lead to a distorted, inaccurate picture of the interviewee.

Use short, quick phrases for probes

If the interviewer is relaxed and spontaneous, the interviewee will be relaxed and spontaneous. Suppose the interviewer wants to probe the interviewee's statement, "I thought it was a good company to work for." If the interviewer follows this with the formal phrase, "What was it about the company that made you feel it was a good company to work for?" he will elicit a formal, stilted response. A better reaction on the interviewer's part is a quick, soft, interested "How so?," "In the sense of?," or "Because?" The interviewee will in this case be more likely to respond as he would in his own work setting, when he will in fact be acting spontaneously.

Consider the two types of interviewing used by a husband and wife below:

Husband: What kind of a guy am I as a husband? (good general question)

Wife: Well, you're all right.

Husband (angrily): Just what the hell does all right mean?

The husband becomes judgmental and punishes his wife. This ensures his goal: not finding out what his wife really does think of him as a husband. A more effective approach:

Husband: What kind of a guy am I as a husband?

Wife: Well, you're all right.

Husband (soft, but with interested inflection): How so?

Now the husband may indeed find out his wife's true attitudes (a fact which, it must be admitted, may punish his good interviewing techniques).

The importance of these short, probing phrases cannot be overemphasized. Such phrases are used to elicit what is frequently the richest material for interpretation. The question, "What kind of a boss was he?" usually elicits a perfunctory "Good" or "He was a good man." Far too many interviewers go on to a different subject at this point, although little can be learned from so superficial a response. However, following the response with "How so?" will generally elicit a revealing elaboration. Moreover, by using short phrases, the interviewer shows that he is interested in the interviewee himself and not merely in eliciting his attention with long-winded, repetitious questions.

Consider the two following examples:

Interviewee: I thought it was a good company.

Interviewer: Because?

Interviewee: I thought it was a good company.

Interviewer: In what sense did you feel it was a good company? You know, there are many facets to a company and I was wondering which ones struck you most about that particular company? Did you feel it was the aggressiveness or the organizational skills of the company? As I'm sure you know, all companies have a distinct personality and I was wondering how you would describe this one? (At this point, the interviewee is wondering how he'll be able to stay awake.)

The first interviewer is focused on diagnosing the behavior of the interviewee, the second on impressing and eliciting the interviewee's attention.

A word about stress interviews might be appropriate here. These typically come in the form of obnoxious questions or in terms of using multiple interviewers at the same time. These types of interviews do indeed indicate how an individual will react to stress. They are probably effective when one is recruiting for the CIA or Army counterintelligence organizations (or for chief-executives who have inferiority complexes and manage by means of ridicule and punishment). In private industry, however, stress interviews suffer from several shortcomings. First, they develop many enemies for the hiring organization. Second, it is unlikely that an applicant will encounter such stress in the work setting; an accurate prediction of behavior under those conditions, therefore, is almost irrelevant. Third, so much rapport is broken that eliciting far more important behavior (organized, detail orientation) is almost impossible. Stress interviewing as opposed to conversational interviewing, it must be said, is a lot more fun—for the interviewer.

Do not attempt to anticipate your next question

An interviewer's questions should be contingent upon the interviewee's responses. One never knows what these responses will be. (If one did, the interview would not be necessary.) If the interviewer is trying to think of his next question, he cannot possibly be listening to the interviewee. (This is one reason people who are intent on impressing others make poor interviewers. Their focus is on how they appear to the interviewee rather than the other way around.)

Attempting to anticipate one's next question will also make the interview stilted and disjointed. The interviewee will frequently go off on a tangent, after which a question that would have been appropriate two sentences ago should no longer be asked.

Interviewer: Whom did you report to then?

Interviewee: To the vice president of manufacturing. (Interviewer is about to ask what kind of a fellow he was, but the interviewee continues.) Of course, I was only in that position four weeks when they transferred me overseas.

The patterned interview is likely to elicit responses from the interviewee that have a low probability of occurring in the work setting. They are contingent upon the interviewer's behavior, not the interviewee's behavior. Moreover, in such a situation the interviewer's focus will be on his next questions, since they are structured in sequence, rather than on the interviewee's remarks. This leads to a stilted, disjointed interview. The interviewer will learn more about the interviewee by allowing him to guide the interview. If a moment of silence occurs, the question, "What happened then?" always elicits a natural, spontaneous response.

Experience in this area is important. As the interviewer becomes relaxed, he will be able to "ride with" the interviewee's direction, just as we all do in social conversations. In the above example, the interviewee's sudden transfer overseas could easily have been responded to with, "How come?" or "Where to?"

In this connection, it is important that the interviewer not ask questions with the goal of determining whether the interviewee engages in specific behavior patterns. The interviewer, for example, should never say to himself, now I will see if he's decisive so I'll ask him, "What was the training program like?" Again, we cannot predict an interviewee's behavior; if we could, we would not be interviewing him. An interviewee's response to this general question can range all over the place and tell you many things about him (organized, too detailed), sometimes everything except whether he is decisive or not.

Probe choice points and unusual situations

Choice points refer to situations in which an individual has made a choice—by changing positions, for example, or by selecting a school or refusing a promotion or transfer. It is in these situations that the reinforcers and aversive stimuli controlling the interviewee's behavior are most apparent. Unusual situations also involve stimuli that are intensely reinforcing or aversive to the interviewee. Why a man left his father's company when he was obviously going to inherit the presidency is a critical question that must be answered. The information is best elicited, not with long-winded or emotionally skeptical questions, but rather, with a soft, quick, interested "How come?" or "Why leave?"

These are, oddly enough, the only two areas an interviewer could be justifiably criticized for not probing. To interview a 40-year-old person thoroughly would take 40 years. Two interviewers should be able to probe and skip entirely different segments of the interviewee's life and arrive at the same conclusions. This is due to the fact that the repetitious behavior patterns of the interviewee should be evident in both instances. If the interviewee is an intensely thorough person, he will be thorough describing an event that took place ten years ago as well as eight years ago as well as yesterday.

Interrupt the interviewee

When we are interacting with people in a relaxed atmosphere, we interrupt them. An interruption may be mildly aversive if the interviewee is intent upon getting a point across. It can also be a strong reinforcer, however, in that it tells the interviewee we are actually listening to him. Silence is not necessarily listening. In fact, it extinguishes the behavior of the interviewee. Listening is an active response involving overt behavior that has an impact on the speaker. When we interrupt the interviewee and ask for clarification on a point we do not understand, we are pairing ourselves with stimuli reinforcing to him.

Silence, of course, can be useful in some situations. Since silence extinguishes behavior, it can be used by the manager to reduce a subordinate's overly strong emotional involvement on a given matter, such as a decision made by management. Suppose, for example, a subordinate bitterly complains about a new company policy. The manager would do well to elicit his subordinate's feelings with good interviewing techniques (nonjudgmental, but probing questions). The subordinate's angry responses should then be met with silent pauses by the manager. This "ventilation" will usually decrease the intensity of the subordinate's feelings on that issue. Too many managers, however, elicit the feelings and then respond with emotional counter-arguments of their own; these emotional managerial reactions are often reinforcing to the subordinate and increase the frequency and intensity of his complaints.

Reflect the interviewee's statements

Reflecting the interviewee's comments is another way of telling him we are listening to what he is saying. This is only true, however, if the reflection sounds interested and concerned, as in the example below. If we reflect in a flat monotone, we may well be pairing ourselves with a stimulus aversive to the interviewee, which will decrease the probability of his responding in the interview.

Interviewee: So I was pretty excited over the promotion.

Interviewer (with concern): It was an exciting moment. (Reflection)

Reflections of negative events should always underplay the aversiveness of the situation. That a reflection is effective is determined by whether or not the interviewee accepts it. If the interviewer makes the reflection too aversive, the interviewee will reject it.

Interviewee: So I was a bit disappointed that I didn't get the job.

Interviewer: It was a pretty disappointing moment. (Overstated reflection)

Interviewee: Well, not really. I had two other job offers at the time. (Reflection rejected)

Interviewer: You were a little disappointed at the moment.

Interviewee: Yeah, it would have given me a chance to see Europe. (Reflection accepted)

Respond with emotional interest

If the interviewee's eyes light up and he takes obvious pleasure in talking about one of his accomplishments and its consequences, the interviewer must respond with the appropriate emotion. Suppose, for example, the interviewee has told us about an extensive study he made on a given project. He then states, "As a result of my input, they gave me total responsibility for implementation of the entire project!" Here the interviewer must respond with an appropriate reinforcer. He might, for example, smile and say with an enthusiastic inflection, "Really!" This is just the reinforcer the interviewee was attempting to elicit. If the interviewer does not react at all or reacts in an uninterested monotone, he will extinguish the interviewee's response and decrease the probability that the interviewee will again respond in a spontaneous, open manner.

PRINCIPLES OF INTERPRETING BEHAVIOR

The purpose of the interview is to elicit a sample of the interviewee's behavior for interpretation. The first ten or fifteen minutes of the interview should be used to relax the interviewee. Interpretations in this initial phase are much more tentative than those made in the later stages of a good interview.

The goal of interpretation is to determine the interviewee's most probable response patterns in the work setting and the stimuli that are most reinforcing and aversive to him. Again, two interviewers should be able to probe two completely different time periods in an individual's life and arrive at the same conclusions regarding his probable response patterns and the reinforcers and aversive stimuli influencing him. This is because an individual's behavior and interpretation of past events are determined by what he is now.

Difficulties in interpretation originate more from poor interviewer questioning than from lack of knowledge of interpretation principles. If we have difficulty interpreting interviewees, we naturally feel we need training and help in interpretation principles. This is rarely the case. Consider the following typical factual interviewer questions:

What was the name of the company you joined?

Where was the company located?

What was the date you joined the company?

What was your position title?

How long did you stay with the company?

Did you hold any other position with that company?

What were the titles of these positions?

What was the date you left the company?

The most highly trained and skilled interviewer in the world would have difficulty making relevant interpretations based on a typical interviewee's responses to these questions. Yet too many interviewers focus on interpretation principles when it is really their poor interviewing skills that preclude them from gaining insight into the interviewee.

The real problem stems from the emotional difficulties involved in interviewing. It can be frustrating listening to another person's point of view without being able to venture your own opinions, or tell him how wrong he is or how stupid his judgments are. This frustration and the resulting interview ineptness are apparent in both selection-promotion and daily manager-subordinate interviews. Eliciting the behavior of another person is a rare and invaluable skill in any position in an organization.

Interpretations should always be put into written form for two reasons. First, the written interpretations should be used to check the efficacy of each interviewer. This is accomplished by correlating the interviewer's interpretations with the interviewee's behavior on the job several months later. Second, permanent stimuli should be made available which will have a constant impact on the interviewee's manager months after the interview has been concluded. These written interpretations should be a constant reminder to the man-ager that he must focus on the person and his shortcomings rather than solely on the consequences of those shortcomings. Most organizations transmit interpretations by word-of-mouth. This approach is worse than ineffective, because everyone straddles the fence. If the interviewee succeeds, everyone recalls his positive interpretations; if the interviewee fails, everyone remembers his negative interpretations and doubts.

Keeping these points in mind, let us now consider three basic principles governing the interpretation of interviews.

Be hypercritical in your interpretations

Pleasing the interviewer is one of the strongest reinforcers to the interviewee. All his efforts will be aimed toward this goal. If the interviewer notices a negative trait during a two- or three-hour interview, imagine how blatant this shortcoming will be when the interviewee is spending forty hours a week in the work setting, where he is not always intent on pleasing anyone. Good interviewers are highly critical people. They are therefore rare people, since it is aversive to most individuals to have to criticize someone who has never hurt them. This is especially true of the typical personnel specialist who is in this position precisely because he is such a "nice" fellow.

Base your interpretations, whenever possible, on the obvious

The obvious response patterns are those most likely to recur in the work setting. If the interviewee is obviously loud and boisterous, describe him as loud and boisterous! Do not look for deep, hidden meanings in a person's behavior. Because an individual crossed his legs does not necessarily mean he is sexually inhibited. Interpretations should, moreover, be based on the most frequent response pattern of an individual, not on his possibly true, but infrequent, response patterns. In fact, *any valid interpretation should be confirmed in at least three instances of behavior during a normal interview*.

The most valid interpretations will be based on the interviewee's behavior during the interview, not on the content of his verbalizations

This is a subtle, but critical, point. It is the essence of correct interpretations. If we ask an interviewee to describe a previous boss, we have no way of knowing whether his description is accurate nor should we care. We do know, however, what the interviewee emphasizes in his description, and this is the material to use for interpretation. Likewise, if an interviewee elaborates at length on his having worked full time while completing his bachelor's degree at night, we must base our interpretation on his need to elaborate this point, his need to impress us with this information. That he worked full time and completed his bachelor's degree at night is a fact we do not know is true; even if it were true, it could be influenced by many variables the interviewee is not telling us about.

Few interviewees are going to tell us they were fired from their last job, nor should we expect them to. Indeed, that they were fired may be more a reflection of their previous manager than of them. To judge the situation would be impossible and irrelevant. That the interviewee, however, frequently and repetitiously pairs

superiors with aversive stimuli during the interview is relevant and important. People can easily change the content (and always do) of what they say. It is very difficult, however, for a person with a strong need for precision not to be precise in the interview. ("I was with that company fourteen months; no, actually it was a little over fourteen months.")

Suppose we ask an interviewee to describe the atmosphere of a company he worked for ten years ago. We do not know if his description is accurate, nor is this important. We do know what he is emphasizing in describing the atmosphere of his former company, and his answer (which, for example, may be well organized, overly detailed, or indecisive) therefore tells us a good deal about his behavior.

A hypercritical interviewee has difficulty controlling his tendency to criticize when he is discussing situations aversive to him, and this tendency is a relevant factor in the selection decision. Too many interviewers become interested in the content of what the interviewee is saying and swing their focus to the company the interviewee is describing rather than the interviewee's behavior itself.

• • •

The variety of human behavior is infinite. To attempt to categorize various response patterns by assigning them to specific personality types would be difficult, if not impossible. It will be more helpful to consider some examples of effective interviewer questioning and interpretation during an interview. The interpretations in the following examples are obviously tentative and would require confirmation in several more instances of behavior during the remainder of the interview.

EXAMPLES OF INTERVIEWING AND INTERPRETATION

Interviewer: Well, could you tell me a little about your business background? You might start the day after school if you like.

Interviewee: Did you want me to start the day after high school or the day after I graduated from college? (He answered a question with a question.)

Possible interpretations: Ambiguous situations are aversive to the interviewee and make him uncomfortable; he actively seeks structure and clarification in such situations, and precision and accuracy are reinforcers to him. This could be a problem if the interviewee is assigned to work under a manager who expects independence and initiative and does not direct subordinates closely.

Interviewer: What was the atmosphere of the company like? (Good broad, general question)

Interviewee: Well, it was pretty good. (Must be probed)

Interviewer: How so? (Quick, short, probing question)

Interviewee: Well, people pulled together. There wasn't a lot of this backbiting you see in a lot of companies. When someone needed help, we all pitched in to get the job done. (Focuses on interpersonal

relations; we still really know nothing about the company, nor does this matter.)

Possible interpretations: The interviewee finds competition with his peers an aversive stimulus; he should not be involved in internal company contests or competition. Support and cooperation from people around and over him are reinforcers that can have a strong motivating impact on him. He must feel he is an integral member of a team; being an outsider or isolated from his group is aversive to him. He should not work under a manager who encourages competition between his subordinates.

Interviewer: What happened then? (Good broad question)

Interviewee: I was promoted to supervisor of accounts receivable.

Interviewer: This was your first crack at management? (Following the lead of the interviewee)

Interviewee: That's right.

Interviewer: How did it go? (Good broad question)

Interviewee: Pretty well. I had a lot of older people under me and, as you know, they can be difficult to deal with.

Interviewer: In the sense of . . . ? (Gentle, quick probe)

Interviewee: Well, we tried to put in some new methods, but changing the habits of people who have been doing something for twenty years isn't easy.

Possible interpretations: The interviewee is uncomfortable with authority over other people (aversive stimuli) and lacks a commanding presence. He is more likely to allow people to go their own way than to lead them. He would have difficulty managing aggressive people (aversive stimuli) and would therefore probably select weak people as his subordinates.

Interviewer: How many people were you over?

Interviewee: About twenty-five.

Interviewer: How were they? (Broad, value-judgment question)

Interviewee: What do you mean? (Unusual response—most people feel comfortable with general questions because they can read into them what they want; the ambiguity, however, makes this interviewee uncomfortable.)

Interviewer: Good or bad?

Interviewee: Good! Everybody got along well with everybody else. Not a single person left the department in the year and a half that I managed them.

Possible interpretations: Maintaining positive interpersonal relations is a strong reinforcer to the interviewee; on the other hand, disruptive interpersonal relationships are overly aversive to him. He has difficulty taking adverse action when necessary and is probably too lenient and superficial in evaluating subordinates (it's unlikely that twenty-five people are all good).

Interviewer: How many people were under you?

Interviewee: About twenty-five.

Interviewer: How were they?

Interviewee: Good; they did their job and we met almost all the deadlines in getting the work out. Oh, there were a few rotten apples in the barrel, as there always are.

Interviewer: Did you have to fire anyone?

Interviewee: Yes, I had to let three people go.

Interviewer: Because?

Interviewee: Well, one would never come in on time. Another one was always complaining, always bitching. I sat down and talked to him about it three or four times but I couldn't seem to change him around. The third one was just lazy.

Possible interpretations: Practical results are reinforcing to the interviewee. He is not uncomfortable with authority over others; he can be a firm manager who will take adverse action when necessary and recognizes the importance of giving feedback to subordinates. He attacks problems in a direct manner and does not go off on superficial tangents (based on his direct, concise behavior in the interview, not on the content of what he is saying).

Interviewer: What happened then?

Interviewee: I left the company.

Interviewer: Because?

Interviewee: It just wasn't the type of company I wanted to work for.

Interviewer: How so?

Interviewee: Well, there were three things I disliked. First, the whole place was disorganized. Second, the pay was quite low. Third, there was no place to go in the organization.

Possible interpretations: The interviewee places strong emphasis on organization (not because he criticizes the company about being disorganized, but because he lists the liabilities of the company in a systematic, one-two-three manner). His responses in the interview are well organized.

Interviewer: How long were you in that position?

Interviewee: About eight years.

Interviewer: Why so long? (Interested, not challenging, tone of voice)

Interviewee: Well, it's not really that long a time (defensive when criticized). Besides the company was quite stable in those days and there was nowhere to go.

Interviewer (later in interview): What are your goals in life?

Interviewee: I want to go as high in an organization as I can. I'd like to be president of my own organization some day.

Possible interpretations: The interviewee, in spite of his last remark, is not ambitious, nor does he move aggressively to attain positions of greater power and prestige; he is overly content with situations as they exist. He has little initiative and poor insight into his own behavior. Impressing people is more reinforcing to him than is taking action (tries to impress interviewer with last comment).

Interviewer: What position did you report to at that time?

Interviewee: Vice president of operations.

Interviewer: What kind of a guy was he?

Interviewee: Good, one of the best managers I ever had.

Interviewer: How so?

Interviewee: Well, he let you do a job the way you saw fit. Then if he felt you were doing something the wrong way, he wasn't afraid to tell you about it. You knew where you stood with him. I probably learned more about myself from him than from any other boss I ever worked for.

Possible interpretation: The interviewee finds constructive criticism and an open atmosphere reinforcing. He is motivated to develop his own personal skills and needs a confident, decisive manager over him who will delegate responsibility.

Interviewer: What kind of a manager was your boss?

Interviewee: All right, I guess. He was a bit sneaky, though.

Interviewer: How so?

Interviewee: Well, he'd take credit for things you had done. But, boy, if anything went wrong, your name was the first thing out of his mouth.

Interviewer: He was pretty quick to put the blame on people under him. (Reflection)

Interviewee: He sure was.

Interviewer: He was somewhat like that other boss you talked about in that respect.

Interviewee: That's right. I haven't had too much luck with my bosses.

Interviewer (later in the interview): What kind of a person was your father?

Interviewee: I never really knew him that much. If he wasn't working, he was out bowling or golfing or, frankly, gallivanting around with women.

Possible interpretation: The interviewee has an authority problem; anyone in a position of authority over him is an aversive stimulus he will attack by pairing with aversive stimuli (which he did in the interview).

Interviewer: What do you look for in people?

Interviewee: I like to see technical competence.

Interviewer: Really? Don't you think the ability to handle people is much more important? (Poor question—shows too much of the interviewer's bias.)

Interviewee: Oh, sure! I meant, from an

educational standpoint technical competence is important. But handling people right is a much more difficult job.

Possible interpretation: The interviewee is too easily swayed by the views of people in positions of authority. He is also more oriented toward technical problem-solving than toward managing people (pairs managing people with an aversive stimulus: "a much more difficult job").

Interviewer: What school did you attend?

Interviewee: The University of Chicago. How about yourself? Where did you get your degree?

Possible interpretation: Dislikes being in a subservient role and actively attempts to dominate others. (Incidentally, never answer an interviewee's question. "Well, we can talk about me later if you'd like. How did you like the University of Chicago?")

Interviewer: How was the company?

Interviewee: Well, it had good and bad points.

Interviewer (later): What kind of a guy was your boss?

Interviewee: Not the best I've had, but not the worst either.

Possible interpretations: Indecisive.

Interviewer: How was the company?

Interviewee: Lousy! The people didn't know their head from a goddamn hole in the wall.

Possible interpretations: Too intense emotionally. Overly direct, blunt, and abrasive.

SUMMARY

This small sample of interviewing interactions should give the reader some conception of a conversational interview. The most important variable in interviewing and eliciting behavior is probably the interviewer's tone of voice when using broad, general questions. The most important rule in interpretation is to base one's judgments, as far as possible, on the present behavior of the interviewee, not on the content of events he says happened two years or even two days ago.

Many companies relegate interviewing to an unimportant level, despite lip service to the contrary. This is because of their lack of focus on the people in their organization. This attitude usually originates with the chief executive officer who often finds it more rewarding to focus his attention up (board of directors) and out (big customers or presidents of other companies) rather than down (on subordinates, where it should be). The other reason interviewing is assigned an unimportant role is that there are so few good interviewers around who carry out the function effectively. This attitude results in fifteen to thirty minute interviews that lead to a high error rate.

Good interviewing is an emotionally difficult process, made even more difficult by the frustrations involved. Yet, if the purpose of interviewing is to elicit relevant behavior and interpret that behavior, in what area of life is it not essential? Good interviewing is a way of life, a way of relating effectively to people. It would eliminate many of the problems in interpersonal relations. It is essential in selection-promotion decisions, daily management interactions, counselling, sales calls, and especially in marital and parental relations. The individual who uses interviewing techniques out of habit will find his decisions in life much wiser indeed.

CLASSROOM EXERCISES

1. Interview your partner for 15 minutes, then describe your partner's personality to the class. Note the difference between personality descriptions and factual data ("he was born in . . .").

2. Have class members ask a student interviewee any factual questions they wish for 30 minutes. Then have them write up a description of the interviewee recommending or not recommending him for a job as class instructor.

3. Repeat No. 2 with another student with the stipulation that no factual questions can be asked.

4. Invite in an executive and have the students interview him for one hour, then have each student write up a description of him.

5. Break the class into groups of four. Pick a topic (e.g., drugs, the President, premarital sex). Pick one student as interviewee. Have the three other students interview the interviewee separately concerning his views on that topic. Have the interviewers write up the interviewee's attitudes on the topic and note thoroughness, discrepancies, and so forth.

6. Have each student do a full (one to two hour) interview of another student and write up a full description of the personal assets and shortcomings of their partner. (These reports will be used after Chapter 8.)

7. Break the class into groups of four. Have one student give a five minute lecture on any topic. Then have him interview the other four concerning their reaction and suggestions for improvement (making no judgments during the interview).

SUGGESTED READINGS

Fear, R. A.: The evaluation interview, New York, 1973, McGraw-Hill Book Co.
One of the best books on interviewing.

Guion, R. M.: Personnel testing, New York, 1965, McGraw-Hill Book Co.
Covers a range of assessment techniques and research in the area of personnel selection.

Mandell, M. M.: The selection process, New York, 1964, American Management Association, Inc.
A broad overview of the selection process at all levels of an organization.

CHAPTER 8

Performance reviews

the art of constructive criticism

Without tact you can learn nothing.
DISRAELI
Endymion

I am part of all that I have met.
TENNYSON
Ulysses

The primary responsibility of a manager is the behavior of people below him; their behavior determines whether or not his department meets its objectives.

Dealing effectively with behavior requires a manager to give feedback to subordinates. Much managerial feedback comes, as we have seen, in the daily interactions with subordinates involving work-related topics. There should be numerous occasions, however, when the manager focuses his discussion *solely on the subordinate's behavior*. Ineffective behavior requires the attention of the manager in and of itself, not simply in relation to a specific project or problem. Moreover, it should be discussed frequently, not once or twice a year.

If, instead, the manager deals only with the consequences of behavior in specific situations, the behavior will continue. The manager will then find himself on a tread-mill, devoting too much of his time to straightening out situations that would never have occurred had he dealt directly with the behavior itself and its causes.

TIMING OF FEEDBACK

Most managers give feedback at the worst possible time—when they are most motivated to do so. Suppose a plant manager finds that his plant superintendent has misread the blueprints of a given job and is assembling the job in the wrong way. It is at this point that the plant manager is most motivated to give his superintendent critical feedback. This is especially true if the superintendent's mismanagement of the project will cost the company money and reflect on the competence of the plant manager. Nevertheless, this is the worst possible time to give critical feedback. The plant superintendent is not motivated toward learning; he is feel-

119

ing defensive, and anything the manager says will be an aversive stimulus to him. In fact, he is about to engage in avoidance behavior.

Most important, the superintendent has paired himself with a stimulus intensely aversive to the plant manager (mismanagement of the project). As a result, the stimulus most reinforcing to the plant manager at this moment would probably be seeing the superintendent hurt. The manager's comments and critical remarks will therefore be spoken in a negative tone of voice with the goal of hurting, rather than helping, the superintendent. He will, in effect, punish the superintendent and, if the superintendent brought the mistake to his manager's attention, that is the response that will have been punished. Few subordinates will bring mistakes to the manager's attention subsequently.

Obviously, the plant manager must immediately point out and rectify the superintendent's mistake. For the moment he must focus on the effects of behavior and not on its cause, but his interaction should be factual and kept to a minimum. If he is irritated, any attempts to "develop" his subordinate at that moment are doomed to failure.

The best possible time to develop subordinates through feedback is when everything is running smoothly; that is, when the manager is least motivated to do so. When a subordinate is not an aversive stimulus to us and we are intent upon helping him grow, we will give our criticism in a helpful manner. Unfortunately, these are the times we are least motivated

to criticize. To overcome this hesitancy toward giving critical feedback, most organizations have adopted a policy of forcing their managers to give annual or semi-annual performance reviews.

PERFORMANCE REVIEWS

There are two basic shortcomings to the maintenance of a performance review policy. First, while most managers will have discussions with their subordinates at regular intervals, they do so to avoid their superiors' aversive stimuli. What actually takes place, however, in these so-called performance reviews is quite another question. If the manager finds criticizing a subordinate aversive, he will continue to avoid it even though ostensibly he sits down with a subordinate and reviews him. Second, it is naive to assume that behavioral changes can be effected and maintained through the use of annual or semiannual reviews. The real changes in behavior come about only as a result of daily subtle interactions between a manager and his subordinates. Compared with these, one or two meetings a year have little impact.

The function of a performance review, giving constructive feedback to a subordinate, is important. It should be done far more frequently than once or twice a year. Moreover, it should be made reinforcing to managers through adequate training in the nature of human behavior. Punishing a manager for neglecting a performance review will only make the process more aversive to him; it will not lead him to do it well.

Self-defeating policies

Most organizations would do well to examine their policy concerning performance reviews. The ostensible goal of a performance review is behavioral change and growth on the subordinate's part; yet the real reinforcer to top management often consists of having on file a recent evaluation of the subordinate. These two goals may be quite incompatible. Realistic criticism of subordinates is more aversive to managers when it must be submitted in written form to top management. Since managers are already far too lenient in evaluating subordinates, a written assessment accessible to top management makes it even less likely that the subordinates will get effective feedback.

Another self-defeating policy is that of combining the performance review with a salary review. Making financial compensation contingent upon a manager's evaluation of a subordinate at a given moment is not the best way to motivate the subordinate to view his own shortcomings objectively. The primary goal for most subordinates under these circumstances will be changing the manager's mind about negative points in the evaluation in order to maximize their salary increase; they will not focus upon the points themselves. For this reason, the salary review should properly be held one or two months *prior* to the performance review. (Reversing the two sets up the same contingencies as does holding them together.)

The primary purpose of a performance review is to increase the effectiveness of the subordinate in the work setting. As mentioned, this goal is incompatible in many respects with providing management with written assessments and salary reviews. It is compatible with giving a manager experience in focusing his attention on his subordinates. Indeed, the greatest benefit of performance reviews may well be the vehicle they provide, not for the subordinate's development, but for the manager's development.

PRINCIPLES

Having looked at the problems connected with performance reviews, we will now consider the principles governing their constructive use. These principles, in fact, should be applied to all situations where critical feedback is necessary; their usefulness is not limited to performance reviews alone.

Establish rapport

Any time two individuals meet in a performance review situation, there is some minor apprehension or nervousness, even if the individuals have been interacting for two or three years. These minor aversive stimuli should be extinguished before the actual review starts. This is best accomplished by "chit-chat." The subordinate might be asked about his family, the home baseball team, or any other nonwork interest or innocuous work activity with which he is involved. Stimuli that are aversive to the subordinate must be avoided at this stage. Discussing some recent mistake he has made, for example, will only increase the aversive tension present.

Following these preliminaries, the manager should move easily into the performance review with an introductory comment like, "As you know, Jim, I wanted to sit down and share my thoughts with you about your performance here at work." This introduction is crucial. Since minor, subtle stimuli from the manager can have a dramatic impact on the atmosphere of the performance review, a mere change in phrasing on his part can set the stage for an aversive encounter. If, for example, instead of saying, "I wanted to . . .," the manager had said, "As you know, Jim, the company requires us . . .," he would have paired the entire situation with aversive stimuli (and indicated his true feelings about the company and its policies as well).

It is important that the manager be relaxed and comfortable during the review. If he is not, this too will pair the entire session with aversive stimuli; his tenseness will be expressed in his tone of voice, his facial and body gestures, and the words he uses. The subordinate will quickly perceive that the situation is aversive to the manager and will become uncomfortable himself.

An understanding of human behavior should reinforce the manager during a performance review. Indeed, a full discussion of a subordinate's shortcomings, given with the goal of helping the subordinate rather than hurting him, can be one of the most reinforcing interchanges two people experience. It can establish a strong sense of trust, openness, and confidence. It can also be a powerful motivating force for both participants, since a sound interchange reflects mutual concern. It can also lay the groundwork for other exchanges in day-to-day interactions, be they a five-minute conversation in the hallway or a three-hour dialogue in some bar.

Always start with stimuli reinforcing to the subordinate

Two influences determine our reactions to an individual. The first is the past history of our interactions with him and whether or not he has paired himself with stimuli reinforcing or aversive to us. The second is the most recent pairing we have experienced with the individual. For example, a man may have experienced numerous and frequent pairings of reinforcers with his wife. If, however, she is fifteen minutes late in picking him up at the train depot, she will be an aversive stimulus to him at that moment. Within a short time (several hours), if no further interactions take place, the overall history of the previous pairings will take precedence over the most recent pairing, and the man will again "fall in love" with his wife.

The manager, unfortunately, does not have several hours without interaction during a performance review. He must, therefore, take the initial moments of the review to pair himself with stimuli reinforcing to the subordinate. He does this most easily by pointing out some of the subordinate's strengths. (Every individual has some strengths.) He might say, for example, "Jim, I feel you're quite thorough when you work through problems; I feel you watch details closely, and the precision in your work is excellent. I have little doubt but that when you're given a job to do, it's going to be done properly." These statements pair both the performance review and the manager himself with stimuli reinforcing to the subordinate. The probability of constructive behavior in the future and the positive atmosphere of the review are enhanced by pairing the effective behavior patterns of the subordinate (precision) with other reinforcers (excellent). The purpose of the review is to not only weaken shortcomings, but to strengthen strengths.

We are assuming here that "normal" stimuli are reinforcing or aversive to the subordinate. There are, however, occasions when positive traits are aversive and negative traits are reinforcing to people. Reviewing an evaluation with one individual, for example, elicited ready agreement to negative traits and strong arguments against positive traits. This person lacked confidence and was quite tense when given new responsibilities. He subconsciously attempted to avoid these aversive situations by constantly downgrading himself to top management. In this way he also elicited the friendship of people around him (reinforcer), since most people like individuals with "humility."

The manager must, of course, sincerely believe his own reinforcing statements about the subordinate. If he does not, the fact will be apparent in his tone and gestures. This will quickly be perceived by the subordinate, for whom the manager and his comments will then become aversive stimuli rather than reinforcers.

Use tentative, soft language when criticizing

After his initial reinforcing statements the manager is ready to "level" a criticism at the subordinate. The purpose in presenting the criticism is not to reduce the subordinate to tears nor to make him jump out of his chair screaming. It is to effect permanent, constructive behavioral change. Aversive stimuli cannot be avoided

in criticizing a subordinate, but they can be made so mild that the subordinate will seriously consider the criticism rather than withdrawing or attacking the manager. The manager, after all, has enormous power over his subordinates; when a manager whispers, most subordinates hear it as a shout.

Let us assume that a manager feels his subordinate is indecisive. Using tentative, soft language, he might say, "Jim, I feel at times you're a bit too indecisive." The tentative phrases are "at times" and "a bit." Since the manager has softened the aversiveness of the criticism, the subordinate, unless he is unusually sensitive, will be able to consider it seriously. Contrast this with the managerial statement, "Jim, you're just too damn indecisive, too weak, too wishy-washy!" This comment may be so intensely aversive to the subordinate that he agrees with it only in order to escape. If, on the other hand, the subordinate has successfully stopped aversive stimuli in the past by attacking them, he will attack the manager who has paired himself with so severe an aversive stimulus. One thing is certain: The subordinate's focus will not be on his own indecisiveness; it will be on his manager and either fleeing from him or fighting him.

Some "strong" line managers rebel at the suggestion of using soft, tentative language. Their commitment to "calling it as you see it" takes precedence over effective behavioral change in subordinates (not behavioral change in the review setting, but in the subsequent work setting). Their philosophy sometimes reflects a stronger desire to impress people with their aggressiveness than in getting results. This is often confirmed by their readiness to criticize someone in a direct, blunt manner, which is matched by their reluctance to compliment someone with the same emotional force. Their commitment to truth is rather one-sided.

Use a concerned tone of voice when presenting criticism

A harsh, authoritative tone of voice has a deadly effect on critical comments. The tone of voice must be concerned; it must persuade the subordinate that the manager is intent upon helping him. Indeed, the manager's major reinforcer in a performance review must be helping the subordinate to "grow." If his major reinforcer is seeing his subordinate hurt, on the other hand, this will show in his choice of words and tone of voice.

Furthermore, the manager must avoid "coupling" the reinforcers with aversive stimuli (criticisms). He must not, for example, say, "Jim, I feel you do precise work that is excellent, but I feel you're not quite as decisive as you should be." Such a pairing of reinforcers and aversive stimuli would simply turn the reinforcers into aversive stimuli. The manager's sincere reinforcing observations would subsequently have little impact on the atmosphere of the review session. The subordinate would always be waiting "for the other shoe to drop." Positive comments must stand on their own; they must be said in a way that

indicates they are as important to the manager as negative statements, and they should be paired with reinforcers to increase the strength of the behavior. A short silence should follow each positive statement, both to allow the subordinate to respond if he wishes, and to break any possible pairings with subsequent criticisms.

Always elicit feedback from the subordinate immediately after your criticism

Following the presentation of the criticism, the manager must elicit a response from his subordinate. Without this feedback, the manager does not know what the subordinate heard or what is going on in his mind. The simplest eliciting stimulus is a direct question: "How do you feel about that?" Again, tone of voice is a prime variable. It can indicate that the manager wants his subordinate to agree with him so both can be done with the whole disagreeable business. Or, without changing the words themselves, it can indicate that the manager is concerned enough about his subordinate's behavior to want to discuss it with him.

So far, the manager has said only the following: "Jim, I feel at times you're a bit too indecisive. (pause) How do you feel about that?" And yet he has already had an impact on his subordinate's behavior. By telling the subordinate he is too indecisive, the manager has paired indecision with aversive stimuli. Moreover, his tone of voice, while soft, is slightly derogatory when discussing the shortcoming. Finally, the mere fact that the manager brought up the shortcoming at all indicates that he finds the trait aversive. Thus the manager has already decreased the probability that his subordinate will engage in indecisive behavior.

Do not interrupt silence

Most subordinates will react to the question, "How do you feel about that?" with a short period of silence. This is partly because the manager is discussing what is one of the most important things in the world to the subordinate—himself. It is also, unfortunately, because, while they have frequently discussed the effects of the subordinate's behavior (the report he wrote, the sales calls he did not make), previous superiors have rarely discussed the subordinate himself.

Many managers find this short period of silence aversive. They attempt to avoid it by jumping into the conversation with another remark. This is a mistake. By allowing the silence to continue uninterrupted, the manager shows the subordinate that this issue is important to him and he will take all the time necessary to discuss it properly. Also, the silence helps pair the criticism with the aversiveness of the silence. (The manager should never ask the subordinate how he feels about a positive statement; the statement itself is reinforcing, but asking him how he feels about it is aversive.)

When the subordinate disagrees

Whatever the reason for the disagreement, and there are many, the manager must be aware that his presentation of the criticism, or the criticism itself, was too aversive to the subordinate. Suppose the subordinate disagrees by saying, "Well, I really feel that's not quite correct. I feel I make decisions when they're called for." Ironically enough, this is the point at which

the manager should throw out a *mild* reinforcer. Why? First, because his goal is to increase the probability of the subordinate being decisive; it is not to get the subordinate to agree with the criticism. Second, by disagreeing with the manager's criticism, the subordinate has indicated that the criticism and the manager himself are aversive stimuli to him, hence a manager-reinforcer pairing would be helpful.

The perfect mild reinforcer at this point would be a reflection. The manager should softly say, "You feel, then, that when a decision is called for you will make it." By pairing the subordinate with decisiveness, this comment on the manager's part will increase the probability of the subordinate engaging in decisive behavior in the future. The reflection must be spoken in an accepting rather than a questioning tone of voice, however. If the manager's voice rises at the end of the reflection, it will be a challenging question, hence an aversive stimulus.

It is true that by throwing out a mild reinforcer to the subordinate when he disagrees with criticism, the manager also reinforces disagreement responses to criticisms and thereby increases the probability of such responses in the future. This is a small price to pay if the subordinate leaves the office a more effective person and if the manager has paired himself with stimuli reinforcing to the subordinate. Notice that the manager has not changed his opinion; he has merely reflected the subordinate's reaction.

The manager might even use a stronger

reinforcer to increase the probability of his subordinate's decisiveness. In response to the subordinate's disagreement, the manager might say, "Well, Jim, maybe I'm wrong. I'm not sure. But if indeed you are decisive, I take my hat off to you. I hope you keep up a decisive orientation, and I'm sure I will notice it." This will almost ensure decisiveness on the subordinate's part, at least when he is in the presence of the manager. (This flexibility is not possible, of course, when a written statement of the review must go to top management.)

Consider the alternative to reinforcing disagreement. The subordinate disagrees with a criticism, and the manager responds with a strong aversive stimulus: "Oh, for God's sake, Jim. I can get ten people in here who will agree you're indecisive." This increases the probability that Jim will respond to the manager as he would to any intense aversive stimulus. Indeed, Jim will probably sit at home that night thinking, not about himself and decisiveness, but about his manager and how he can "get back at him," or about how he might transfer to another department or another company. The key point is that the subordinate has both disagreed and said he is decisive in one response. The manager who punishes the response is doing so because disagreement is aversive to him. By punishing the subordinate at this moment, however, he is also decreasing the probability of decisiveness.

If, on the other hand, the manager is only interested in eliciting agreement from

his subordinate, he might try a different approach. The subordinate is disagreeing with him partially because he is an aversive stimulus to the subordinate. To overcome this problem, the manager must simply pair himself with several stimuli reinforcing to the subordinate. He might say, for example, "Jim, as I mentioned before, I feel you're a thorough, conscientious person. I feel you do a job properly when you assume responsibility for it, and I think you have excellent initiative in moving out to get the job done. I feel your relationships with other people in the company are beyond reproach. Everyone likes you and respects you. But I do wonder at times if you may not be quite as decisive as you could be." Most people will be surprised at the frequency with which this chain of reinforcers elicits from the subordinate the comment, "Well, maybe you're right."

Agreement should not be the manager's primary goal, however. Certainly, when a subordinate disagrees with a criticism, it is a good indication that the manager has become an aversive stimulus to him, but this fact is secondary to the effective manager. His primary goal is to make the subordinate more decisive, not to elicit agreement or "love" responses. Indeed, the subordinate's behavior in the review session should be of minimal importance to the manager. It is the subordinate's behavior in his subsequent daily activities that the manager is attempting to influence.

Do not discuss specific situations

Of all the suggestions in this chapter, this one will be the most aversive to the most people. A fairly common response to the manager's question, "How do you feel about that?" will be, "Can you give me an example of what you mean?" Let us first recognize the question for what it is, a disagreement with the manager's criticism. In the above example, the manager reinforced disagreement. What he was really attempting to reinforce, however, was the individual's constructive statement, "I am decisive." Asking for a specfic example is not a constructive response, however. Hence, the manager should follow it with a mild aversive stimulus in order to decrease its probability of recurring. He should then bring the subordinate back to the issue by repeating his initial statement. Thus he might say, "No, I'm not thinking of any one thing in particular. I just feel that at times you're not quite as decisive as you could be. How do you feel about that?"

There are three reasons the manager should not go into specifics. First, the subordinate who asks for examples is attempting to avoid aversive stimuli (criticism and his manager) by discussing a stimulus other than himself (avoidance behavior). Suppose, for example, the manager falls into this trap and says, "Well, yesterday at the meeting you refused to give any recommendations on buying that equipment." The subordinate then responds with, "The reason I didn't give any recommendations was that I couldn't get the figures from Bob," to which the manager must reply, "Why couldn't you get the figures from Bob?" In short order, the subordinate and his manager will be discussing Bob, his procrastination, and his inability to communicate the figures when needed.

An individual will always have one-hundred sound reasons for engaging in a specific type of behavior in a given situation. The subordinate may indeed be indecisive on many occasions, but discussing any one in particular will always lead him to justify his indecisive behavior in that situation. In short, the manager will always lose these arguments. More important, the interaction will no longer center on its proper goal, changing the behavior of the subordinate. By focusing his manager's attention on a specific situation rather than on its causes, the subordinate successfully avoids aversive stimuli. Many managers are only too happy to be sidetracked in this manner.

The second reason to avoid specifics is that a specific focus may lead the subordinate to change the behavior involved, but it will lead him to alter his behavior in that particular type of situation only. This is because the pairings involve a specific situation, not the person's behavior. In the above example, by focusing his attention on the subordinate's inability to commit himself at the meeting, the manager may well increase the probability that the subordinate will make recommendations in meetings, since this is the stimulus with which the manager's aversive comments are paired. However, the subordinate will continue to be indecisive in virtually all other situations in which he finds himself. Again, telling a man he is not detailed enough in his work and then discussing this fault in reference to a report he turned in in which he omitted punctuation marks will lead him to include punctuation marks in subsequent reports. His lack of orientation to detail will continue to be apparent in his other activities. The stimulus to pair with aversive stimuli (criticism) is the behavior reflecting a lack of orientation to detail, not the habit of omitting punctuation marks.

Stimulus generalization will affect a broad band of behavior if the manager pairs a general behavioral trait with aversive stimuli, but it will affect only a narrow band of behavior if the manager pairs specific stimulus situations and the subordinate's behavior in those situations with aversive stimuli. The subordinate who is overly sensitive about being treated unfairly can be treated unfairly in a thousand different ways. To discuss his reaction in a specific situation may tone down his sensitivities in that situation, but it will have little effect on his overly sensitive reaction to the hundreds of other situations he encounters in which he is treated unfairly. The manager should focus on behavior, not on specific episodes.

The third reason not to discuss specifics is that the manager should not even be thinking of a specific situation. A performance review should deal with *repetitious* behavior, responses the manager has observed many times in many situations. Behavior that is atypical for the subordinate has no place in a performance review. If an individual is consistently attentive to details, but makes a careless mistake on one occasion, there is no possible justification for accusing him of not being detail-oriented. The manager who does so is usually getting revenge for the pain he has suffered because of his subordinate's atypical mistake.

There are two occasions appropriate for discussing specifics. The first is during the actual event, when the continuance of an ineffective behavior pattern will lead to more lost time, money, or energy. If a man is cutting the wrong corner off a widget, he must be told to stop immediately and the process corrected. This does not, however, relieve the manager of the need for thinking about the causes of this behavior and later dealing with them in a constructive manner. The second appropriate time to discuss specifics, if it seems necessary, is during the salary review. It will do little good or harm, however, since the subordinate's focus will then be on what to him is probably a strong reinforcer at the moment, money, so arguments will run hot and heavy anyway.

When the subordinate agrees with the criticism, ask him, "Why?"

If the manager is a reinforcer to the subordinate, if he has made his criticism only mildly aversive, and if the observation squares with reality and is relevant, the overwhelmingly probable response will be agreement by the subordinate. The conversation will run something like this:

Manager: Jim, I feel at times you're a bit too indecisive. How do you feel about it?

Subordinate: Well, I think you might be right. I feel I am a bit too indecisive at times.

It is at this point that many good managers blunder. They feel they might be hurting the subordinate (aversive stimulus) and forcing the subordinate to hurt himself. They therefore cut this aversive situation short by reinforcing the subordinate with a remark like "Well, on the other hand, you are quite thorough and precise when you work through a problem." This, of course, reinforces the subordinate's indecisiveness! Many managers are really reinforcing behavior that is reinforcing to themselves—agreement by their subordinate.

When the subordinate agrees with his criticism, the manager's response should instead be a simple question: "Why? Why do you feel you might be a bit too indecisive at times, Jim?" The subordinate has no answer to this question. He does not know why, and it is unlikely that he will say, "It is because my mother did not hug me to her bosom when I was three years old." By asking the question, however, the manager indicates to the subordinate that he is not merely attempting to elicit agreement; he is also trying to help the subordinate explore this shortcoming. Moreover, he pairs the shortcoming with more aversive stimuli (tone of voice when asking why), thus making indecisiveness an even more aversive stimulus to the subordinate. Finally, he mildly punishes the subordinate when the latter states, "I am too indecisive," by prolonging the conversation on a topic aversive to the subordinate.

Even though the subordinate does not know why he is indecisive, the manager should have some hypothesis to propose. As we have seen, the causes of any behavior pattern usually stem from the behavior of other people. Now is the time the manager must bring the principles of influencing behavior into effect. This particular subordinate's indecisiveness, for example, may well be a reaction against other people's criticism directed toward him when he did commit himself to a judgment. The manager should have his best possible guess ready before the review session begins. He should then suggest it to the subordinate at the appropriate moment: "I wonder if it's because you might feel at times that someone might criticize your decision?" This suggestion may well be a presentation of aversive stimuli the individual has been successfully avoiding, but fearing, all his life. By not pairing it with other aversive stimuli and by speaking about it openly and nonchalantly, the manager is starting to extinguish "criticism from others" as an aversive stimulus.

The manager's next move should be to pair criticism from other people with stimuli that are reinforcing to the subordinate. Hence, he might say, "You know, Jim, when someone criticizes you, he is frequently telling you that he likes you. When someone takes a shot at you, he is often saying he cares enough about you and your views to argue with you. Someone arguing with you can mean he respects you." This pairing of the aversive stimulus (criticism from others) with a reinforcer (respect from others) will, as we have seen, decrease the probability of the behavior controlled by the aversive stimulus, in this case, indecisiveness. Moreover, by using reinforcers, the manager pairs himself with these reinforcers, leading the subordinate to "feel good" about the review discussion and his manager.

It is also at this point that the verbal equivalents of behavior should be used in pairings. "I really think the indecisiveness hurts you. I think it leads people to avoid you at times" (indecisiveness-aversive pairings). "I feel that if you were more decisive, you'd feel better about it and I know I would. I think a little more decisiveness on your part would lead the people under you to look up to you more often" (decisiveness-reinforcer pairings). Operant principles will also come into play. The subordinate will often suggest that he will make greater efforts on his part to be more decisive; this should be reinforced.

Pair defense mechanisms with aversive stimuli

Some subordinates, although relatively few, will use an infinite variety of defense mechanisms to avoid the criticism of their immediate superior. These may range all the way from bland acceptance of anything the superior mentions to outright opposition to everything the manager brings up, be it good or bad. In either case, the manager must stop the review, point out the defense mechanism he observes being used, and pair it with aversive stimuli. When a subordinate is responding with a superficial acceptance of everything the manager says, the manager might remark, "You know, Bill, I feel you're just accepting everything I say in order to get this discussion over with. I feel I'm wasting my time here." This will usually bring forth a quick denial by the subordinate and a more serious involvement on his part. A similar pairing of oppositional behavior with an aversive stimulus is also usually effective: "You know, Bill, I get the feeling that no matter

what I say, you're going to disagree with it. I almost get the feeling that if I were to say black is black, you would say black is white. I wonder if you're taking this approach because you're a bit too sensitive to criticism."

MANAGERIAL REACTIONS TO PERFORMANCE REVIEWS

Most subordinates desperately seek feedback. Most live out their vocational lives with gross misconceptions of what their managers think of them. And yet most managers are uncomfortable in a performance review situation. It is aversive to them to play God and to make judgments about those things that are so important to their subordinates. Nevertheless, there is no alternative. A manager cannot abdicate his responsibility and the judgments necessary when he assumes authority over other people. Failure to give a subordinate any feedback at all is a far greater abuse of managerial power than is giving him feedback that is erroneous. Many people have adopted and maintained ineffective behavior patterns which could have been alleviated or eliminated had their managers taken the trouble to discuss their problems frankly. Allowing an individual to continue on an ineffective course of behavior is also playing God, after all; the manager's judgment in this case is a particularly damning "I will do nothing about it."

The manager who sits in his office and refuses to interact with his subordinates is not, in any case, avoiding the responsibility of influencing their behavior. He is engaging in a massive extinction process, the results of which will be frustration, irritation, and finally, lethargy on the part of his subordinates. Likewise, the manager who confines his discussion to work-related topics still uses classical and operant stimuli that have an impact on the judgments, attitudes, and general behavior of subordinates. This impact may be effective or noneffective but it is intrinsic to a managerial position; it cannot be avoided.

SUMMARY

The points put forth in this chapter have been placed in the context of a performance review. However, a manager must, as we have said, focus constantly on developing his subordinates and on the daily impact his behavior is having on them. When Jim's manager, for example, notices a tentative thrust at decisiveness on Jim's part, he should be ready to jump in with a stimulus that is reinforcing to Jim. In effect, he must be ready to shape, through the appropriate use of reinforcers, his subordinate's constructive behavior. Without doubt, this is a complex task. No one expects the manager to be perfect in his dealings with subordinates, and even a slight improvement can be dramatically reflected on the profit statement of his organization. The techniques in this chapter should be part of the manager's repertoire, to be used every day, not once or twice a year. They might be used during a five-minute chat over coffee or in a complex, three-hour meeting. We will look at examples of their daily use in the next chapter.

In a real sense, a performance review is a misnomer. A real performance review is a person review. It is a recognition that most things in the company flow from the behavior of people. It is a recognition that the behavior of the person is a key management responsibility, no matter how frightening that responsibility may be.

Performance reviews can be one of the most rewarding, motivating interactions between a manager and his subordinate. They can lead to sincere, and sometimes dramatic, attempts by a subordinate to adopt more effective behavior patterns in the work setting. These attempts will be wasted, however, if the manager does not follow them with appropriate reinforcers. Without follow-up, an annual performance review is useless. With follow-up, the performance review can initiate a developmental process that eventually leads to striking personal and organizational growth.

CLASSROOM EXERCISES

1. Have each student pick someone he knows well in the class and tell him his two worst shortcomings.
2. Following the full interview (Chapter 7), have each student give feedback to his interviewee using all the principles of reinforcement theory to strengthen strengths and weaken weaknesses.
3. Have several students give feedback to others about their behavior in the classroom. If asked for specifics, the students should give them and note what happens subsequently.
4. Break the class into groups of three. Have one student give feedback on assets and shortcomings of second student, using all the principles of reinforcement theory. Then have third student give feedback to the *reviewer* on how well he did, again using all the principles of reinforcement.
5. Invite in an executive. Interview him for one

hour. Then have several students give him feedback, using all the principles of reinforcement.

6. Have each student tell the instructor how he might better run a course, using all reinforcement principles to "shape" him into doing so.

7. Have each student pick a shortcoming of someone close to him in his personal life. Have him attempt to change that shortcoming and report to the class on how he went about it and the results.

SUGGESTED READING

Blum, M. L. and Naylor, J. C.: Industrial psychology, New York, 1968, Harper & Row, Publishers.
Chapter 7 covers research in the performance appraisal area.

CHAPTER 9

The management process

analysis of case studies

Rhetoric is the art of ruling the minds of men.
PLATO

We are now ready to consider examples of manager-subordinate interactions that will illustrate and utilize the principles we have learned. The manager is not expected to emulate the styles of the managers depicted here, only the principles their behavior reflects. One manager can say, "What the hell did you do that for?" and make it an intense aversive stimulus to a subordinate, while another can say the same words to the same subordinate in such a manner that it constitutes a reinforcer.

The goal is implementation of the principles, not the concrete actions depicted here. In these examples, we will try to use the principles of reinforcement, interviewing, and behavioral feedback as they might occur in day-to-day managerial interactions. Because of the complexity of behavior, we will assume "normal" stimuli are reinforcing and aversive to the participants.

CASE STUDIES

The first illustration we will examine is an interaction between a general sales manager and his subordinate, a regional sales manager. The regional sales manager is responsible for a specific geographic territory and has eight salesmen under him covering the territory. One morning the general manager, who has not seen the regional manager for about a week, passes his subordinate's office and notices that he is alone and working on some papers. Recognizing that his primary responsibility involves face-to-face interactions with his subordinates, the general manager walks into his regional manager's office, and the following interaction takes place:

Manager (smiling and enthusiastic): Hello, Jim, have you got a minute? (The manager has paired himself with several reinforcers—the smile, the enthusiasm, and the respect implicit in asking if the subordinate is busy. Most of us are very much aware of the subtle cues an individual emits when greeting us that tell us whether we are a reinforcing, neutral, or aversive stimulus to him.)

Subordinate: Sure, Paul, have a seat.

Manager (slouching low in chair to create a relaxed atmosphere): How's everything going? (A good interviewing question, broad, general, and designed to elicit from the subordinate his most probable responses. Had the manager instead announced, "I want to talk to you about your expense report," his statement would have confined his subordinate's behavior to a narrow spectrum; he might also have failed to notice whether the subordinate was undergoing any stress that needed to be discussed.)

Subordinate: Oh, pretty well. Actually, I just found out our sales are running 14 percent ahead of last year for this time period.

Manager (sitting up in chair quickly, and with strong inflection): Are they really! Fourteen percent increase? Excellent! Beautiful! (It is obvious that this manager has, during previous interactions, paired practical results [sales] with reinforcers; if, on the other hand, he had paired lowering the expense account with reinforcers, the subordinate might have said something like, "Our expenses were down ten percent for the month." In this instance, the manager is not only pairing practical results with reinforcers, he is also following his subordinate's accomplishment of increased practical results with reinforcers, thereby increasing the probability that his subordinate will focus on practical results in the future. How many managers would sit blandly by, or ask a question on a different topic ["which areas were up

most?"] after a comment like the one this subordinate made?)

Subordinate: Yeah, we're all pretty happy about it.

Manager (again with enthusiasm): I would be too! You and your people are doing a hell of a good job, Jim. Why don't you bring them all in and take them out to dinner with their wives to the Athletic Club at company expense? (Here the manager is pairing his compliments with a concrete reinforcer. If he were to use verbal compliments continually as reinforcers without pairing them periodically with other reinforcers, their effectiveness would soon extinguish. His suggestion should not, of course, have been made if the subordinate were a withdrawn individual for whom taking his salesmen out socially was an aversive stimulus.)

Subordinate: Do we have enough money in our budget to do a thing like that?

Manager: For that kind of a performance we do. (Follows his subordinate's "concern for the budget" response with a reinforcer and pairs performance with a reinforcer)

Subordinate: Good, I'll do it.

Manager: How's everything else going? (This type of question, if sincere, can be quite reinforcing and motivating. It indicates a concern for the listener by focusing on his affairs rather than on those of the speaker. It is, moreover, a good, broad, general question.)

Subordinate: Well, I'm having a little trouble with the superintendent of our plant down in Atlanta.

Manager: How so? (A good, concise, probing question. The manager did not launch into his own negative experience with the plant superintendent several months ago, a reaction that would have prevented him from finding out about his subordinate's problem. Managing people is altruistic; the effective manager's focus is almost always on the other person's successes and problems, not his own.)

Subordinate: Well, one of my salesmen's customers has been calling the superintendent and complaining about our late deliveries. The superintendent got hold of my salesman and read him the riot act, hauled him over the coals. He told my salesman to handle his own customers and keep them off his back. The salesman was pretty shaken up about it.

Manager: What happened then? (Still doing good interviewing)

Subordinate: I went over to the plant and told the superintendent what I thought of him talking to my salesman.

Manager: Good. (Reinforcement, thereby increasing the probability of aggressive [and probably internally destructive] behavior by the subordinate toward the plant superintendent) What did he say?

Subordinate: He said our salesmen shouldn't be having their customers call him. I told him if he had any complaints about the salesmen he'd better talk to me about it or keep his damn mouth shut.

Manager: Good. (Reinforcement of hostility toward operating people) That guy always has been a big mouth. (Pairs the plant superintendent with an aversive stimulus)

Subordinate: I don't think he'll be such a big mouth any more. I really pinned the runt to the wall, and some of the plant guys saw it. (The subordinate's hostile remarks have been shaped to greater intensity through reinforcement; he has gone from "told him what I thought of him" to "really pinned the runt to the wall.")

Manager: Well, if you have any more trouble with him, tell me, and we'll both go out there. (Reinforcement. This comment not only operantly reinforces hostility toward the superintendent, it almost ensures future clashes. The manager has classically paired "you have any more trouble with him" with a strong reinforcer "tell me and we'll both go out there." The regional manager has increased the likelihood of negative interactions with the superintendent in the future.)

In this sequence, the manager has shaped and increased the probability of a hostile response from his subordinate toward the plant superintendent and operations people generally. In particular, he has increased his subordinate's dislike of the plant superintendent by pairing the latter with aversive stimuli in his comments. Likewise, he has decreased the probability that his subordinate will attempt to build rapport with the plant superintendent or even be amenable to others' suggestions to this end. The sequence has therefore widened the chasm between operations and sales, a chasm that always starts at the top through interchanges such as this one. The regional manager is now likely to reinforce negative interactions between his salesmen and operations people.

Why did the manager reinforce this behavior? Because any behavior by others that hurts operations people is reinforcing to him. Why? Because his manager (vice president of sales) reinforces hostility toward operations people. Why? Because the president reinforces hostility in the vice president of sales toward operations people.

Manager: Anything else happening? (Good interviewing question)

Subordinate: No, that's about it. (He feels satisfied; he has been amply reinforced.)

Manager: How's Ed (one of the salesmen under the regional manager) coming along? (Any response an individual emits that has not been elicited by a discernible stimulus indicates a topic of importance to that person. In this case the manager is indicating that his subordinate's salesmen are important to him. Since questions frequently function as aversive stimuli or reinforcers, this question will be one or the other, depending on whether previous discussions between the two about Ed were aversive or reinforcing to the subordinate. Questions carry important information.)

Subordinate: Oh, he's coming along all right. (An avoidance response; previous discussions about Ed must have been aversive to the subordinate.)

Manager: Is he still carrying those negative attitudes with him? (Good response. The manager does not stop the aversive stimulus after his subordinate's superficial answer. Too many managers would have said, "That's good," and gone on to another topic, thus increasing their sub-ordinate's superficial behavior concerning Ed.)

Subordinate: Apparently. My secretary told me the other day he told her God himself couldn't survive on the money this company pays. (Attempts to stop the aversive stimuli by shifting his manager's focus to a specific situation concerning Ed, and away from his own handling of Ed)

Manager: Have you talked to him about those attitudes? (The manager doesn't "take the bait." Many would have done so. Since Ed is not present, however, a long discussion about him will have absolutely no impact on his behavior. Discussions of Ed, therefore, should only be held relative to the regional manager's behavior. The general manager had adeptly kept the aversive stimuli going because the regional manager has not yet made a constructive response.)

Subordinate: No, I haven't been able to get to him yet.

Manager (wincing): Aw, Jim, I asked you to talk to him about his attitudes three weeks ago. (Punishment. The manager has followed the response of "not talking with a subordinate" with an aversive stimulus. He has also followed an honest response by his subordinate with an aversive stimulus. He has decreased the probability of his subordinate avoiding a discussion with Ed and, admittedly, he has decreased the probability of his subordinate telling him he has not talked to someone; there is no alternative here, however. How aversive this stimulus was will usually be determined by the subordinate's next response.)

Subordinate: Well Christ, I haven't had time.

Manager: Oh, come on, Jim. You know, procrastinators are like chickens; they both sit on things and hope they will hatch on their own momentum. (Effectively punishes a rationalization. The aversive stimuli are still "on." Also pairs people who delay taking action with aversive stimuli.)

Subordinate: You know, it takes a little time and effort to boost sales the way we're doing. (The manager's response was too aversive; had it been a bit milder, the subordinate might have responded with, "I know, I'll get to it Friday." The subordinate is now defensive. His last response was fairly constructive, however; it is, therefore, time for the manager to "turn off" the aversive stimuli and pair himself with reinforcers to reestablish rapport.)

Manager: I know you've been working your heart out, Jim. I know you're putting in as many hours as anyone in the company, and, frankly, you've done a hell of a good job in straightening this territory out. (The manager, sensing that he has become an aversive stimulus to his subordinate by pairing himself with too many aversive stimuli, overcomes this problem by pairing himself with what to the subordinate are strong reinforcers. He also follows the responses of effort and putting in long hours with the cessation of aversive stimuli and reinforcers. How effectively he has paired himself with reinforcers will again be determined by his subordinate's subsequent response.)

Subordinate: Well, I suppose there should always be time to sit down with a guy who has bad attitudes and straighten

him out, but . . . (The manager was partially successful.)

Manager: I appreciate your saying that. (The manager throws out a quick reinforcer and blocks a potential negative statement. His subordinate has admitted a mistake; to prolong this topic would probably make both the topic and the manager too aversive, so the manager promptly reinforces a constructive response, even though it means interrupting his subordinate. This manager knows that the use of a "but" or "however" almost invariably means that a reinforcer is going to be paired with an aversive stimulus. He therefore jumps in at the "but" and reinforces the use of the reinforcer while, at the same time, blocking the aversive stimulus. He then moves quickly on to another topic.) Say, how are we coming with Preston Corporation? Have we made any sales over there yet?

Subordinate: Oh, Christ, I haven't been able to get over there either since you asked me to three weeks ago.

Manager (laughing): You louse, I don't think I have any impact on you at all. (The manager had to use an aversive stimulus, but he made it mild by combining it with reinforcers of humor and self-deprecation.)

Subordinate (laughing along with the manager): Why, you know you're all I live for. I'll get over there before the week is out. (The manager's aversive stimulus was not too strong, hence the subordinate responded in an effective manner.)

Manager: If you go over there, I know we'll get the sale. (Pairs the verbal equivalent of the desired response and himself with the reinforcer) You know, the people at Preston think a good deal of you. (Pairs the customer with a reinforcer, a pairing many managers have difficulty using, especially if they used to call on the account. The subordinate may not have gone to Preston because it is an aversive stimulus to him.) Anything else we should be discussing? (A reinforcing question. These interviewing questions allow the subordinate to feel he is controlling the interchange as much as the manager—which, indeed, he should be.)

Subordinate: No, that about covers it, I think.

Manager (getting up): Well, back to the grind for me, then. (Pairs himself with a good reinforcer, implying that activities other than talking to his subordinate are aversive to him)

This was a generally effective manager-subordinate interaction. The manager, whether he is aware of it or not, has been subtly guiding his subordinate's behavior. Many managers feel guilty about such interactions; they feel they are not earning their keep with mere "chit-chat." As a matter of fact, such conversations should occur at least once or twice a week; indeed, they are a manager's primary responsibility.

Consider what the manager has accomplished in this interchange. First, by suggesting dinner at the Athletic Club, he has increased the probability that the subordinate will reinforce his salesmen's efforts.

Second, he has increased the probability that his subordinate will tone down negative attitudes in one of his salesmen. (These two accomplishments alone will result in increased sales, since the salesman's negative attitudes are undoubtedly hurting the other salesmen's attitudes and motivation and his own sales calls.) Third, the manager has increased the probability that his subordinate will call on Preston Corporation; without this interaction, that sales call might never have been made. In fact, the conversation had only one unfortunate result. The manager has also increased the probability of poor communication, animosity, and lack of cooperation between sales and operations, a situation which his own manager had better "chit-chat" about with him.

Because he is an emotionally expressive person, this manager is able to give his subordinates a good deal of feedback. By the frequent use of reinforcers and mild aversive stimuli, he lets his subordinates know what is expected of them. Most managers, however, are great sources of extinction. They rarely go out of their way to elicit behavior from their subordinates, and when they do, they rarely respond in any meaningful fashion to that behavior. Hence, there is truth to the frequent complaint of most subordinates that they "don't know where they stand"—even after a two-hour meeting with the manager!

•   •   •

In our second example, we will assume that an outsider has been brought into an organization as vice president of operations (manager). He has responsibility for five plants around the country. He has been on board about three months and knows that he is an aversive stimulus to one of his plant managers (subordinate) because this particular plant manager wanted the vice presidency. This is his third visit to this plant manager's location.

Vice president: Hello, Dick, how's it going?

Subordinate: Well, we've had an upsurge in grievances recently, and there's been some talk of a wildcat strike.

Vice president: Oh, my God, that's all I need. (Since the vice president is an aversive stimulus to his subordinate, his discomfort constitutes a reinforcer to the subordinate; therefore, this response will increase the probability that the plant manager will continue to place emphasis on problems in the plant. As irrational as it sounds, the plant manager's subsequent behavior in the plant may actually increase the problems, since they have such a negative, hence reinforcing, emotional impact on his superior. For example, the plant manager may well be a little more brusque, a little more abrasive with his subordinates, after this interchange with his superior.)

Subordinate: Well, it looks pretty serious, Frank. The word has come from several sources in the plant. We haven't been able to pin the instigators down yet, but we will. (The plant manager is indicating that employees out on the floor are also aversive stimuli to him; vague references to "sources" and "instigators" are aversive stimuli used to refer to people who are aversive to the speaker.)

Vice president: What the hell do you think is causing all of this?

Subordinate: I don't know. I wish I knew.

Vice president: Do you think it might be Jerry (plant superintendent)? You know he's always treating the foreman and the hourly people like they were something to be tolerated, something to look down on. (The vice president pairs Jerry with stimuli aversive to himself, but not necessarily aversive to the plant manager.)

Subordinate: No, I don't think so. (Extinguishes or mildly punishes the vice president's suspicions concerning Jerry.) Overall, Jerry's doing a fine job. (The plant manager shares the plant superintendent's views about the people on the floor. Indeed, the superintendent probably got these views from his boss in the first place; hence he is a reinforcer to the plant manager, because he has paired himself with attitudes the plant manager likes.)

Vice president: Have you talked to him about the way he treats his people? (Good focus on the behavior of the only person he can influence at that moment; avoids discussing the superintendent except insofar as it relates to his immediate subordinate's behavior)

Subordinate: Yeah, we've discussed it a bit. (Extinction) He feels he's getting the most he can out of the people with the rotten equipment we have here. (The vice president's question is an aversive stimulus to the plant manager, who is attempting to avoid further interaction along these lines by shifting the conversation to another topic, the equipment. The plant manager's feelings toward the company are implicit in his use of the aversive stimulus, "rotten equipment," which he no doubt blames on the company.)

Vice president: Well, there's not much we can do about the equipment. We don't have much cash for capital investments now. (The vice president, in an attempt to stop his subordinate's aversive stimuli, "takes the bait," then pairs himself with weak, uncomfortable responses, all of which are reinforcing to his subordinate. He should have asked, "What did you actually say to Jerry?")

Subordinate: Well, I don't know how the company can expect anything with equipment that should have been junked thirty years ago. (Blatant pairing of the company with aversive stimuli. There should be little doubt now as to the origin of any negative attitudes in the plant. The subordinate's negative attitudes have also increased in intensity because the vice president's uncomfortable feelings are reinforcing them.)

Vice president: I know. I'll do everything I can to get some money for this plant. (The plant manager is now controlling the interaction, a not infrequent situation when one remembers that interpersonal factors take precedence over other stimuli, including position titles, in influencing behavior. He is able to assume control because "someone complaining" is an overly strong aversive stimulus to his superior, who has apparently stopped previous aversive stimuli by "passive agreement" responses.)

Subordinate: I'd sure appreciate that. (The subordinate adeptly reinforces his man-

ager's passive subservience and, more important, stops the aversive stimuli inherent in his previous complaining responses.)

(Let us assume that this conversation is interrupted by a call from the president to the vice president. The president asks the vice president what is going on in this plant, since he has heard rumors that a wildcat is imminent. The vice president says he is exploring the situation. The president says, "I know what the problem is, it's that plant manager out there. If you're too weak to do something about him or get him the hell out of there, you're going to have real trouble yourself." The president has just paired the plant manager with an aversive stimulus and "lack of action" on the vice president's part with intense aversive stimuli. The vice president walks back into the plant manager's office a "tougher" manager; he now knows that the plant manager is an aversive stimulus to the president and that he must take action to save his own skin. He has been "transformed" into a tough manager.)

Vice president: Anything else happening? (Good "concerned" question, a concern that is aversive to the subordinate)

Subordinate: No, that's about it. (Attempts to extinguish his manager's behavior and presence)

Vice president: Exactly what did Jerry say when you talked to him about his negative attitudes toward the people on the floor? (His subordinate's displeasure, an aversive stimulus to this manager prior to the president's call, is now a reinforcer.)

Subordinate: Just what I mentioned.

Vice president: You didn't mention anything. (Punishment; an aversive stimulus that knocks out the subordinate's previous response and sets the stage for further attempts at avoidance behavior. The aversive stimulus here is not only the manager's "attack" response, but also his new, confident manner.)

Subordinate: Well, we discussed the people and how they weren't putting out. (Avoidance behavior. The subordinate attempts a subtle switch to another topic, the people in the plant rather than Jerry. Again, a blatant pairing of people in the plant with aversive stimuli, a certain precursor to, and indicator of, a drop in productivity.)

Vice president: I didn't ask you about your discussions about the people. I asked you about your discussions with Jerry and *his* negative attitudes. (Punishment; an aversive stimulus that again knocks out the subordinate's previous response.)

Subordinate: I don't think his attitudes are quite that bad. (What was aversive prior to the president's call is now a reinforcer to the vice president. That is, the subordinate's uncomfortable feelings, aversive to the manager a short while ago, are now reinforcing his "attack" responses.)

Vice president (angry): Do you know why you don't?

Subordinate (angry): No, why?

Vice president (angry): Because you have the same attitudes. Because he gets his lousy attitudes from you. Because you're the guy who's causing us all our problems out here. (A correct diagnosis of the subordinate's behavior would have shown negative emotional reactions by others to be reinforcing to him, a fact explaining most of the problems in the

plant. The vice president's discomfort and irritation are reinforcers to his subordinate; hence the subordinate's rebuttals are now being reinforced again. To have punished the subordinate and decreased the probability of further "attack" responses, the vice president could have smiled and quietly stated, in a calm, confident manner, "My friend, our discussion is over.")

Subordinate (angry): Well, if you don't like me here, why don't you fire me? (Still attacking, because he is being reinforced)

Vice president: I know what my prerogatives are. I don't need you to tell me. I want this plant straightened out and your negative attitudes stopped or some action will be taken. (The vice president is still reinforcing his subordinate with negative emotional reactions. His behavior reflects the severity of the president calling him too weak; he is thus engaged in avoidance behavior that, typically, goes too far and is too rigid.)

Subordinate: That's fine with me.

For long-term development, the vice president would need to pair "negative emotional reactions" by others with stimuli aversive to this subordinate. He does not really have time to do this, however, since the plant is in serious trouble. He should, therefore, have accomplished one last pairing by saying to the subordinate, "You seem to find people getting upset quite rewarding—for that reason, you are no longer working here, you're fired." He should then have gone to the plant superintendent and said, "People are expressing too many negative feelings around here, so I've fired the plant manager, and if these negative reactions continue, you won't be around long either." To be truly aversive, these statements would have to be made calmly and quietly. This particular vice president, however, probably does not have the confidence nor the ability to carry out his responsibilities.

An adequate diagnosis of problems in an organization must conclude at two points. First, since problems almost invariably originate in the behavior of people, an accurate diagnosis will only have been made when the cause of the problems has been assigned to one or more persons. A machine breaking down is caused by a poor maintenance supervisor, or a poor planning department, or a poor operations department, or a poor capital investment committee, and so forth. To focus only on the machine, however, usually means more problems ahead because the cause has not been cured.

The second concluding point of an accurate diagnosis occurs when the assigned responsibility for problems is put at its highest originating level in the organization. Anything short of that will not result in long-term solutions. In the above study, for example, little would have been gained by blaming the hourly people for a wildcat. While it is true that the plant superintendent (Jerry) and the plant manager fostered a wildcat by their managerial behavior, little long-term effect will result from firing them. The vice president is not ca-

pable of handling the situation and that may be where the trouble lies. The president, on the other hand, may be the ultimate cause, as determined by the frequency with which he is abrasive toward subordinates, pairs employees with aversive stimuli, and hires weak vice presidents. In sum, long-term solutions only result from accurately assigning responsibility for problems to people at the highest level from which the problems arise.

• • •

In our final example, let us look at an interaction between a new vice president of administration and his subordinate, the director of communications. The subordinate, in this case, is a meek, passive, indecisive fellow whom the vice president has given himself three months to develop or he will have to let him go. The director of communications does not know this, however.

Manager: Well, Bill, how's it going?

Subordinate: Oh, pretty well.

Manager: How's the new computer running? (Extinction; should have said "Good!" then asked the question.)

Subordinate: Well, it seems to be doing all right.

Manager: Seems to be? (The manager has emitted a stimulus aversive to the subordinate, thereby punishing the subordinate's weak response to the question and subsequent questions.)

Subordinate: Well, I mean the work's getting out.

Manager: Then the computer is running fine.

Subordinate: Yes, it's doing a good job.

Manager: Excellent! (The manager's delight seems to refer to the functioning of the computer, but actually, since it follows a firm statement by the subordinate, it reinforces firmness on the subordinate's part.)

Subordinate: Will we be getting some extra help when the system is up and running?

Manager: Will you need some extra help?

Subordinate: Well, I'm not sure. If the system runs smoothly, we probably could get away without hiring anyone. But if the system breaks down, we could be in an awful lot of trouble. (The manager remains silent, thereby extinguishing his subordinate's indecisiveness.) I suppose we might ask the people to work overtime if the system breaks down.

Manager: Excellent idea! (Reinforces initiative in the subordinate, who has committed himself to a plan of action without guidance from others)

Subordinate: I don't know if they will do it, though. It depends on how long we ask them to work, I suppose. (The manager remains silent and extinguishes this indecisive response.) I guess we wouldn't have too much trouble. They would sure enjoy the extra pay.

Manager: I think you're absolutely right. (Reinforces a more optimistic, decisive response by the subordinate with a good you–reinforcer pairing)

Subordinate: I'll have some overtime schedules drawn up that we'll implement if the system doesn't function as well as we'd like.

Manager: Sounds good. I'll give you all the help you need with people from other areas, too. (The manager has selectively and successfully reinforced and shaped

an affirmative action program on the part of his indecisive subordinate.) How's Paul (the director's subordinate) coming along? (Paul has been drinking heavily for two years, and the vice president wants his director of communications to fire him. Firing the man is intensely aversive to the subordinate, however.)

Subordinate: Well, not too good. He missed two days last week.

Manager: Oh, God! Missing days at a time like this is inexcusable. (The manager has punished his subordinate for bringing him bad news, decreasing the probability that the subordinate will tell him "bad" things in the future. However, the aversive stimulus was entirely appropriate; using it confirmed the importance of someone missing days to the manager, hence to the subordinate. The manager has also paired Paul's behavior pattern with an aversive stimulus. Moreover, he has presented an aversive stimulus to the subordinate which the latter must now stop.)

Subordinate: I know. I'm going to talk to him about it this afternoon. (An attempt to stop the presentation of aversive stimuli by the manager)

Manager: Talk to him? What the hell good is that going to do? We've already talked to him twenty times about it. (The manager has followed "talking to Paul" with strong aversive stimuli and effectively punished a response pattern that should normally be reinforced, but not in this case because of its history. He has also, however, paired himself with the same intense aversive stimuli, a pairing that is almost certain to elicit a hostile remark, even from this passive subordinate.)

Subordinate (with some anger): I know you want me to fire him, but you know that's the easy way out. (The subordinate is pairing both the response he does not want to make, firing the subordinate, and his manager with an aversive stimulus, "the easy way out.")

Manager: Well, I don't really feel it's quite that easy. (In a gentle tone of voice): I think firing someone can be quite difficult. (Bad response, although it may win the argument; by pairing "firing someone" with an aversive stimulus ["quite difficult"], the manager has made this behavior more aversive to his subordinate. He probably focused on winning the argument when his subordinate became aversive to him by using the phrase "easy way out.") I know I'm scared to death, when I have to do it. (The manager's last comment, by pairing fear with himself, makes an admission of fear on his own part less aversive to the subordinate and also pairs the manager with what to this subordinate is probably a reinforcer, the admission of fear.)

Subordinate: I know, I get a little uneasy about it myself.

Manager: What is it about the situation that makes you a bit uneasy? (Good performance review question)

Subordinate: I don't really know. I'm sure Paul expects it.

Manager (softly and with concern): You know, I feel at times you might be a bit reluctant to hurt someone. How do you feel about it? (Good performance review approach)

Subordinate: Well, I think you might be right.

Manager (in a concerned soft voice): Why? Why do you feel you might be a bit reluctant at times to hurt someone?

Subordinate: I don't really know.

Manager: I wonder if it might be that you're anticipating their reaction a little bit. But I wonder if when we fire someone we often are doing them a favor. I know a lot of guys who have been fired and said it was the best thing that ever happened to them. In fact, by firing Paul, you might be doing him the greatest favor anyone has ever done him. It might lead him to reassess his life style and maybe stop drinking so much. I wouldn't doubt but that if you fired him, he'd thank you for it some day. (The manager is pairing the verbal equivalent of firing the individual with reinforcers, thus making this response less aversive to his subordinate.)

Subordinate: Well, I'm not sure what his reaction would be.

Manager (knowing that being labeled a "coward" is intensely aversive to this subordinate): I'll tell you what—I'll be in town on Friday next week; why don't we both sit down with him and do it? (The manager has punished his subordinate's concern for other people's reactions.)

Subordinate: That's all right, I'll probably get to it before Friday. (Punishment has reduced subordinate's concern for others' reactions.)

Manager: Well, you're the boss and it's your ballgame. (Stops the aversive stimulus and reinforces the response he wants)

Some managers may feel these interactions do not give the subordinate enough credit. They may feel that a more "rational, logical" approach would be just as effective and certainly more respectful toward the subordinate. In the example above, for instance, it might be argued that the manager should point out to his subordinate the low probability of a cure in cases involving alcoholics, the bad effect the alcoholic is having on others in the department, and the possibility that the stress of the man's responsible position is causing the alcoholism. These arguments are absolutely right. But this "rational, logical" approach actually accomplishes what we are suggesting in our use of behavioral principles— and accomplishes it in a less effective, less precise manner. Each "rational" suggestion pairs "keeping the man on his job" with stimuli that hopefully are aversive to the subordinate (low probability of a cure, bad effect on others, stress of job contributing to alcoholism).

The difficulty with the so-called rational approach is two-fold: It makes unwarranted assumptions about human behavior, and it lacks precision. Pointing out to an individual the "bad effects of an alcoholic on others in the department" may be quite reasonable. It may also have little impact on a subordinate to whom these "bad effects" are not an aversive stimulus. Indeed, it may even have a deleterious impact on some subordinates, to whom these "bad effects" are really reinforcers. Those who espouse a rational approach to management are really assuming that stimuli that are reinforcing or aversive to themselves are reinforcing or aversive to

everyone (at least, everyone who is "reasonable"). Much of this book has been devoted to showing that this is an "unreasonable" assumption and far from the truth.

CONCLUSION: THE INFLUENCE OF AUTHORITY

Most people in positions of power use that power to retain their power. Yet the vast majority of managers, because their focus is so strongly oriented upward toward their superiors rather than downward toward their subordinates, grossly underestimate (without diminishing) the impact their own behavior has on the behavior of their subordinates.

Our society is founded upon the concept of authority. Throughout life, we learn that doing those things that please our parents, teachers, policemen, government officials, and others in authority will lead to pleasant experiences. More important, we learn that *not* doing those things that please people in authority will lead to unpleasant experiences. Few, if any, people are in a stronger position of authority over us in our daily adult lives than are our immediate superiors in the work setting.

This phenomenon of "authority impact" has a critical influence on the profits of an organization. It starts at the top with the chief executive officer, whose attitudes, opinions, and philosophy quickly permeate the organization down to the lowest level (hence, the "labor" problems of England and Italy). The chief executive who believes all decisions should be made in his office will selectively pair "decisions by others" with aversive stimuli and "following orders to the letter" with reinforcers in the presence of his vice presidents and department heads. The latter will, in turn, engage in similar behavior with their subordinates. Independent subordinates to whom merely "following orders" is strongly aversive will leave the company, as will subordinates to whom "making their own decisions" is intensely reinforcing. Within a surprisingly short time, virtually everyone within the organization will adopt cautious, conservative behavior patterns, behavior that will eventually show up on the loss column of the profit sheet.

This impact is true of all organizations, be they governmental, academic, military, nonprofit, or profit-making. *No decision an organization makes, consequently, is more important than the one involving the selection of its chief executive officer. This is not the result of the impact the chief executive has on formulating strategic policies and procedures; rather, it is the result of the impact he has on the behavior of other people in the organization.*

Confidence and competence are the mark of a good person. Liking confidence and competence in others is the mark of a great person. We presently live in a world in which success, competence, good fortune, and confidence are aversive stimuli to many people when they occur to, or in, other people. We presently live in a world in which failure, fear, lack of confidence, dependency, hostility toward others, and misfortune are reinforcers to many people when they occur to, or in, other people. Who will change this sad state of affairs? The institutions of religion and government do not appear to have had much success. Managers in private industry, however, are powerful authority figures who have the tools to change basic attitudes. To the extent that they are successful, they will help the individual, their organization, and society.

There is a parlor game which asks each person to respond to the following question: If there were a nuclear holocaust (not an improbable event) and you were one of only several survivors, what technical skills would you want in the others? Most people name such professions as "an engineer," "a medical doctor," or "a chemist." Yet, because of the enormous influence he is capable of having on the behavior of others, surely the greatest need of all would be for an individual skilled in one of the most difficult arts known to man—an effective manager of people.

CLASSROOM EXERCISES

Have each student "manage" five other students in a meeting (on videotape or in front of full class). Define the situation in various ways:

   Manager is a dogmatic entrepreneur
   Subordinates have negative attitudes toward
      manager
   Manager is weak and indecisive
   All subordinates issue an ultimatum
   Everyone dislikes another department
   All subordinates are lazy and don't care about
      the quality of their work.

SUGGESTED READINGS

Drucker, P. F.: Management, 1974, New York, Harper & Row, Publishers.
A definitive work on management by one of the foremost consultants to organizations.

Rand, A.: Atlas shrugged, Bergenfield, N.J., 1957, New American Library.
A long, sometimes tedious novel that offers excellent insights into the behavior of people in the work setting and society generally.

ADDENDUM

Since the original publication of this book, Dr. Thompson has written a number of articles. We are including several of those we feel might be of special interest to the reader.

Management by objectives in sales

Great expectations—Great frustrations
(or Never try to teach a pig to sing;
it wastes your time and annoys the pig.)
DAVID THOMPSON, Ph.D.

They were the best of time; they were the worst of times. They were the best of times because Jim had recently achieved his goal of becoming a Commercial Loan Officer; expectations were high and the future looked bright. They were the worst of times because Jim was not meeting quota hence the present state of reality was low.

This description is no doubt applicable to many of our lives at one time or another. It is a description worthy of analysis for two reasons. First, its commonality is indicative of the pervasiveness with which people, especially in business and industry, are subjected to goal and objective setting, be it management by objectives (MBO) or any other paradigm. Second, the description should be analyzed because it contains within it the seeds of frustration and failure, two frequent phenomena in our competitive society (especially in the newly emphasized sales area of banking).

EXPECTATIONS

The most effective approach might well be a closer look at what an expectation is and from whence it comes. This examination also seems warranted by the fact that so many of our own attitudes, feelings and behavior are determined by the expectations others have of us.

Many years ago, a fellow named Pavlov discovered that associating a bell with food soon gave the bell the power to influence a dogs behavior. This principle of association is so profound that it has been virtually ignored since its discovery. It is the basis upon which expectations are built. To drive expectations to high levels, one merely has to associate a future event with those things a particular person finds rewarding.

Suppose, for example, our friend Joe was going to the movies to see "Apocolypse Now" and we said the following to him:

You know, I saw that movie two weeks ago. I would consider "Apocolypse Now" one of the best movies I've ever seen. From the moment it came on the screen, you could hear a pin drop in the theatre. That movie just grabbed the audience! It actually rivets you from the start and give you more emotional reactions than any experience I've had in five years. By the time the

A-2

movie was over, everyone was just completely drained.

Now there are few, if any, movies capable of eliciting so intense an emotion. Yet, at that point, "Apocolypse Now" is just such an event to Joe. It is a future event to be anticipated with joy and interest because it has been associate with strong positive things to Joe. It is an expectation!

Since few movies could be that good, Joe's reaction to the actual movie is likely to be less than enthusiastic. Questioned after the movie, his reaction may range from a mild, "It was alright.", to a more negative, "It wasn't that good!" (depending on his level of tactfulness).

Did our associations, which determine his expectations, increase Joe's *negative* reactions to the actual movie? Emphatically yes! How? By associating an event with stronger reinforcing associations than the event realistically warranted. Do these overly strong prior associations lead to increased frustration when the actual event is experienced? Yes! It should be noted that the reverse also holds: associating an upcoming event with negatives leads to joy if reality does not confirm the negatives. Tell someone, for example, of the intense pain caused by a visit to the dentist; if that person's subsequent visit requires no dental work at all, greater relief will be the result.)

EXPECTATIONS AND REALITY

The point here is that we are really talking about two experiences, each being separate and distinct from the other. One involves associations about a future event and the other involves the event itself. Both experiences are important. Indeed, of the two, the association experience, which determines expectations, is probably the more important since it will strongly influence the effects of subsequent reality on the person.

Management by objectives, goal setting or any other rubric under which the process transpires is, in effect, associations about upcoming events by managerial personnel to their subordinates. Nowhere is this process more emphasized, clear-cut and crucial in banking than in the sales area. The expectations communicated by managers to their Commercial Loan Officers and Business Development Officers will have a strong influence over the reactions of these Officers to reality, their bank, its customers and even themselves. This reaction will soon appear on the bank's profit and loss statement.

The ultimate key then, is the relationship between the two experiences of managerial goal-setting and reality. Are they incongruous and, if so, by how much? If they are relatively incompatible, then one will be pleasant and the other unpleasant —by definition. Which will be which will depend on the verbal associations made by another person prior to the event since reality itself can rarely be controlled or changed. Because most people (especially managers in banking) want to be liked and respected, these pre-event associations or goal-setting sessions will usually become overly complimentary, optimistic and positive, thus leading to Great Expectations from both the Officer's territory and from the Officers themselves.

"I think you'll handle this heavier customer load beautifully because you're one of the best people I have."

"You did such an excellent job on the Mackson account that we want you to handle this one too. Its more complex but I'm sure you can do as great a job pleasing top management on this one as on the other one."

"There are some economic downsigns now but you have excellent rapport with your customers and I think a 10% increase from your territory by year's end would really put you at the top of the sales force."

"I think that setting and meeting these high goals will do your career at the bank a lot of good."

What is wrong with these associations? Nothing—if they are realistic! Everything if they are not!

GOAL-SETTING MOTIVATIONS

Why should people want to set up unrealistic expectations in the minds of others? Some to please people over them (subsequent failure can be blamed on others), some to see people fail, some to elicit the liking of others (as mentioned, high expectations often involve compliments), some to merely please and/or impress people at the moment, many to see their own unrealistic desires fulfilled. In short, many pre-event associations (goal-setting) have little to do with the future event to which they ostensibly relate; unfortunately, they often have a good deal to do with interpersonal relationships at the moment they are being discussed and arranged.

To see the damage that is done by setting goals too high, one must determine what characteristics are desirable in the bank sales force. It would certainly seem that confidence and competence are two essentials. It would also seem apparent that confidence and competence in a Loan Officer or Salesperson is contingent upon that person liking the two things with which they must always deal and interact effectively—themselves and other people. A manager's behavior in the now critical area of sales in banking can, therefore, best be judged by the impact it has on those under them, i.e., does it help them like themselves and others more? (It was Watson, the great manager of IBM, who said, "I've found that if a salesman doesn't like the customer, he usually doesn't get the order.")

Now the most common reason given for setting high goals is the notion that doing so motivates people to strive harder and stretch further. Oddly enough, this will only be true if the goals are attained, for success increases motivation, confidence and competence. If the goals are too high, however, failure (by definition) results; then frustration, anger, fear, blaming others, excuse-making and other deleterious forms of behavior result. Overly high goals may impress top management momentarily, but they often lead to few, if any, successes, thus leading to frustrated employees and its consequences (including high turnover).

To conclude: setting up expectations without a strong commitment to reality will soon backfire for reality, like gravity, eventually dominates everything.

It is the responsibility of managers to increase the confidence of their subordinates since few factors will increase the profits of an organization more readily than a truly confident, hence realistic, aggressive group of profit-oriented employees. Nowhere is this now more true than in the Sales Force of a bank, where people are being asked to influence other people (often strangers) despite the fact that they have no power over them. Encouraging success is the most effective vehicle for reinforcing and strengthening this confidence, this love of oneself, what one does and other people. Few things will result in realistic success and, consequently, constructive behavior more readily than managerial expectations that are agreed upon because of well-considered, thoughtful goal and objective setting which was determined, not by wishful dreams nor interpersonal desires to impress people, but by an objective and considerate assessment of reality.

Fear: the dark force

attaining those things you want least

BARBARA JONES and DAVID THOMPSON, Ph.D.

Bob dated Kris for eight months. He feared losing her and, as a result, he smothered her. Thus he lost her. Jim fears others will find him insignificant and not pay him any attention. As a result, he goes to great lengths to impress people. Thus, people avoid him and he does not get the attention he so desperately seeks. Mary is fearful of being criticized by others. Consequently, she does not commit herself to a decision until she has some idea as to how everyone else feels. For this, people criticize her. Mike is fearful of being seen as a failure. As a result, he ridicules anyone whom he feels represents competition to him. Thus, he lacks interpersonal skills, is not promoted and is seen as a failure by most people.

The above examples reflect an important phenomenon in life: *fear increases the likelihood we will experience the very things we fear.* Determining how and why this self-destructive mechanism works and what we can do about it are the questions addressed by this article.

Our first task should be to determine what we are fearful of when we experience the relevant, common fears which motivate most of us virtually everyday. These daily fears usually consist of such things as ridicule, rejection, criticism, being ignored, being seen by others as a failure or as weak or passive or frightened, being seen as dependent or unattractive, being looked down on or seen as inferior or insignificant, unimportant, being disliked or disrespected. The behavior influenced by these fears may take different forms in each of us, but is pervasive indeed in all of us. Its influence is manifested in all areas of our life, from the work setting to our personal relations, from parenting to academia, from leisure activities to our consumer behavior.

While the list of these motivating fears seems endless in variety, one is struck by two characteristics common to all of them: *first, no matter what specific form they take in each of us, our common, everyday fears always center on the behavior of other people with whom we interact. Second, virtually every behavior we fear others will exhibit toward us involves anger on their part* (again, in one form or another).

Since we have determined that our fear

increases the likelihood of our experiencing those things we fear, our next step might involve determining the motivation of those who would treat us with disrespect, ridicule, criticism, and so forth, i.e., of those who are angry at us. (This does not mean we were necessarily responsible for the anger; some people, for example, are angry at, and consequently ridicule, everyone). Now an angry person is a person who wants to hurt others, to see them emotionally upset, to see them in a state of discomfort, i.e. to see them in a state reflective of fear.

Both common sense and the psychology of interpersonal interactions indicate that the way we respond to people will either strengthen (reinforce) their behavior or weaken it. Different things are, of course, reinforcing to different people and even to the same person at different times. But to an angry person, a fear reaction by the person upon whom they are venting their anger (in whatever form) will reinforce that anger. *And to reinforce behavior is to increase its frequency.* Thus does our fear increase the likelihood of our experiencing, in ever increasing frequency, the very things we most fear. Thus does our fear turn an occasionally ridiculing person into an excessively ridiculing person. Thus does our fear turn an occasional pouting or complaining spouse into a constant pouting or complaining spouse. Thus does our fear turn people in our lives, in increasing frequency, to look down on us, avoid us, criticize or treat us with disrespect.

SOME EXAMPLES

The overly protective mother, because of her fear of losing her children, anticipates their every desire while reminding them of her sacrifices on their behalf. Does her smothering indulgence, born of fear, assure their love? Not likely. Does her fear-induced behavior lead to a loss of their respect and an increased likelihood they will leave her? Probably. Does the spouse who fears his/her partner might leave and abandon them develop a firmer bond between them with the suspicions and jealousy such fear usually elicits? Hardly. Does the constantly placating person successfully avoid the dislike of others so feared; or does their constantly subservient orientation lead most people to dislike them?

Does the employee who fears being controlled or looked down upon by management avoid these reactions by his fear-induced attacks on management for any directive they may issue? Does the manager who fears criticism avoid criticism by refusing to delegate any authority and adopting an overly precise, detailed, cautious orientation because of these fears? Does the manager who fears subordinates liking each other and not being dependent on their boss (a common phenomenon among all managers) reinforce negative attitudes in each toward the other? What fears account for the frequency with which sales and operations clash?

SOME SUGGESTED SOLUTIONS

1. The first step in ridding ourselves of these compromising weights is to deter-

mine just what our particular fears are (a more difficult task emotionally than one might initially think). What are we most fearful of people thinking of us? Of people doing in our presence or to us? Candid answers from close friends should be encouraged and reinforced, not punished with outraged incredulity.

Now the mark of fear-driven behavior is its excessiveness. Since those things we fear from others could occur at *any* time, we must be on guard *all* the time. The overly detailed, precise person who fears criticism is excessively detailed because criticism can occur at any time so protection must be present all the time. Thus, we must ask ourselves what our most frequent behavior is in the presence of others and if it is possible that the behavior is intended to preclude the possibility of some behavior in others. The macho person, for example, excessively brags about his physical prowess, not because being seen as strong is rewarding to him, but rather, because being seen as weak is frightening to him. Awareness of this fact may soften his excessive macho behavior.

2. The second step, albeit a most emotionally difficult one, is to discuss our fears as openly as possible with others. Oddly enough, this should be done initially with people we know least well since this situation will be less threatening than such candid discussion with those close to us. Such an open discussion will usually dissipate the fear somewhat when we realize no dire consequences resulted from our openness. When the macho person openly concedes his fears of being seen by others as frightened, when the intensely ambitious person speaks freely of her fear of being seen as a failure, when the excessively aggressive person openly discusses her fear of being seen as passive, then will these fear-driven behaviors become less intense, less influential and less destructive.

3. Silence is golden. Most interactions of a negative nature can be anticipated, either because of the situation (your boss wishes to see you; his/her request coincides with a recent mistake on your part) or because of the people involved (Mike frequently ridicules your ideas in meetings such as the upcoming one tomorrow). Now we have determined that our fear reinforces the negative behavior others direct at us. Thus, although we still feel fear, we must adopt a different behavior pattern that is effective but within our capabilities at the moment (fear destroys competence in all situations).

Silence is our best shot! When the yelling starts, when the ridicule begins, we must stare at the perpetrator calmly and fixedly—and not say a word! The most critical point in this scenerio will occur when the angry speaker stops, for it is then that our shuffling feet and shifting eyes reflect *our* fear, *their* reinforcement. But a calm, silent stare not only deprives them of their joy but actually creates anxiety in them. For the greatest fear of most people and certainly angry people, is not knowing what the other person is thinking, especially of them. Silence on our part increases this fear reaction on their part. Indeed, some people will become so uncomfortable over the silence that they will start asking us questions in order to elicit some reaction. All such questions should be calmly and softly answered with, "I don't know. I'll have to think about it."

4. To help us tone down our fears and engage in the silence that creates the punishing ambiguity to our angry tormentor, we would do well to *analyze* the behavior of the other person (people) as it is occurring. This analysis encourages a calm, thoughtful appearance on our part for one reason—we are actually thinking! And nothing dissipates the cauldron of felt emotions such as fear, more readily than thinking.

   Why is that person saying that thing at this time? What effect is he/she trying to have on me? On others? What is this speaker's greatest fear (most anger is based on fear)? What is this speaker's behavior indicative of in the organization? Attempting to answer these questions during interactions is an all consuming task that requires effort, observation and thought and leaves little room for fear and its consequences.

5. There is another way to handle the angry person, a most effective way that

our fear, unfortunately, precludes in most of us. We have determined that, to an angry person, our fear is reinforcing. What then might be punishing? Fear's opposite—our happiness, our good cheer!

A prefunctory analysis will also indicate that the angry person, in trying to hurt us, would find our calm, cheerful agreement with their comments punishing indeed. Since hurting us is the goal, our agreement will often stop the assault and cause the angry person to rethink his/her approach; after all, the intended denials and arguments reflective of our fear did not occur.

When do we know our fears are conquered? When we can use the above approach of cheerful agreement in response to a normally fear-inducing interaction.

Colleague (in front of others): Hey Jim, where do you get the guts to wear those ugly shirts?
Instead of looking down embarrassed, we might laughingly say: If I didn't wear them, my good looks would just overwhelm people.

Thus does our confidence, our good cheer, our happiness, our lack of need to defend, argue and deny place us in a position of control. This is the ultimate criterion for lack of fear. It is a stringent one which few of us attain but which in striving toward, leads all of us to grow.

Our confidence and good cheer will, if consistently maintained, not only punish and decrease the frequency of the anger of people around us, it will lead such people to avoid interacting with us over time. Eventually, it will lead such people to fade from our lives, to be replaced by confident, competent people of good cheer who like confident, competent people of good cheer.

One final consideration. Most lives involve relatively few major decisions and choice points. Yet these will impact that life in many ways for many years. Which school to attend, which person to marry, which job or career to pursue, having children, which friends to see frequently, and so forth are issues of this nature.

Now, we have found that fear is a debilitating emotion that not only compromises our competence and effectiveness, but actually increases the likelihood of our getting the very things we feared. We feel it is essential, therefore, that fear be eliminated as much as possible from one's mind when making these major decisions. This is most efficiently done by purging our minds, during these decision-making times, of any concern over what others think of us. This is a most difficult task. Yet a concentrated effort to not care what others (especially those significant to us) think of us, even for a few moments, will often lead to decisions that are most constructive and beneficial for us and those around us.

Confidence and good cheer, therefore, are the secrets of the good life, not only in daily interactions, but also during major decision-making periods. To the extent that we develop them in ourselves, to that extent will we help develop them in others—and doing so would seem to be a life well-served.

Self-development

a guide for personal growth

DAVID THOMPSON, Ph.D.

Jim is a frightened person. He fears criticism from others so he is indecisive and has bogged down in irrelevant details in his life. Susan is a frightened person. She is passive and self-effacing because she fears people will dislike her. Mike is a frightened person. He acts tough and macho too often and at inappropriate times because, subconsciously, he fears people will see him as a frightened person.

The organization that Jim, Susan, and Mike work for pay a heavy price for these fears (as do their colleagues, bosses, subordinates, friends, relatives and anyone else with whom they interact frequently). So we must help them to change. How? Through professional help? Hardly. Such help is slow, expensive and of questionable efficacy. Through our own efforts with them? Hardly. We are unable to help because Jim, Susan, and Mike are us—and our lack of recognition of that fact precludes our effectiveness with them.

Self-development, therefore, must start with two basic premises. First, we must confront directly those things that determine our thoughts, feelings and attitudes. Second, for obvious motivational reasons,

we must be responsible for our own self-development.

CAUSES

One of the most pervasive fears that most people experience concerns itself with the possibility that they have little control over their own lives, i.e., that their feelings and attitudes are influenced, if not controlled, by other people and external events. To fear such external causes is self-defeating, destructive and incompatible with reality. For the fact is, our feelings and attitudes *are* influenced, if not controlled, by external events, especially by the most important external events in our life—the behavior of people with whom we interact frequently. To fear this fact, therefore, leaves one with the disadvantage of fearing reality. It is as effective as going through life fearing the force of gravity (it does not eliminate gravity, but does give us the added burden of fear).

1. *Focus on the behavioral impact others have on you.* Given a realistic acceptance of external influence, one must focus on just what effect the behavior of others is having on us (this often conflicts with our

intensely pervasive concerns about what others are thinking of us).

Now most people elicit from others the behavior they truly want. Hence it is important to determine what the people with whom we interact frequently want in others because that's what they are often going to elicit from us.

This analysis can result in sobering conclusions indeed. Our boss continually tells us he wants more independent initiative; closer analysis indicates he subtly punishes us when we engage in behavior that reflects an independent initiative. Top management continually extolls the virtues of positive attitudes; closer analysis indicates that top management subtly reinforces our ridicule of customers or our complaints about co-workers. Our spouse feels our boss is unfair to us; closer analysis indicates our spouse is competing with our boss for our time and attention and does not want us to like him (or anyone else for that matter).

To feel we can avoid the consequences of these influences is also incompatible with reality and self-defeating. Interacting over time with people such as the above will eventually lead us to compromise our independent initiative, to ridicule and criticize customers and co-workers, and to feel our boss is unfair.

The first principles of self-development, therefore, is: know what types of behavior the people around you really like and want in others. If it is fear, dependency, indecisiveness, anger toward others and so forth, minimize your interaction with them as much as possible. When you have to deal with them, consciously analyze their behavior as you do so; this has the effect of blunting the emotional impact their behavior will have on you (nothing cools down emotions more quickly than thinking). More importantly, make a concerted effort to find those people who like those things in others that you would like in yourself, that you would like to be. Seek out and interact frequently with people, for example, who like competence, confidence, a liking of people and things in others; express yourself freely to them and let their behavioral impact wash over you. Are they difficult to find? Certainly, but it's well worth the effort.

2. *Interact with people you dislike and have avoided.* All objects in the universe have inertia; that is, they remain in their present state unless acted upon by an *external* force. People have inertia. Behavior is stable because most of us avoid interacting with people who represent an external force that is different from those presently influencing us and maintaining our state of inertia. The withdrawn person feels outgoing salespeople are phony— and avoids them. The negative, complaining and depressed person feels positive, optimistic people are naive and pollyanish —and avoids them. The indecisive person feels decisive people are arrogant—and avoids them. The dependent person feels independent people are cold and uncaring —and avoids them.

Yet, in each of the above instances, interacting with these avoided people could lead to quick, surprisingly beneficial and eventually stable changes in the people they impact. But inertia wins. Like gravity, its force is pervasive and overwhelming. Those who combat it, however, and risk change in themselves will take a second look at people they have disliked and avoided. From a more objective orientation, they may eventually come to see these people as, not only likable, but also as constructive change agents who bring with them much happiness for the people they influence.

3. *Reinforce a positive self-concept.* The relativity of all things in life is due, in large part, to the fact that the human mind rarely judges anything in isolation. It judges almost everything in terms of a comparison with something else. And the thing the mind most often compares with everything and everyone else is itself. That is why a positive self-concept is so important (who wants to always come out on the short end in an evaluative comparison with others?).

Now we have determined that influences on us are external. This is especially true in regard to our self-concept. It is imperative, therefore, that any positive remarks directed at oneself by others be amply reinforced, thus increasing their frequency and ensuring some subsequent semblance of self-worth on our part. In short, we must stop the all too frequent habit of punishing the few people who are kind enough to compliment us and enhance our feelings of self-worth.

The Other: You really did an excellent analysis!

Our Old Self: Well, it really wasn't that good.
Our New Self: Thank you! I appreciate your saying that.
The Other: That's a beautiful shirt you have on.
Our Old Self: It's really quite old.
Our New Self: It's my favorite shirt, and I try to wear it on the days I'll be seeing you.
The Other: I think you deserve the promotion.
Our Old Self: There are probably a lot of other people who deserve it more than me.
Our New Self: Knowing you feel that way is about as important as the promotion itself.

The principle being stated here is that while we are able to influence ourselves minimally, we can impact others (we are external forces to them) with a view of guiding them toward having a constructive influence on us. Nowhere is this more important than in their impact on our self-concept. To create an environment in which we are respected and cared for, therefore, requires us to reward such behavior in those with whom we interact frequently. The result will be respect and caring for ourselves by ourselves, i.e., a positive self-concept.

There are, of course, few people who are willing to compliment others, including us (because such behavior has often encountered punishment, such as from our Old Self). One special global orientation on our part will increase the probability of eliciting these important accolades—*liking other people.* There are few people who can resist a positive orientation toward someone who likes them. Before an interaction with someone important, therefore, one should think of all the likable characteristics of that person. Then, and only then, should one interact with that person, expressing oneself freely; the benefits will usually be readily apparent. (Again, when they come in the form of positive statements about you, please reinforce the speaker.)

4. *Rid yourself of ghosts.* This principle can have more beneficial impact on an individual than all the others combined. Each of us goes through life with ghosts. A ghost is a fear we hold that other people will think a specific thing of us or view us in a certain way. Some of the more common ghosts are: being seen by others as weak, or frightened, or passive, being seen as a failure or as dependent or as being unimportant or insignificant, being disliked or criticized or rejected, being ignored or left alone in the world.

Ghosts rarely, if ever, occur; we are driven only by the fear that they might. Since they might occur at *any* time, we are being driven by the fear virtually *all* the time.

Thus, ghosts lead to behavior that is excessive (and inappropriate). Excessively macho behavior reflects a ghostly fear of being seen as frightened, excessively ambitious behavior a fear of being seen as a failure, excessively emotional behavior a fear of being insignificant to others, excessively independent behavior a fear of being dependent, excessive passivity a fear of being disliked, excessive rigidity a fear of being criticized, excessive dependence a fear of being left alone, excessive criticalness a fear of personal closeness and vulnerability.

Frequent, repetitive behavior is the mark of a person. Excessive behavior is their achilles heel. Nothing will free one for self-development more than the elimina-tion of the ghosts in their life. How is it done? By first determining the specific ghosts involved. This is not a particularly difficult task (although the intellectual insight achieved will not change anything). Second, but most (emotionally) difficult, eliminating ghosts is best achieved by trying to bring the ghosts to life, i.e., by trying to sincerely and honestly convince people you are what you fear they might think you are.

Example: Mike is 'tough' in every sense of the word. He will back down from no one and many have backed down from him. He brags excessively about his tough, hardnosed approach to life and people.

Ghost: Mike is frightened of being seen by others as frightened.

Self-development: Mike must embark on a campaign of convincing people (starting with those least important to him since they are the easiest) that he is indeed a frightened person at times. (Difficult for him to do?)

Example: Jim is a cold, analytical person. He has considerable intellectual skills which he uses excessively to criticize people, rarely expressing any positives.

Ghost: Jim is frightened of close, personal relationships (he is frightened of liking anyone because he was punished so often in the past when he did).

Self-development: Jim should *not* be encouraged to express positive warmth toward others (he will find it too difficult and fail). He should be encouraged to sincerely convince others that he is frightened of close, personal relationships. (Difficult? Yes, but after he has done so and found the earth did not explode, he will then be in a much better position to express positive warmth sincerely and successfully.)

Example: Susan is an overly passive person who excessively and too readily agrees with anyone's point of view.

Ghost: Contrary to popular view, being *liked* may be

of little importance to Susan; being *disliked* is the ghost she is avoiding.

Self-development: Susan must try to convince people of her fear of *not* being liked by people (sincerely, not as a vehicle to elicit sympathy) and she should try indeed to be disliked by some. (Difficult? Yes, but after she has brought these ghosts of fear to life and found they don't bite, she will start disagreeing with people *when appropriate.*)

Raising our ghosts of fear and bringing them to life through open discussion is not an easy thing to accomplish. Yet it is not that difficult if one starts with mild ghosts, brings them to the light of reality and experiences the exhilarating freedom of seeing them evaporate.

What is it we fear most in the minds of others as to how they view and think of us? What do we devote most of our energy toward convincing others we are not? Turn the Tables. Convince them you are that, speak to them of these fears —then you will be able to go on to more important, constructive things since your fear will have been dissipated by the reality you created.

To accept reality rarely hurts since, like it or not, reality (like gravity) has a way of always being around in one form or another. To accept the fact that the people with whom we interact most frequently have a strong influence on what we think and feel is to accept and adapt to reality. It is the first step of the never-ending, but constructive and personally rewarding road toward self-development.

ADDENDUM

The joy of reinforcing others

DAVID THOMPSON, Ph.D.

Jim told his boss that sales were down 5% in his territory because general economic conditions were bad. His boss offered him praise for his efforts and encouragement for the future. A colleague of Jim's told his boss (the same boss as Jim's) that sales were down 5% in his territory because general economic conditions were bad. His boss told him that was an excuse, unacceptable and, if sales did not increase soon, his presence in the company would be unacceptable.

Bill and Mike sell the same commodity type product for competitors. Delivery and quality of service are similar but Bill gets far more orders than Mike. Hilary and Beth do similar work (although Beth's is really better) but Hilary gets more attention, raises and promotions than Beth.

Clearly something subjective is happening in these all too familiar and typical situations. Our reactions to them can be indignation and anger over the injustice of people or it can be a closer look at why many people who do high quality work fail to grab as many rings as some who do work of lesser quality. Those readers who like to wallow in their anger over the obvious inherent unfairness of life and people might do well to stop reading here. Those who wish to explore these situations with a view toward becoming more effective interpersonally and grabbing more rings might wish to continue.

REINFORCERS

Suppose Bill asked you the question, "Are you going to the meeting at three?" And suppose Art asked you the question, "Do you know that you have one of the quickest, most agile minds I've ever encountered?" Barring the possibility of psychosis on your part, whom do you feel you will like more? Whom do you think has better judgment, is more confident, adopts a more effective stance toward life and its problems? There are two reasons we would feel more inclined toward attributing these fine characteristics to Art rather than Bill: first, he asked us such an insightful, penetrating question, and second, so few others do.

That we are tilted positively toward Art is the result of Art having used a reinforcer, that is, something pleasing, rewarding, happiness-inducing to us. Now reinforcers have an overwhelming psychological consequence: they pair or associate their

A-16

positive effects with those who express them. That is, just as Pavlov's dogs grew to like (salivate to) a bell associated with food (if you can stomach the analogy), so too do we grow to like (salivate toward) people who associate themselves with what are reinforcers to us. More important, if we use reinforcers with others, they will experience pleasure and salivate when we appear. Now that is control!

Let us therefore dedicate our lives to reinforcing others. Let us freely express positives such as: Your hair looks beautiful. You did a better job on that report than I could have. Your social skills are outstanding. You are one of the most athletic, coordinated people I've ever met. I think most people are awed by your command of the language. Your analyses are the best I've ever seen.

This is not to say that we will lie nor that we will inundate anyone at any one time with all these reinforcers (for surely they would drown in their own bodily fluids). We will only express reinforcers when we sincerely mean them. The alternative approach would appear "phony" to the recipient and would not be a reinforcer (if we were truly adept at lying we would be successful politicians and would not need training in this area anyway). Also, people get tired of the same reinforcer over and over again. Therefore, we will use them sincerely and sparingly (but at least one per interaction with a person). These relatively low criteria, however, will lead people to like and seek us out, to give us

raises and promotions, to fill our sales quotes and make us, in general, socially popular, admired and wealthy.

Then why haven't we done it? Ah, why indeed! Why is it so difficult to mouth these sounds which might please others? Why are we so inhibited in emotionally expressing reinforcers to those about us (an inhibition many of us rarely feel over expressing negatives). Why do we see that impressing others requires us to be impressed by them; that appreciation by others for our fine mind is more readily attained, not by our insightful analyses, but by our expressed appreciation of *their* outstanding attributes?

THE GROWING OF INHIBITIONS (or how I learned that expressing positives was negative.)

Given our premise, therefore, that our reluctance over expressing positives is self-destructive in the long term, let us explore how such reluctance is nurtured and encouraged.

We live in a competitive world in which the fittest survive. We live in a world which taught us early on that people we liked, if they liked someone else, ignored us or even ganged up on us. We learned that when people liked us *only*, their attention, cooperation and even subservience was more easily elicited and maintained. In short, we learned that people liking each other could be threatening to us and our well-being.

Now reinforcers should be personal and, as such, are powerful. The more powerful they are to the recipient, unfortunately, the more negative they usually are to a third party. Affection between parents is often reacted to negatively by children. A teacher's compliment to a pupil frequently elicits ridicule by the pupil's friends. Telling your boss that he is one of the best managers you've ever worked for may please him indeed; it is unlikely to please anyone else present (be the third party one of your colleagues, your subordinates, your boss' colleagues, your boss' boss or even your boss' spouse). Telling a subordinate he made an outstanding presentation often elicits an underlying competitive anger from his or her peers. The sales manager is expected to call on customers with salespeople. If the manager gets involved effectively in the sales call, he will often reinforce the customer and build a mutually positive relationship, a relationship that can be threatening to the salesperson (sometimes the manager will implicitly assume credit for subsequent orders).

These third party reactions to the use of reinforcers are often more active than the above examples would indicate. That is, they usually involve the use of punishment in one form or another (e.g., the ridicule of the child by school-mates has its counterpart in the 'soft-quota' or 'windfall' reaction of many in the sales force to a contest winning salesperson). This punishment is often directed at both the giver and receiver of reinforcers. Thus are our inhibitions over expressing reinforcers grown!

Because of this important phenomenon, one crucial principle must always be adhered to: *Never reinforce any person in the presence of another person.*

No doubt there are exceptions to this rule. They are so few, however, and the

negative consequences of bucking the principle so great that, like a beautiful, vituous woman, it should never be violated.

The punishment given a *receiver* of reinforcers by a third party also has a subsequent effect on the giver of reinforcers. Behavior that is not reinforced gradually weakens and decreases in frequency. Because of previous punishments, few people will have the confidence to accept, acknowledge and reinforce someone for giving them reinforcers. It is therefore often true that our expression of reinforcers will be met with shuffling feet, hung heads and an awkward silence—a somewhat less than reinforcing reaction for us. Thus, our constructive reinforcing gestures are almost always doomed to undergo the weakening effects of extinction.

Our second rule when expressing reinforcers, therefore is: *Do not expect nor want nor give the recipient time to emit a reaction to our reinforcer.*

The best approach when expressing a reinforcer is to go to another topic *immediately.* Besides being punished by third parties for accepting reinforcers, most people have learned that others *give* to *get,* that the expression of a positive is meant to elicit a positive from them "I love you" is often said, for example, to elicit a commitment from the receiver, i.e., "I love you too." Thus, the awkward silence following the expression of a reinforcer is often a reflection of the recipient's suspicion and wariness, reactions well founded in the past (and often strengthened by incompetent salespeople).

"That's a really beautiful blouse you have on! Say, are you going to the meeting at three today?" This is the effective way to use reinforcers. It will have an impact. Yet it has *eliminated* the embarrassing silence, our own destructive expectation of a reciprocal reinforcing reaction and the other person's suspicion that we are only giving them a reinforcer in order to elicit one, then and there, for ourselves.

A third obstacle to our intelligent use of reinforcers lies in the fact that, as mice judge all things by cheese, so to do we judge all people by ourselves. As a result, we assume that what is reinforcing to us is reinforcing to others. This error is compounded by our all too pervasive fear that others will think poorly of us, which is a quite different orientation from our hope that they will think well of us. As with most fears, our behavior usually elicits the reaction we most fear. Thus, the person who fears being seen as a weakling constantly tries to prove how strong he is, the person fearful of being seen as frightened how brave he is, the person fearful of being seen as passive how aggressive he is. All of these behaviors may be reinforcing to the speaker, but rarely to the listener.

"I know alot of important people" is the remark of someone who fears others will find him insignificant. Because it is based on fear, it usually does just that! (and if the comment doesn't, reality will—see article on expection). "You certainly seem to know alot of important people" is the remark of someone confident and capable enough to look beyond his own needs. "I'm a very coordinated person" will *decrease* the likelihood others will see you as such. "*You* seem to be a very coordinated person", *increases* the likelihood the recipient will see you as such.

Behavior motivated by the fear of what bad things others might think of us, therefore, leads us to engage in the expressive behavior of trying to convince others we are not those things. This usually leads people to feel we probably are or, at a minimum, to become uncomfortable around us. Behavior which freely and sincerely expresses appreciation for the strengths of others, conversely, usually elicits subsequent appreciation for ones' own strengths.

Our third rule: *People will be more readily impressed with those who openly express the fact that they are impressed with other people.* This rule requires, however, an ability to dismiss our own needs and fears when assessing others. It requires us to realize that some people love a pat on the back, others hate it; some people love to be told they are the best or they are loved, others fear it; some people love attention, others dread it. Before attempting to interact with someone, therefore, it is important that we engage in a most difficult pasttime—thinking. And this thinking must be objective, i.e., freed from our own biases and prejudices.

Why is it so difficult to express these reinforcers to others? Do we really believe that telling someone they "did a better job on the project than we could have" is going to make them feel superior to us, or leave us, or ignore us? Quite the contrary! They will find it easier to like us, to seek us out, to express appreciation for our strengths. Expressing sincere reinforcers to others at appropriate times is the mark of the truly confident person. It is also the mark of the person who more readily elicits coopera- tion, constructive attitudes and the willingness to put forth effort. In short, the ability to express sincere reinforcers is the mark of the Effective Manager.

Dr. David Thompson, presenting a live seminar on Reinforcement principles, is now available on video- tape. For further information, contact:

MTR Corp.
1807 Glenview Rd.
Glenview, IL 60025
312-998-4650

References

Azrin, N. H.: Aggression, paper presented at the American Psychological Association convention, Los Angeles, 1964.

Azrin, N. H.: Effects of punishment intensity during variable-interval reinforcement, J. Anal. Behav. **3:**123-142, 1960.

Azrin, N. H.: Effects of two intermittent schedules of immediate and nonimmediate punishment, J. Psychol. **42:**3-21, 1956.

Beecroft, R. S.: Classical conditioning, Goleta, Calif., 1966, Psychonomic Press.

Bijou, S. W., and Baer, D. M.: Child development II. Universal stage of infancy, New York, 1965, Appleton-Century-Crofts.

Bitterman, M. E.: Techniques for the study of learning in animals: analysis and classification, Psychol. Bull. **59:**81-93, 1962.

Blake, Avis, and Mouton: Corporate darwinism, Reading, Mass., Addison-Wesley Publishing Co.

Blum, M. L., and Naylor, J. C.: Industrial psychology, New York, 1968, Harper & Row, Publishers.

Bugelski, B. R.: Extinction with and without sub-goal reinforcement, J. Compar. Psychol. **26:**121-133, 1938.

Camp, D. S., Raymond, G. A., and Church, R. M.: Temporal relationship between response and punishment, J. Exp. Psychol. **74:**114-123, 1967.

Campbell, J. P., Dunnette, M. D., Lawler, E. E., and Weick, K. E.: Managerial behavior, performance, and effectiveness, New York, 1970, McGraw-Hill Book Co.

Catonia, C. A., editor: Contemporary research in operant behavior, Glenview, Ill., 1968, Scott, Foresman and Co.

Coleman, J. C.: Abnormal psychology and modern life, ed. 3, Chicago, 1964, Scott, Foresman and Co.

Dinsmoor, J. A.: A discrimination based on punishment, Q. J. Exp. Psychol. **4:**27-45, 1952.

Drucker, P. F.: Management, New York, 1974, Harper & Row, Publishers.

Drucker, P. F.: The effective executive, New York, 1967, Harper & Row, Publishers.

Drucker, P. F.: The practice of management, New York, 1954, Harper & Row, Publishers.

Estes, W. K.: An experimental study of punishment, Psychol. Mon. vol. 57, no. 263, 1944.

Estes, W. K., and Skinner, B. F.: Some quantitative properties of anxiety, J. Exp. Psychol. **29:**390-400, 1941.

Fear, R. A.: The evaluation interview, New York, 1973, McGraw-Hill Book Co.

Ferster, C. B., Culberston, S., and Boren, M. C. P.: Behavior principles, ed. 2, Englewood Cliffs, N.J., 1975, Prentice-Hall, Inc.

Ferster, C. B., and Skinner, B. F.: Schedules of reinforcement, New York, 1957, Appleton-Century-Crofts.

Gellerman, S. W.: Motivation and productivity, New York, 1963, American Management Association.

Guion, R. M.: Personnel testing, New York, 1965, McGraw-Hill Book Co.

Guthrie, E. R.: Reward and punishment, Psychol. Rev. **41:**450-460, 1934.

Harris, F. R., Wolf, M. M., and Baer, D. M.: Effects of adult social reinforcement on child behavior. In Bijou, S. W., and Baer, D. M., editors: Child development: readings in experimental analysis, New York, 1967, Appleton-Century-Crofts.

Hartman, T. F.: Dynamic transmission, elective generalization, and semantic conditioning. In Prokasy, W. F., editor: Classical conditioning: a symposium, New York, 1965, Appleton-Century-Crofts.

Hilgard, E. R., and Bower, G. H.: Theories of learning, ed. 4, Englewood Cliffs, N.J., 1975, Prentice-Hall, Inc.

Hilgard, E. R., and Marquis, D. M.: Conditioning and learning, New York, 1940, Appleton-Century-Crofts.

Honig, W. K., editor: Operant behavior. Areas of research and application, New York, 1966, Appleton-Century-Crofts.

Hulse, S. H., Deese, J., and Egeth, H.: The psychology of learning, ed. 4, New York, 1975, McGraw-Hill Book Co., chaps. 1-5.

Karsh, E. B.: Effects of number of rewarded trials and intensity of punishment on running speed, J. Comp. Physiol. Psychol. **55:**44-51, 1962.

Keller, F. S., and Schoenfeld, W. N.: Principles of psychology, New York, 1950, Appleton-Century-Crofts.

Kimble, G. A., editor: Foundations of conditioning and learning, New York, 1967, Appleton-Century-Crofts.

Kling, J. W., and Riggs, L. A.: Woodworth and Schlosberg's experimental psychology, ed. 3, New York, 1971. Holt, Rinehart, & Winston.

Lieberman, D. A., editor: Learning and the control of behavior: Some principles, theories, and applications of classical and operant conditioning, New York, 1974, Holt, Rinehart & Winston.

Margolius, G.: Stimulus generalization of an instrumental response as a function of the number of reinforced trials, J. Exp. Psychol. **49:**105-111, 1955.

Marrow, A. J., Bowers, D. G., and Seashore, S. E.: Management by participation, New York, 1967, Harper & Row, Publishers.

Mandell, M. M.: The selection process, New York, 1964, American Management Association, Inc.

McDonald, F.: The Phaeton ride, Garden City, N.Y., 1974, Doubleday & Co.

McGregor, D.: Leadership and motivation, Cambridge, Mass., 1968, The M.I.T. press.

McGregor, D.: The human side of enterprise, New York, 1960, McGraw-Hill Book Co.

McGregor, D.: The professional manager, New York, 1967, McGraw-Hill Book Co.

Mednick, S. A., and Freedman, J. L.: Stimulus generalization, Psychol. Bull., **57:**169-200, 1960.

Pavlov, I. P.: Conditioned reflexes, London, 1927, Clarendon Press.

Premack, D.: Toward empirical behavioral laws: I. Positive reinforcement, Psychol. Rev. **66:**219-233, 1959.

Premack, D.: Reversibility of the reinforcement relation, Science **136:**255-257, 1962.

Rand, A.: Atlas shrugged, Bergenfield, N.J., 1957, New American Library.

Razran, G.: A quantitative study of meaning by conditioned salivary technique (semantic conditioning), Science **90:**89-91, 1939.

Razran, G.: Stimulus generalization of conditioned responses, Psychol. Bull., **46:**337-365, 1949.

Razran, G.: The observable unconscious and the inferable conscious in current Soviet psychophysiology, Psychol. Rev. **68:**81-147, 1961.

Reynolds, G. S.: A primer of operant conditioning, Glenview, Ill., 1975, Scott, Foresman and Co.

Skinner, B. F.: The behavior of organisms: an

experimental analysis, New York, 1938, Appleton-Century-Crofts.

Skinner, B. F.: Two types of conditioned reflex and a pseudotype, J. Gen. Psychol. **12:**66-77, 1935.

Solomon, R. L., Kamin, L. J., and Wynne, L. C.: Traumatic avoidance learning: the outcome of severe extinction procedures with dogs, J. Abnorm. Soc. Psychol. **48:**291-302, 1953.

Spiker, C. C.: The effects of number of reinforcements on the strength of a generalized instrumental response, Child Devel. **27:**37-44, 1956.

Ulmann, L. P., and Krasner, L.: A psychological approach to abnormal behavior, Englewood Cliffs, N.J., 1969, Prentice-Hall, Inc.

Watson, G.: Social psychology. Issues and insights, Philadelphia, 1966, J. B. Lippincott Co.

Index